First published in Great Britain in 2011 by Canongate Books Ltd,
14 High Street, Edinburgh EH1 1TE

www.canongate.tv

1

British Library Cataloguing-in-Publication Data
A catalogue record for this book is available on
request from the British Library

ISBN 978 085786 384 3
Export ISBN 978 0 85786 385 0

Typeset in Minion Pro and Helvetica

Printed and bound in Great Britain by Clays Ltd, St Ives plc

JULIAN ASSANGE
THE UNAUTHORISED AUTOBIOGRAPHY

CANONGATE

Edinburgh · London · New York · Melbourne

CONTENTS

A NOTE FROM THE PUBLISHER

On 20 December 2010, Julian Assange signed a contract with Canongate Books to write a book – part memoir, part manifesto – for publication the following year.

At the time, Julian said: 'I hope this book will become one of the unifying documents of our generation. In this highly personal work, I explain our global struggle to force a new relationship between the people and their governments.'

In the end, the work was to prove too personal.

Despite sitting for more than fifty hours of taped interviews and spending many late nights at Ellingham Hall in Norfolk (where he was living under house arrest) discussing his life and the work of WikiLeaks with the writer he had enlisted to help him, Julian became increasingly troubled by the thought of publishing an autobiography. After reading the first draft of the book that was delivered at the end of March, Julian declared: 'All memoir is prostitution.'

On 7 June 2011, with thirty-eight publishing houses around the world committed to releasing the book, Julian told us he wanted to cancel his contract.

We disagree with Julian's assessment of the book. We believe it explains both the man and his work, underlining his commitment to the truth. Julian always claimed the book was well written; we agree, and this also encouraged us to make the book available to readers.

And the contract? By the time Julian wanted to cancel the deal he had already signed his advance over to his lawyers to settle his legal bills. So the contract still stands. We have decided to honour it – and to publish.

What follows is the unauthorised first draft. It is passionate, provocative and opinionated – like its author. It fulfils the promise of the original proposal and we are proud to publish it.

Canongate Books,
September 2011

JULIAN ASSANGE

The Unauthorised Autobiography

'If you want to build a ship, don't drum up people together to collect wood and don't assign them tasks and work, but rather teach them to long for the endless immensity of the sea.'

Antoine de Saint-Exupéry

1

SOLITARY

I consider myself lucky to have been born to curious people who filled the air around me with questions. One day I would meet my enemies and they would hate me for wanting the truth. You could almost forget your own name in all the name-calling. Yet I know well enough who I am and hoped I could tell you myself. My name is Julian Assange. And one day the police wanted me in London. The story could end there, were it not for the complications of time and history and personhood. They say the past is another country, but so is the future if you'll only let it be: speeding along in the back of an English police van you begin to see the world.

They were shouting my name. Shouting slogans. And the press photographers were scrabbling around the windows like crabs in a bucket. It felt like the van was being beaten and that it might turn over, but it was just the press trying to get pictures. I crouched down and held my head between my knees, not wanting to be cast as a criminal. At one point I looked up and saw the cameras being thudded against the tinted glass and angled so as to catch me. I covered my head with my arms. Then suddenly the vehicle gathered speed and was off. Some of the other prisoners shouted out in their own cubicles, unaware of who I was, evidently shocked at the smashing of the van. Others laughed at the commotion. The show was over. It took about forty minutes for us to reach the gates of Wandsworth Prison. It was 7 December 2010.

I felt weirdly confident at the entry point. I suppose some of that came from knowing my predicament was being scrutinised. I knew the world was watching and that made my plight worthwhile: it serves the cause to be the one visibly taking the flak. Some part of me was horrified at the idea of being branded a criminal for doing our work, but I knew enough to appreciate it could only highlight the issue of justice. There's no bravery involved in such a position, only cunning. I was asked to sign in my personal belongings, which amounted, on this good day, to a single Biro pen and about £250 in cash. I was instructed to strip, which I did, immediately donning prison garments of a grey pullover and grey pants. Oscar Wilde, when he was transferred to the same prison in 1895, created a noble stir when he found that his waistcoat was missing. 'Pray pardon my ebullition of feeling,' he said to the warder. I'll try to keep the words 'like Wilde' out of this, and say nothing about my own poor stock of waistcoats, but the Irishman couldn't fail to come to mind in that rank Victorian slammer. My lawyer later said I had been languishing in Oscar's cell: I'm not sure, but the spirit of the man, his fight against prejudice, was indwelling. He was treated horribly and kept in conditions as inhumane as they were heartbreaking, and I have to say it was other prisoners, past and present ones, who were on my mind at Wandsworth.

I thought a lot about Bradley, the young American soldier who was suffering harsh treatment in an American jail, summarily condemned, in my opinion, for allegedly raising the alarm on an illegal war. He was on my mind a great deal in the confines of the cell.

One of the things that happens almost automatically is that you begin to pace up and down. Like a panther in a cage, you have to find an outlet for constrained action. I walked up and down and was sort of planning what to do, trying to get attuned physiologically to this small space. I knew it was ugly and terrible in there, but it wouldn't be for long. You tell yourself these things and try to focus. On the outside world, as they call it, my lawyers were working overtime to get me out, but their world seemed light years away as I walked in circles and felt, like never before, the meaning and the substance of the word 'solitary'.

To reduce the noise, and maybe the cold, my cell's previous occupant had covered the air-vent with a piece of A4 paper. Later, when the warders turned the lights out, I realised that the worst thing, after all, was to be out of communication. I live for the arts of connection, and I suddenly knew how hard it was going to be in there, not hearing, and not being heard. Especially hard given the position of WikiLeaks: we were engaged in communications warfare with a number of opponents, and these were situations that needed directing on an hourly basis. When the light came up in the morning, I knew the first thing I had to do was discover how to make calls. Surely they'd make allowances and give a guy some Internet access? I know, not likely. But my default position is always to hope that the impossible is only the impossible until your imagination proves otherwise. So I kept thinking and kept hoping and eventually I pressed the emergency button.

They allowed me to see the Governor. He decided I should be in the Onslow Wing with the 'at risk' prisoners. Several storeys high and several cells deep, the wing has its own culture within the prison. It seemed I should go there because, in the Governor's opinion, I was at risk of being attacked by other prisoners. It was a strange assumption, because the prisoners I met were quite clearly on my side. In Onslow, the landings were filled with rapists and paedophiles, crime bosses, the occasional celebrity. I was alone in the cell and still had no phone allowance. No phone and no writing materials and no chance of talking with my colleagues. I stood in the cell feeling defiant but ill equipped.

The cell was down in the basement, about two metres by four, with a bed, a washbasin, a toilet, a desk, a closet and off-white walls. Much of the wall space was taken up by a drab grey plastic structure that formed the water and ventilation system for the washbasin and toilet. These were designed to minimise the possibility of self-harm, but this also meant that everything was dull, smoothed off, and hidden. There were no taps in the washbasin, no flush handle on the toilet, no cistern. Everything was automated or operated by touch. There was a medical emergency button on the wall by the bed and a curtain to pull around the toilet. At the top of one wall was a small window, with bars across it at four-centimetre intervals, that looked out onto the prison exercise yard, a small space enclosed by a high mesh fence, topped with layers of razor wire. Sometimes in the mornings I would see the legs of prisoners in the yard passing by the window, hear shouts, snatches of

jokes and conversation. Above the cell door an infrared surveillance camera looked into the room, armed with a bank
of LED lights that glowed a dull red throughout the night,
constantly watching. The cell door was unmarked apart
from a single spyhole in its centre, covered on the outside
by a metal flap.

The other prisoners were curious about me, so the metal
flap on the cell door was constantly being flipped up as they
looked in to see what I was doing. There's a film of Robert
Bresson's called *A Man Escaped*, a beautiful film, but really
a feat of sound engineering, where a spoon struck against
brickwork can seem orchestral. Every sound was like that
in Wandsworth: full of echo and emptiness. The metal flap
scraped as it was lifted and I sensed an eye. Yes. They wanted
to see what I was up to in my cell. Or what I was like. No
situation nowadays can be considered immune from the
celebrity-seeing eye, and soon there were whispers at the
cell door. Whispers at volume. 'Be careful who you speak
to.' 'You'll be okay.' 'Don't trust anyone.' 'Don't worry about
anything.'

I felt I was in a kind of deviant's *Barbarella*. I wanted to
be out doing my work as a journalist, not stuck here playing
the martyr, and my life's training had made it impossible for
me to stomach the bureaucratic hell of prison and the stig-
matising horror of being reduced by blind authority. Every
hour of your time in prison is a kind of guerrilla warfare
against encroaching paperwork and stultifying rules. In just
applying to buy a postage stamp you risk hypothermia in a
snowstorm of forms. After they moved me to the separa-
tion unit, I continued with my campaign to make calls. It
was Stalinist. It took me most of my time there to win a
phone call to my lawyer. To make such a call you had to be

calling an approved number on a previously submitted list of numbers and you had to have phone credit. There were two types of credit, domestic and foreign. Different forms for that. And the forms were both hard to get hold of and hard to get attended to. I filled in the same forms so many times that the process became like the case of Jarndyce and Jarndyce in *Bleak House*. Unending. I then had to supply the name, telephone number, address and birth date of the person I wanted to call. You had to fill out a form to get a PIN corresponding to your domestic telephone account and another PIN corresponding to your foreign account. It went from being a farce to being a nightmare to being a form of torture. The forms kept coming back and forth or being lost. Once you finally get to the phone you're only allowed to speak for ten minutes. Then you can't make another call for five minutes. They record all the calls except the ones made to lawyers, but further steps have to be taken to prove the speaker is a lawyer. As part of this approval effort the prison will only accept office numbers, not mobiles, despite the fact that lawyers spend their lives on mobiles. And so it goes on, a Kafkaesque miasma of passive aggression and hindrance.

In the end I got to speak to my mother and to my lawyer. I also tried to speak to Daniel Ellsberg, the man who brought the Pentagon Papers to the world. He wasn't in. Turns out he was off chaining himself to the gates of the White House. (They removed his handcuffs to make it impossible.) 'G'day, Dan,' I said to his voicemail. 'Just dropping you a note from the bottom of a Victorian slammer. The message is to other people: "Wish you were here."'

As the days wore on documents began to appear under my cell door, some of them delivered at night, ushered in by whispers. A lot of them were newspaper clippings or articles downloaded and annotated by the prisoner. 'Is Rape Rampant in Gender-Equal Sweden?' said one article. Conspiracy abounds in the confines of a prison, but so does lawyerly empathy: the incarcerated ones have experience, obviously, and many are tough on themselves and tough on the system that surrounds them, taking it for granted that the prison culture can seek to exploit you. Many among my traffic of correspondents – my placers of things under the door – were veritable experts in the miscarriage of justice, which soothed me in the wee small hours. It would be an indulgence to think that all prisoners are innocent, but some of us are, and I felt the documents and letters were a kind of solidarity. There's a lot of anger, too, and I felt angry as I tried to exercise in that small space, walking in a figure of eight like a demented bee.

One morning an envelope arrived with nothing inside. I stood at the window and saw it was still snowing. I think it was 10 December. I later found out the envelope had origi-nally contained a copy of *Time* magazine. My face was on the cover with an American flag covering my mouth. The leader article called me 'an exceptionally talented show-man'. Maybe I am, but I didn't feel like it at that moment. Instead of reading *Time*, I had to do time, and to break the monotony I continued to look for other things in the draughty space beneath the door, the stuff meant for Pris-oner Number A9379AY. That's how it works, keeping you quiet, keeping you in the dark, reducing you to a serial number, while you look for the light that's beneath doors and beyond walls.

One of the most enlightening articles posted under my door came from a prisoner called Shawn Sullivan. It was a copy of 'the Extradition Treaty Between the Government of the United Kingdom of Great Britain and Northern Ireland and the Government of the United States of America', signed by David Blunkett and John Ashcroft in March 2003. Article 7 related to Capital Punishment, suggesting that a state of whom extradition is requested might refuse if the requesting country considers the offence to be punishable by the death penalty. American politicians had already called for my extradition to face charges under the espionage act. Congressman Peter T. King wrote to Hillary Clinton to say that I was at the head of a 'terrorist organisation' and should be treated as such – the same Peter King that used to shake his little collection tin up and down the streets of New York City raising money for the IRA, the self styled 'Ollie North of Ireland'. It amazed me to think about how these guardians against 'offences' were themselves so offensive. I read the document and realised again that I was, no matter what they said of me or invented about me, merely a figure in something much larger than myself. I could only keep my head clear, absorb the flak and the caricaturing of my nature and my motives, and continue working.

Letters arrived, and I sent some, too, but always with difficulty, as the bureaucratic machine ground on. A jail is like an island, on which the inmates can seem unreachable; it is also a concrete, living idea of abusive power, and the letters helped me to feel cared for during those difficult days in Wandsworth. The letters showed another country from this England of slopping out, where people realised that they themselves must embody the arguments for their own liberty. From Hampshire: 'Dear Julian, You will not know me. I am just one of millions of citizens around the world who know what is going on, and are not blinded to the political games of which you have become a victim.' From Tulse Hill: 'You must always remember that the achievement of WikiLeaks is vital for the development of our world. P.S. Sending a puzzle book to keep you thinking.' From Basingstoke: 'I support your stand and feel you are being victimised and harassed by powerful forces.' From Yorkshire: 'Can you hear the sound of falling masonry? Keep up the good work. You are welcome in North Yorkshire any time. Excellent broadband in this part of the world, too.' From Essex: 'I think your case has made many people sit up and think a little more deeply about power, politics and corruption.' From Merseyside: 'We thought about you last night and hoped you were safe in that unpleasant place. When you are released, can you come up to the North West and explain to people the importance of freedom of thought, speech and information?'

Some of the mail came in the form of Christmas cards, simply signed 'An Old Lady', or 'A Friend'. Perhaps less friendly, though delivered around the same time, was a cutting from the *Washington Times*, 'Assassinate Assange?' The author of this alliterative pleasantry, one Jeffrey T. Kuhner, placed a chill on the warm cards. 'Mr Assange is not a journalist or publisher,' he wrote; 'rather he is an enemy combatant – and should be treated as such.' If there could be any doubt as to Kuhner's meaning he dispelled it in his concluding sentence: 'We should treat Mr Assange the same way as other high-value terrorist targets: Kill him.'

I suppose I should have been shocked to find myself subjected to this sort of rhetoric from a fellow journalist, but I had learned long before that too many journalists are nothing more than stenographers for the powerful. Why should I be surprised to read that Jeffrey Kuhner wanted me dead when I had already been called 'an anti-American operative with blood on his hands' by the TV star and governor-impersonator Sarah Palin? And if the Attorney General Eric Holder thought I was 'an enemy of the US', why be shocked to read that the Fox News neocon Charles Krauthammer wanted me looking over my shoulder every time I walked down the street? Former Bush advisor Jack Goldsmith may have thought he was praising the US media when he said that their 'patriotism' made it easy for the government to work with them, but if I ever received such a 'compliment' I think I would resign.

On my way from exercise yard to cell, or from library to cell, I found my fellow inmates staring at me. The authorities were paranoid about the possibility of a prisoner taking a picture on his mobile phone. They're not supposed to have mobiles, but many do, and it seemed likely that a picture would end up in one of the newspapers. So the Governor appointed a guard who accompanied me everywhere. 'They think everyone is out to get me,' I said to him.

'Who?'

'The authorities.'

'Well,' he said, 'everyone has a price and these people have nothing.'

I met with a Catholic chaplain in one of the meeting rooms. There wasn't much in the way of spiritual guidance, not that I'm the perfect candidate, but the man was from Uganda and I felt a connection and we laughed as we talked. On the way back through the hallway I spotted Solzhenitsyn's *Cancer Ward* on a bookshelf. I took it back to my cell and got lost in it, just the old wisdom about inhumanity and the solace of the gracious book. An educated, middle-class woman appears in the story; her husband is in a labour camp and she wonders what she should tell their son. "'The truth's enough to sink a grown man, isn't it?" she says. "It's enough to break your ribs. Or should I hide the truth and bring him to terms with life? After all, the boy's got eyes of his own, he can see."

"Burden him with the truth!" declared Oleg.'

On the outside there were acres of press coverage. I heard as much from my supporters, and it gave me pause for thought: Cablegate now represented the biggest release of classified material in history. And I paused too over the costs and causes of the Swedish affair. By not ringing those women back, had I really left the door open for hatred? Time may unfold sequentially but experience does not always. I was thinking in prison about the shape of my life, about these opportunities, these crises, and in the end my mind was taken up with the world beyond them. Had I made an error of judgement, or was it all proportionate in terms of what I was trying to achieve? Had I kicked the Yanks in the shins too hard? The case would pass, after much tribulation for all those involved, I supposed, but it would pass, and I would learn from what had occurred that shocking year. Yes. In solitary confinement I felt I had enough anger to take me through a hundred years, but my task was to get on with our publishing work and to watch the world respond.

My bail hearing took place at the City of Westminster Magistrates' Court on Horseferry Road on 14 December. The court was packed and so was the street outside as I approached in a police van. Someone said the roads around Victoria were treacherous, and I smiled, thinking, 'I've known treachery, so let the roads be at peace with themselves.' The Prosecution was keen to oppose bail under any circumstances and to portray me as some kind of James

Bond villain, well connected and full of computer wizardry, likely to outfox the forces of surveillance. It was implied by them that I would hack into the system of tagging. I'm sure we could, but, as usual, the Prosecution, like much of the press, was falling for the lesser kind of fiction. They needed a villain with silver hair, some kind of cat-stroking nutcase bent on serial seduction and world domination. It was interesting – it was alarming – to see how much they allowed a sense of justice to be confused by the many fantastical headlines surrounding me. There was no point opposing it. An impression had been created, and I had neither the skill nor the will to outflank it. But I always knew my lawyers would have to struggle with a Prosecution, and a press, who thought they were watching a movie as opposed to trafficking in a person's life.

The judge at one point berated the public gallery for using Twitter. That seemed symbolic enough. When it comes to the British courts, it is often contempt that breeds Contempt, and there was always what you might call a generational refusal at the heart of my case. (Eventually, a council of elders at the High Court decided, after the fact for us, that the use of Twitter was permissible in court.) There was a lot of fuss about bail money, too. Although I'm an activist and head of a not-for-profit organisation, the film-script headlines encouraged them to set my bail at an eye-watering £240,000. I was still thinking, 'I'm not going to be a victim of this situation. I am not a criminal.' That same feeling had been very strong as I arrived in the van that afternoon. The cameras were banging again on the glass and I looked up, holding my fingers in a 'peace' sign. That photograph made all the papers, but it was just an impulse, an attempt by me to say, 'You will not turn me into a cowering criminal.'

They had tried to crush me in that little prison, but I came to the court that day sure that the narrative was coming together, not on their terms, but on those of my supporters and me.

I was still in danger, though. I was beginning to realise that danger was probably where I lived now. But I stood in the dock pitching my sense of decency and truth against theirs; in my own mind this was a show trial and where they couldn't pick holes in our arguments they would drive horses and carriages through my character. I was learning the game. But I stood there in the dock with a certainty they didn't know me. Maybe I was a figment of their own fearful imaginations; the Prosecution, like many a politician in many a country, saw in me a threat, where a great many ordinary people saw in our organisation an opportunity. I looked at my supporters in the gallery and waved.

I was granted bail on the 14th only to be told that the Swedish authorities had appealed against the decision and that I would have to be sent back to Wandsworth. It was hard to take, having to leave my friends and supporters behind once again, having to leave the talking to my lawyers, having to sit inside the prison van once more as it crawled through the media scrum. It was hard to enter my cell once more and hear the door shut behind me. But as I had told my mother before the hearing, my convictions were unfaltering and my ideals were not shaken by my circumstances.

After two more nights in jail I was back in court, the High Court this time, on 16 December. Those two days in court became about technical requirements. I have nothing profound to say about the judge, except to suggest that he behaved throughout as if there was a correspondent from the *Times* perched on his shoulder. It was hard otherwise to see why he reckoned my bail should be so high and my tagging so severe. In his mind I was some kind of shadowy, movie-style kingpin, likely to disappear at any minute in a puff of smoke, a souped-up helicopter, or a hail of laser-fire. In fact, my circumstances were more ordinary than he could have known. I had no home and no car, I had hardly any possessions, and a bag of phones. He just didn't get it, and meted out punishment as though it might be pre-emptive. I had no charge against me and was wanted for questioning in a country whose motives I presently had no reason politically to trust. That was it.

Finally, the money raised for bail by my supporters came through, and the Swedish appeal was rejected. I was about to be free. How long that freedom would last was question-able. I was to be kept under a kind of house arrest at the home of a supporter in Norfolk pending the extradition hearing in February. But at the High Court the moment was for jubilation. In a private way, I felt the time in jail had been traumatic, emboldening and instructive; I finally saw the size and the scale of what WikiLeaks was doing. The experience sent me reeling back into my own past, and it confirmed the future. We were now officially up against the power of the old order, up against its assumptions, up against its power to silence people, up against its fears.

I appeared on the steps of the court just before 6 p.m. This would be good for the live feed to the evening news. My lawyers beside me, I immediately heard the cheers and saw a mob of photographers and journalists. It was dark but the whole scene was bright with camera flashes. Such a lot of people, and you couldn't see beyond about ten feet because of the dark and because of the snow that was falling heavily. I stood there, and everything eventually quieted down, and I thought of what to say. I had a lot of people to thank and, in a way, while it was a time for celebration I was also thinking of those men and women around the world still in jail, still in solitary confinement, ignored by the media, with no one to put up bail money and with no prospect of release.

Doesn't snow have a way of softening things, of calming the rush of life and muffling the sound? I definitely thought so as I stood there and clarity came. The snow was backlit with hundreds of cameras flashing. I just looked into it for a few seconds and it occurred to me on the steps of the court that I had travelled a very long way to see such snow.

2

MAGNETIC ISLAND

For most people, childhood is a climate. In my case, it is perfectly hot and humid with nothing above us but blue sky. What I recall is a feeling on the skin and the cool nights of the tropical savannah. I was born in Townsville in North Queensland, Australia, where the trees and the bush crowded down to the sea and you looked over to Magnetic Island. In the summer the rains came and we were always ready for floods. It was beautiful, actually. Heat like that goes down into the bones and never leaves you.

The people of Townsville lived in suburban housing, many of them living the 'Australian dream' of a small house and car. In the late 1960s there was an army base nearby. The population was about 80,000 and the local economy dealt in wool and sugar, or in minerals and timber from the region. For some reason there were a lot of Italians, many of them working on the cane farms, and I remember the closed sense of community that existed among them. Italian was the second most spoken language. It must have been a conformist kind of place in many ways, filled with quietly industrious people growing bored in the constant sunshine. You could say it was a distant province in a country that was itself a distant province of the world. That would describe how it seemed to my mother's generation. By 1970, she was keen to see the world, or at least to see it changed.

That year my mother bought a motorbike. She was a bright and creative girl who loved to paint, so quite soon, aged eighteen, reeling from the mediocrity of her schooldays, Christine hopped on her bike and drove the 2,000 miles to Sydney. She was a country girl, though, and she later told me Sydney was too much. But life was happening right in front of her, as it tends in all our cases to do. She was standing one day on the corner of Oxford Street and Glenmore Road in Paddington, just opposite the Victoria Army Barracks, when she saw a massive anti-Vietnam War demonstration slide past her like a modern history tableau. Though she didn't understand much about it, my mother wanted to join this great tide of feeling. As she stood there, what she remembers as a gentle voice appeared at her ear. It belonged to a twenty-seven-year-old, cultured guy with a moustache. He asked her if she was with anyone and when she said 'no' he took her hand.

About 60,000 Australians were involved in the war in Vietnam. It turned out to be the longest conflict they'd ever got involved in: 500 men lost their lives and 3,000 were wounded. In May 1970, around the time my parents met, the anti-war demonstrations were at their height in Australia; about 200,000 people marched in the major cities, some of them being arrested, as the law then allowed, for not having a permit to hand out leaflets. The 1970s are now routinely called 'the decade of protest' in Australia (Gay Pride happened in Sydney in 1973) and my parents – the bright young creative girl and the cultured demonstrator who walked into her life – were dyed-in-the-wool protestors. There was something theatrical about it, a conservative society finding its voice, and I must have taken it in with my mother's milk, the idea that non-conformity is the only real passion worth being ruled by. I believe I was conceived in that spirit.

Back in Townsville on 3 July 1971, my mother was taken to the Basel Hospital, and I was born around three in the afternoon. She says I was round, dark-haired, loud, with the look of an Eskimo.

It would be safe to say that Christine, my mother, has – and had then – a natural disinclination towards doing what she was told, and I soon picked it up. My grandmother remembers my sense of dreamy wonderment, and I'm not in a position to argue with her, though it seems reasonable to assume I might have been dreamily wondering at an early age what was happening at the Townsville army base. In any case, my grandmother rocked me to haunting Greek melodies recorded by Maria Farandouri and I quieted down. When I was a few months old my mother moved us to a cottage on Magnetic Island, to a house with mango and eucalyptus trees outside the windows.

Forgive me for going all Proustian, but I believe my mother bred a sensualist in me, and, somewhere in my mind's eye, I can see the many patterned scarves she hung over the bassinette. The light would pass through them, casting shapes over my hands and legs. When I had grown just a little, my mother took me around in a sling or in a backpack that I loved and soon took to calling Peck Peck. Early childhood is so important, I think. It gives you all your capacity for wonder. My mother had a gift for love and for making life no less interesting than it was. You can't take that for granted. Some people press their children into dullness before they've even opened their mouths. And there's probably something to be said for Magnetic Island itself at that time: it was a freedom-haunted place, a beautiful Eden of about a thousand inhabitants, where people who didn't fit in any place else came to live. It might have been a lush and forgotten hippy republic, and I can't discount its early influence; like hoop pines or cabbage palms, a child will tend to hang as he grows, and something of Magnetic Island would stay with me.

My first word was 'Why?' It was also my favourite. And though I didn't love the play pen, I loved the books that my mother would store in there beside me. I learned to read that way, with Ladybird books, supplemented later with Tarzan and Dr Seuss and *Animal Farm*. From the beginning we moved around a lot, but Magnetic Island – named by James Cook, who thought it interfered with his compasses – was a place to come back to. When I was two my mother met a man called Brett Assange, a musician and travelling theatre guy who proved a good stepfather to me. A lot of my family's energy was devoted to the life outdoors. We swam every day and later I fished with my grandfather in the Sandon River or at Shark Beach. I remember rolling down the hills with my mother on her bike, and as we sped along I would stretch out my hands and try to grasp fruit from the trees overhead. We trekked from one place to another, always, for me, with a sense of discovery, the perennial 'Why?' never far from my lips. My parents weren't shy of 'Why?' They would lay out the possibilities and let me decide for myself.

By the time I was five I had already lived in many houses. I think we had a sense of North Queensland being a moveable feast: I carried the climate with me and just breathed curiosity. My mother wasn't a constant activist, but she knew the power of change. Around then, living for a time in Adelaide, we went door-knocking to stop uranium mining. We banned tuna from our house because of the harm the fishing nets did to dolphins, and later, when the blockade forced a change in fishing practices, we rejoiced and felt our own efforts had played a part in producing the result. Another time, in Lismore, my mother was jailed for four days as a result of her participation in a protest to stop logging in rainforests. I'd say it was a gentle but firm education in the arts of political persuasion. We always felt change was possible.

I exhibited my share of cruelty, too. It was a Tom Sawyer kind of childhood in many ways, with long days spent outdoors, learning how to master the environment and conquer danger. I was fond of my magnifying glass and would march through the bush with it. The cruelty was a matter between me and the sugar ants, which trooped across the ground and often found themselves sizzled under my lens. The ants would climb up your trousers and bite you. Worse were the green tree ants, common in Australia among the forests and low-lying places. Not only did they bite, they sprayed a burning fluid from their abdomen onto the wound. There were so many species of ant and none was immune, so far as my infant mind was concerned, from the power of my spying glass. It seemed natural to enhance the power of the sun to punish hostility. The war between five-year-old boys and ants is legendary.

There were others sorts of hostility, too. My parents travelled with a small fold-up theatre – they did shows, little

theatricals, later involving puppets – and I suppose they
were bohemians. They were against the war and had demonstrated; they'd been in and out of the cities. They were
worldly in a way that wasn't always typical in Queensland,
especially among the non-hippy community. My mother
had modelled and acted, and together they designed sets
and read books. To some people it was no kind of life to
live, and I suppose that was my introduction to prejudice.
We came back to Magnetic Island one time and got a house
up in the hills. The atmosphere was clammy and the heat
would make people lethargic; atmosphere is important in
Australia, and in many places, creating not only a physical
state in people but a mental state as well, and when I think
of that house on the island I think of a certain constric-
tion in people that borrows from the weather. Some of our
neighbours were constricted in that way, perhaps especially
in reaction to my parents' notions of freedom.

My parents had a gun to deal with snakes. There were
snakes in the bath from time to time. One day we came
back up the hill to discover the house was on fire. About
twenty local people were standing around as the flames
licked around the veranda. No one was attempting to put
out the fire and suddenly all this ammunition in the house
exploded. I remember one of the neighbours laughing and
saying we couldn't stand the heat. It was all very sinister,
and the fire brigade took forty minutes to come. In many
ways that fire is my first, very big and complicated memory.
I remember lights and colours and incidents from before,
but this was something else. It involved levels of human
complication that would come to fascinate me. The locals
seemed to take a certain delight in the idea of pretension
and daring getting their comeuppance. I noticed, probably

for the first time in my life, how authority could drag its heels to make a point and how bureaucracy could make a stone of the heart. There was something demonic in the way they let 'nature' take its course.

So, here was municipal power. And I was moved by it. It might seem invidious to look for sources of character in your life, but it might be counted forgivable in a journalist and essential in an autobiography. Early on, I became fascinated by how things work. As soon as I could handle the tools, I began picking engines apart. I began building rafts. I loved mechanical Lego. When I was six I tried to make a crude metal detector. That was my earliest sense of the world: as of its being a place where you could work things out, show a little scientific curiosity, build something new.

At an early stage I realised there was a social element to all this. I put a gang together, the better to get things done and have fun while doing it. We used to go to this large, defunct slate quarry. There had been a mine there but everything was abandoned: the storage sheds still stood, the hauling equipment and even, inside the sheds, the logbooks and all the paraphernalia of explosive devices and such. We'd go up there frequently. I suppose we saw it as our domain, a place where we could exist independently of authority. The rocks and abandoned sheds were covered in these scurrying lizards – blue-tongued lizards and skinks – and there were sometimes wallabies up there, too. The quarry was surrounded by a bamboo forest and sometimes I would take myself off alone to explore between the thick hollow trees. I remember fighting my way to the centre of it one very hot day. I felt alone but quite powerful in the effort to get through, and, when I made it, I got out my knife and carved my name on a thick chunk of bamboo. I went back there about eight years ago and was surprised to find how easy it was to move through the forest – although it didn't diminish the power of those memories. My childhood stands out in my mind for its bigness, the vividness of its impressions, and I think that some of my desire to uncover the world's hidden secrets comes from those early explorations.

I went to well over thirty schools in all. It was just that kind of life, in which consistency was a matter of style and values, not of where you parked your car or how you paid your debts. Later on in my childhood, the peripatetic existence became more hysterical. We were later much more like fugitives, my mother and I. But early on, it was heavenly. And it gave me a sense of meeting new challenges all the time. With mum and Brett, it felt like we were gulping down experience without fear. During that early period, I had a happy childhood, and it was partly to do with the joy of discovery and the certainty that rules were there to be broken.

Within the little gangs I headed up we had our share of children's wisdom and a whole stack of prejudice. At one time, I think we felt the Italians were a sort of adversary. They had this habit of paving. They'd buy a house with bougainvillea outside, this wonderful blush of colour, and would immediately clear it all and pave the garden and put up Doric columns. I'm ashamed of it now, but I took against this. It seemed important to me then to take a stand against this thing. I was probably the kind of child who was shopping for things to take a stand against. I remember one day my folks were making dinner and found they were short of tomatoes. The Italian neighbours had loads of tomatoes. My mother had asked for some and had been refused, and this got to me. So the next day I began digging a tunnel from our garden to theirs. I got some of my little gang involved, bringing shovels and candles to get the job done. It was hard work, but we got under the fence in secret and came away with two baskets of tomatoes. I handed one of them to my mother and she had this grin. We waited to see what would happen, and what happened was that two policemen quickly turned up at the door and they, too, were grinning. The policeman just stood there rocking on their heels. It was my first run-in with the law. We handed back one basket of tomatoes, and the scandal reverberated. But I was happy that I still had the second basket of tomatoes hidden.

I don't know if I was eccentric or whatever, but I know I was single-minded. They sent me to some kind of Steiner-style school where it was all about expressing yourself. There was a scooter, I remember, and an obnoxious little girl who wouldn't share. In accordance with the school's philosophy, I decided to express myself without hindrance, so I hit the girl over the head with a hammer. This caused a giant fuss, of course, and I had to leave, although the girl was fine.

We just kept moving. Lismore, about 130 miles from Brisbane, is the place I associate more with my schooldays. You could say Lismore was the centre of the counter-culture in Australia, and it later became a Mecca for backpackers, a place where people seeking an alternative lifestyle came to roost. The second Aquarius Festival, the Aussie Woodstock, was held around Nimbin in 1973, and many people stayed on and set up co-operatives. My parents ran a puppet theatre. Over those years, there was a sense of fight-back against corporate agencies. Dairy farming was under threat from the big company Norco, and the Australian rainforest, famous at one time as the 'Big Scrub', was completely cleared in a way that left a scar on the land. My people cared about these things and I, in turn, came to care, too. School was at the local village of Goolmangar. I liked the idea of people, especially men, who could stand up for themselves and I was nurtured in this by a very excellent teacher called Mr King. In my view, even then, a lot of teachers were prissy, but this guy was strong in a way that seems important. He was this very competent individual and I felt safe with him. I think so much of my personality comes from what you might call congenital temperament, but experience plays its part, and I clung to the idea of manly competence as represented by this one good teacher. But, generally, I found school to be an agony of boredom. I wasn't the brightest person ever, but I was hungry for learning and facts, and the system just moved so slowly. I remember praying to God to make things move more quickly. I said, 'I don't think there's a God, but, if there is, I'll trade you two of my little fingers just to make this whole school thing go faster.'

At the same time I had this interest in generating children's lore, the kind of information, the kind of opinion, that passes for wisdom among the very young. I suppose I was good at it, creating believable factoids that worked their magic on my peers. I loved passing on my discoveries to them, like the time I maintained, quite convincingly, that rolling in the dirt was the perfect way to stop bleeding. I had this view that adults were the gods on earth, my mother the Supreme Being, but naturally I began to see that adults were fallible. Real life kind of begins at that point, when you see how adults in responsible positions are merely powerful and not necessarily in the right. It's the big lesson. I was able to see failures in compassion and sometimes I saw brutality. Australia was still quite provincial then, before the Internet, before cheap air travel, and you would be caned at school for misdemeanours. Going to so many schools, I was always trying to establish myself in a new pecking order. And at the same time I was trying to abolish the pecking order altogether. Brutality crept in, and so did injustice and prejudice: at times I was a font of transgression, and that was a difficult thing to be in rural Australia back then. In one of my schools, I was dragged up to the Principal's office on an unknown charge and was beaten with a cane for some mysterious 'indiscretion'. It later transpired that there had been a theft and my peers had pinned it on me.

I was drawn to books. Books and magnets. My grand-father remembers me coming to summer school with a bag of books, one of them a giant biography of Albert Einstein. That could've got me hated, I suppose, but if you're not in the habit of thinking like that, you never will. There was just this lovely confluence, for me, between the physical world and the life of the mind, and I dived into both at that age. And you could say it has coloured everything I've done since then. Everything. My sense of computers and my sense of justice and my view of authority. It was all there during this period in Goolmangar and I felt the force of my own personality coming out.

I had these ethical adventures in my childhood and they made me bigger. One time there was an anti-war rally and my parents had commissioned themselves to create a piece of live street theatre especially for it. Mum made a Styrofoam M16 rifle, painted black with a shoulder strap. My stepfather was dressed in fatigues from the army surplus place, and we went to the butcher and ordered two pints of blood. I remember the strange looks we got.

We drenched my stepfather in the blood and later that day he got arrested because of the fake gun. Later, my mother helped this guy who was engaged in guerrilla scientific studies of the nuclear test site at Maralinga in the Australian desert, where, with the agreement of the Australians, the British had conducted both 'major' and 'minor' tests of nuclear weapons between 1952 and 1963. The 'minor' tests, in which nuclear bombs were set alight, or blown up in amongst conventional explosives, or placed on aeroplanes that were deliberately crashed, were actually far worse than had been publically acknowledged, scattering radiation over a wide area. The British and the Australian governments, however, denied that there had been, or was, any danger to servicemen or to the Aboriginals that lived in the area. This turned out to be a lie, although they would only admit it years later. So this friend of my mother was searching for the truth, and I remember, one night, we had just come from there and were driving along a highway with this guy at about two in the morning. The guy noticed we were being followed, so we quickly dropped him off, then, further down the road, my mum and I were pulled over by the federal police. The policeman told her she might be described as an unfit mother, out with a child at 2 a.m. He told her she should stay out of politics. And she did after that. But I didn't.

School was a problem, though. Even Mr King, who taught me all sorts of things and was a masculine role model, couldn't make up for this lingering sense of waste that attached itself to school in my eyes. Perhaps I was just bred to hate the system and this was the system. I started wearing my hair long in spite of injunctions not to. Weirdly, I've always been ridiculed or judged on account of my hair, and it started early. My parents advised me to cut my blond mop, just to make it easier for me, but I wouldn't do it and I thrived on a kind of defiance. Before long I was refusing to tie my shoelaces in the normal way. I devised this elaborate system of wrapping the laces round the ankle and tying with a knot rather than a bow, and I began teaching this method to the other kids. Then I decided to dispense with shoes altogether and the teachers considered this to be a crime. I was often the new boy in school. So many times: the new boy. And I'd make my mark with these acts of defiance. We had no TV at home. There was hardly any money. We went to markets sometimes to scavenge for cabbages. I was happy with all this; it was part of the colour of life; it was part of doing things your own way. Only during one period of being a teenager was I ever status-conscious. I didn't want my mother dropping me outside school in an old crap car. But that was an aberration and it didn't last.

We had a feeling for animals. People had a sense of us, usually a disparaging sense of us, as hippies, but really we were just nature-lovers and natural non-conformists. At one time we kept chicks that gave us eggs, and three goats for milk. Our beloved dog Poss had to vie for attention with a veritable travelling menagerie comprising a donkey, a pony, a litter of mice – which my mother directed in candle-lit 'shows' – and at a cottage we once lived at on a pineapple farm our lives were taken over by possums. A large grey bird called a brolga took up residence, too. There was a sense that we were always seeking refuge from modern life. I was deeply invested, I now see, in trying to grow into a system of thinking about the relation between people and things. Years later I would study quantum mechanics and begin to see, but then I just grappled with the world on offer, my parents' world, though I lost myself very happily for a time in keeping my own hive of bees.

My mother and stepfather split up when I was nine. It didn't seem so devastating at the time, but it represents, with the benefit of hindsight, the end of a relatively paradisical period in my life. As I said, there had been a Tom Sawyer feeling at the centre of my young years, a beautiful world of discovery, and the adventures of the near future would be altogether darker. Many of us see the safe environs of early childhood in a halo of light, and, for me, despite our rapid coming and going, our many houses and my hatred of school, those years were lived in a state of natural illumination. The world was fresh and the ocean was clear and the air smelled of the white gum tree. But human nature is more complicated, of course, than its physical setting, and life would not be life if it didn't cede to dark complications. Brett had his own struggles and, eventually, my mother couldn't cope with him any more, so we moved to a flat above a shop-front in Lismore that my mother shared with the Nomad Theatre Company. Mum often earned money as a face painter at markets, and later on my younger half-brother and I would trundle along. For a while I took up a mouth organ and played the pre-adolescent blues.

My mother and I had tried to live respectably in town, but we were about to embark on a peripatetic life largely fuelled by anxiety, drifting once more down the Mississippi. We would see a lot of Australia over the next few years – we'd seen a certain amount already – but for at least five years we felt pursued, and I suppose those years, as much as the happy years before, shaped the kind of person I was to become in the future. Our life with Brett had brought sunshine and art, music and nature, into our everyday experience. Brett's theatre productions, the way they could be rolled out and packed up in no time at all, was good preparation for WikiLeaks, but the next part, the part involving a man called Leif Meynell, would show us what it was like to be pursued by shadowy forces. He was my first tail.

3

FLIGHT

My mother's people came to Australia from Scotland in 1856. The head of the clan was James Mitchell, a tenant farmer from Dumfries, who lived at the same time as the radical Scots poet Robert Burns, another farmer. Burns protested all his life against injustice and tyranny, penning a universal 'Marseillaise' to the human spirit, 'A Man's a Man for a' That'. The poet died in poverty in Dumfries just as my kinsman Mitchell was growing up, and he would have understood the Mitchell family's wish to emigrate. Like him, they were Protestants subject to the laws of the established Church of Scotland, and life was hard for them in the soggy fields.

Hugh Mitchell, with Anne Hamilton and five children, set himself up as a dairy farmer in New South Wales, at Bryans Gap, near Tenterfield. He was well known in the New England district, and died at the age of eighty-four, leaving an estate of £121 and a son, James, just like him, who in time took up a freehold on land at Barney Downs. James was an able horseman and he served as a volunteer in the Boer War. On 2 June 1900, he wrote a letter to his son Albert from Bulawayo in Rhodesia, telling of the hard time he was experiencing in the regiment and saying how frustrated he was not to find himself fighting at the Front. This complaint – the complaint of many a serving soldier – was answered by fate, who saw to it that eight weeks later he was part of a garrison in the Transvaal that came under a heavy Boer barrage, and James Mitchell, a squad sergeant-major, died of wounds. The man who buried him wrote a letter home. 'It was a sad duty for us,' he wrote, 'the saddest I have seen in South Africa . . . This war is a sad, cruel business.' Other ancestors of mine, on my father's side, the Kellys and the Greers, owned the Imperial Hotel at Nundle, after coming from Ireland. My paternal great-grandfather, James Greer Kelly, had four sons who were brilliant sportsmen, well known for their prowess at cricket and football. He also had a daughter, Miriam Kelly, my grandmother, who came to Sydney and married a man called Shipton, and together they had my father.

Our early families pass on life to us, as a matter of science, but do they also pass on their ideas? I can't claim to know them, but I can see that this Celtic journey they made for goods and gear, for plots and for gold, also brought with it the yearning for a new world. Some of them on my mother's side suffered for their idealism, in Gallipoli and elsewhere. My great-grandfather, Alfred Hawkins, was on the Japanese prison ship, the *Montevideo Maru*, when it was sunk by a US submarine in 1942. It was, I believe, our family's first known experience of friendly fire. And not just our family: 1,051 Australian soldiers and civilians went down about sixty miles off Luzon in the Philippines, and the wreck was never recovered. A few years ago, there was one surviving witness, a Japanese sailor, who recalled the terrible cries of the Australians as the ship sank. Others, he said, sang the song 'Auld Lang Syne'. History doesn't record where my kinsman was on the ship that night, and whether Alfred Hawkins was crying or singing, but it should be noted that the song 'Auld Lang Syne' was written by that famous Scottish neighbour of ours, Robert Burns.

My own father was missing from my life, and only became part of it again when I was grown up. I'll come to that. But it meant that Brett Assange was the male figure I related to, the good father. Brett was one of those cool 1970s people who were into guitars and everything that went with the music scene. I've got his name – Assange – an unusual one, which comes from Mr Sang, or *ah-sang* in Cantonese: his great-great-great-grandfather was a Taiwanese pirate. He ended up on Thursday Island and married a local girl and moved to Queensland. The name was Europeanised to escape the rampant discrimination against the Chinese.

When I look back to these people, I see a group of families who moved around Australia from crisis to comfort, and mother's story, and mine, was little different. My mother divorced Brett Assange when I was nine. He had been good to me, and was good in general, but not so good to himself, and the end of their relationship represents the end of a kind of innocence in my life.

My stepfather's place in our family was usurped by a man called Leif Meynell. My mother met him as a result of some cartooning work she was doing for Northern Rivers College of Education. I remember he had shoulder-length blond hair and was quite good-looking; a high forehead, and the characteristic dimpled white mark of a smallpox injection on his arm, which at the time I considered as proof that he was born in Australia in the early 1960s, though these inoculations might have been common elsewhere as well. From the darkness at his roots, it was obvious he bleached his hair. And one time I looked in his wallet and saw that all his cards were in different names. He was some sort of musician and played the guitar. But mainly he was a kind of ghost and a threatening mystery to us.

I was opposed to him from the start. Perhaps that's normal, for a boy to resist a man like that, or any man, in fact, who appears to be usurping his father or stepfather. Leif didn't live with us, though my mother must have been besotted with him at first. But whatever her feeling for him was, it didn't last. She would see him off, but he had this ability to turn up and pretend it was otherwise. Eventually, it was a matter of us escaping from him. We would cross the country and only then suffer this sinister realisation that he had found us. He'd suddenly be back in our lives and this grew to be very heavy. He had this brilliant ability to insinuate himself. He punched me in the face once and my nose bled. Another time, I pulled a knife on him, told him to keep back from me; but the relationship with him wasn't about physical abuse. It was about a certain psychological power he sought to have over us.

We had moved again, in about 1980, to this house on a nice stretch of the northern coast of New South Wales, about fourteen miles inland. It was an avocado and banana plantation gone to seed and we rented this property. I remember tying my kite to one of the fence-posts and watching the green light coming through the banana leaves. It was all a bit like a gothic novel set in the tropics, and Leif, I suppose, was Heathcliff in shorts and thongs, coming back like some dark force. My mother became pregnant by him and, seeing the possible impact of my opposition, he tried at first to be reasonable, pointing out that he was now the father of my brother and that my mother wanted him around. 'But if you ever don't want me around,' he said, 'then I'll leave immediately.' He wanted to stay with us, and did, for a time, but I was conscious of wanting to look after my mother and the baby. She had mastitis, and I nursed her through a fever. I nursed her with orange juice. It was very dark around that house at night, with the moon lighting the way, and there was this tremendous feeling of stillness and isolation.

My mother was in love with Leif. And I was too young to understand what sexual love was all about. I just knew that he wasn't my father and that he was a sinister presence. He tried, again and again, to make the case that I should not reject him and he had this thing with my mother and he was my brother's father and everything. But a time came, at that plantation house, when I told him I no longer accepted this deal. He had lied to us in a way that I hadn't known adults could lie. I remember he once said all ugly people should be killed. He beat my mother from time to time, and you felt he might be capable of just about anything. I wanted him to leave, as he had promised me he would, but he denied that the conversation had ever happened.

Nomadism suits some people; it suits some people's situations. We just kept moving because that's what we did: my mother had work in a new town and we would find a house there. Simple as that. Except that the moving in these years, because of Leif, had a degree of hysteria attached, and that, in a sense, took all the simplicity away and replaced it with fear. It would take time for us to understand what the position was, and it was this: Leif Meynell was a member of an Australian cult called 'The Family'. On reflection, I can now see that his obsessional nature derived from that, as well as his egocentricity and his dark sense of control.

The Family was founded by Anne Hamilton-Byrne in the mid-1960s. It started in the mountains north of Melbourne, where they meditated, had meetings and sessions where they used LSD. The basic notion was that Anne happened to be a reincarnation of Jesus Christ, but with elements of Eastern philosophy thrown in, such that her followers beheld a karmic deity obsessed with cleansing their souls. Anne prophesied the end of the world, arguing, quite comically, though not to her, that only the people in the Dandenong Ranges of mountains east of Melbourne would survive. Anne and her husband got rich on the collections that were taken at Thursday meetings. Although the sect was never very large, they doted on her blue aura (she had a lighting system installed to keep her ever-blue), and many of them were middle-class doctors who had grown dependent. The principal power of the sect was based on a network of influence among its members. They were masonic in this way and could call on favours from high places, which explained, to us, why Leif was always able to track us down.

Leif's real surname was Hamilton. He was one of those who had been 'adopted' by The Family. Eventually, Anne Hamilton-Byrne and her husband would be convicted of falsifying adoption papers but at their height they were able to brainwash the authorities. The use of LSD meant that many of the sect members felt they had enjoyed revelations, so were happy to act as 'aunties' when it came to Hamilton-Byrne's child-acquiring mania. At one point, The Family had acquired as many as twenty-eight children. There were little altars to Anne Hamilton-Byrne all over the house and each child was given a personal photograph of her, as if she was Mao. The cult was obsessed with sex and with cleanliness. Anne herself had, it seems, an insane kind of vanity. She hated ugly or fat people and had recourse to cosmetic surgery.

Leif Meynell was part of that cult. And everything he did relating to us was informed by his association with The Family. At one point, running from him, we were living in the Adelaide Hills and we had to move again, this time to Perth in Western Australia. We went to Freemantle, which is now a cool suburb, but then it was mainly an industrial dockyard area. We had a neighbour who knew all about our situation, and, one day, she came back from the milk bar to tell us that Leif Meynell had been in the street. We had to flee. We ended up that time at a house in the Patch, outside Melbourne, on a long narrow plot that slumped down towards a creek at the bottom of the hill. Once I found a dead sheep in this creek, stinking and bloated. I walked backwards and forwards across the creek, using its back as a kind of bridge. It was a time, perhaps, when all sorts of extraordinary things could come to seem pretty normal. It was a cold winter, the puddles freezing over, and my footprints in the mud would be overlain by a layer of ice. They appeared like the steps of a man on the moon preserved under glass. I had to chop wood and stoke a fire every morning to heat the water that passed through coils in the chimney. My main recreation then was bees that I kept outside the house. Every morning I attended to them and quietly watched as they went about their business.

Bees have a way of dealing with predators. They keep moving and they always die away from the hive. I'm sure the isolation I mentioned before, the sense you get in some parts of Australia that civilisation is elsewhere, caused these cults to thrive. In that farming community, they had a strange attitude towards animals, and there was a satanic vibe thereabouts. I even remember a satanic-ritual shop run by a figure called Kerry Calkin. In those parts, it was all fairly pedestrian, but frightening nonetheless. The atmosphere was like *Lord of the Flies*, and our lives at the time were filled with a combination of paranoia and guilt.

It was becoming so tiring. Just moving all the time. Being on the run. We got some intelligence that Leif was drawing close; they told us he was back near us in the hills outside Melbourne. My brother and I showed a lot of resistance that final time: we just couldn't bear the idea of grabbing our things again and dashing for the door. As a bribe, my mother and I told my little brother he could take his prized rooster, a Rhode Island Red, a very tall, proud, strong-looking bird, and also an extremely loud one. To match that, I insisted on taking my two-storey beehive. Picture the scene: a by-now hysterical mother and her two children, along with the pride of their menagerie, stuffed into a regular station wagon and heading up the dirt track.

I had become something of an expert on beekeeping. Also an expert on how to transport them from one place to another. You have to overlay the entrance to the hive with sheets of newspaper. The bees will eventually eat their way through the paper, but, if you judge it right, they won't get through until you've reached your destination. We're driving from Melbourne to Brisbane and the kids are sleeping in the car and the bees are quietly buzzing in their hive. The sun begins to come up and the rooster wants to alert the world, but I've got it by the throat, and I feel this tremble, this spirit of 'Good morning', and all the while I can hear the bees beginning to get angry as they munch through the paper. 'Come on!' I'm saying to my mother, and the entire scene is a nightmare. 'These bees are going to get through the paper and they're vindictive!'

Eventually, we're desperately trying to find a grassy field to let the bees out for a breather and the rooster out for a shit. And the bees are buzzing more and more and the smell of honey and wax is starting to fill the car and the rooster is crowing and we stop the car by a huge church. The rooster jumps out and dashes off, and I open the back of the station wagon and tell everybody to stand back as I prepare to rip off the tape to the entrance of the hive and let them out. The bees are raging. They need to blame something, hopefully something fluffy and brown. Obviously, they attack the rooster, and I'm secretly quite pleased. The thing is running across the field with a swarm of bees attacking its nether regions. And this goes on every day and every night until finally we reach Brisbane. There's no God, and no sense of universal justice, either, but there is nature's own sweet irony. Not long after we set up in Brisbane, I came out one day to see a row of cane toads, about six or seven of them, big and fat, venomous, repulsive, with bloated poison sacks on their backs, and they were sitting right there eating my bees as they came out of the hive. The Aboriginals are known to dry those poison sacks and smoke them to get high. But there was no pleasure in them for me. I had learned my final lesson in how to survive Australia: build your hives a good few feet off the ground as you travel north.

On the run, we learned a little bushcraft. We learned how to get by on very little money and not enough normality. Being unsettled was our normality and we became good at it. There was an Australian traveller called Nat Buchanan ('Old Bluey'), who travelled light and had a gift for exploring Australia and making something of his independence. A book written by his great-granddaughter Bobbie Buchanan, *In the Tracks of Old Bluey*, reveals a man who knew Queensland, a man who knew how to co-exist with animals and humans, a man whose temperament led him to show courage when faced with life's obstacles. Buchanan was a nomad of Irish stock, just like us, and, also like us, he passed his habits on to his children. Difference is, I suppose, that while Old Bluey was chasing nature and finding himself, we were being chased by a force of nature we could barely contend with, and getting lost. Nat was a pioneer, the first man, as Bobbie wrote, 'to cross the Barkly Tablelands from east to west and first to take a large herd of breeding cattle from Queensland to the Top End of the Northern Territory'. Nat died in 1901, more than eighty years before my mother, my brother and I were driving as fugitives past the Tanami Desert. 'Nat was a colourful, if enigmatic character,' his relative's book says, 'whose story is quite remarkable and needs no exaggeration.'

My mother changed her name. We worked out that Leif must have had contacts within the social security admin-istration – that was how The Family is thought to have worked – so it seemed best to change the names that would be held inside the government computer system. But he was quite a gifted talker and would get friends to supply him with information about our whereabouts and he would always catch up. It was a private investigator who eventually came and told us about his close relationship with the Anne Hamilton-Byrne cult. We were living in Fern Tree Gully, and I was now sixteen years old. We'd come to the end of the road. Also, I was feeling almost a man myself and was ready to front-up to him. Masculinity and its discontents could be addressed here, but let's just say I knew I could waste him and he appeared to know it, too. He was lurking round the bounds of the house and I walked over and told him to fuck off. It was the first and the last time, and something in the way I said it ensured that we would never see him again. He would push, for a time, for access to my brother, but his history spoke against him and he was gone.

Truth be told, my mind was in other places for much of the time Leif was chasing us back and forth across Australia. I had always liked taking machines and pulling them apart and rebuilding them. It was, I suppose, a technical instinct, and I was keen not just to push appliances around or switch them on but to understand them. After the departure of Brett the first period of my life was over and I was ready for some heady advancement. I noticed, in a shop in Lismore, a fascinating new machine that instantly spoke to me of something new. It stood in the window: the Commodore 64 computer.

To modern eyes that computer looks laughably primitive, a chunky, boxy mass of grey plastic that ran on disks more than twice the size of the phone in my pocket with less than one-hundred-thousandth of the capacity. You could look at it now and say that it resembled a cast-off from a *Star Trek* set, a childish impression of what the future might look like. But the thing is, to someone like me in a small town in Australia, this really was the future, and I wanted to understand it.

By the time I was sixteen, the computer had become my consciousness. It was the beginning of a new life. Not that the old life didn't have sway – it did, and still does – but in some way it was the computer I spoke with, or spoke through, reaching past all local concerns to an infinity

point where selfhood dissolves into history. Later on, the
question of selfhood, or my selfhood, would come to obsess
many sections of the press. Was I arrogant or crazy, careless
or manipulative, touchy or thin-skinned or tyrannical? But
the self they were talking about was in their heads. It was
part of their fantasy. I was trying to do my work under pressure and wasn't much aware of myself at all, not in the sense
they mean. People nowadays love the play of selfhood: they
think everything is a soap opera. But I mean what I say when
I say my 'self' lies somewhere behind me: with a computer,
and a lifetime's project, you no longer find yourself chasing
from pillar to post the small business of yourself. You
disappear into something larger and you serve it as best you
can.

Maybe it was a generational thing. And some don't get
it. They want to stuff you into their old fictional categories:
of being Billy the Kid or Dr No, of being Robin Hood or Dr
Strangelove. But I believe a generation came of age in the
late 1980s that didn't think like that. We were weaned on
computers, and we didn't reckon on 'selfhood': we reckoned
on 'us', and, if at all possible, 'us and them'. When it comes
to computers, the cliché was of a geek in a bedroom who
was disconnected. In fact, it was the kids watching TV that
were disconnected, passive, solitary. We might have been
up all night, but the best of us were busy making what we
were watching.

To know what your thoughts really are – to grow beyond
them, into the thoughts of others, a very sweet oblivion – is
about placing a large part of your mind into the space of
your computer. Without being grandiose about it, I would
say this constituted not only a new way of being in the
world, but a new way of being in your own skin. People

would always have trouble with it, wishing us, even now, to fulfil the old remits of the ego. But we learned at a young age how commitment works in the computer age: it works by transfusing your lifeblood to an intelligence system dependent on you, and on whom you are dependent. It used to be science fiction, but now it is everyday reality, and I guess I will always seem alien to many people, because I was part of a generation that dug down into our machines, asking them to help us fight for justice in ways that would fox the old guard, even the protest element of the old guard, such as my parents, who didn't know how to break the patterns of power and corruption that kept the world unfair.

Computers provided a positive space in a negative field: they showed us we could start again, against 'self-hood', against 'society', building something less flawed and less corrupt in these fresh pastures of code. One day we knew they would change the world, and they did. The old guard would come with its name-calling and its media, its embedded sense of 'national interests' and patriotism, its accusations of betrayal, but we always knew the world was more modern than they realised. Cairo was waiting. Tunisia was waiting. We were all waiting for the day when our technology would allow an increasing universality of freedom. In the future, power would not come from the barrel of a gun but from communications, and people would know themselves not by the imprimatur of a small and powerful coterie, but by the way they could disappear into a social network with huge political potential.

That was me at the age of sixteen. I was giving myself to my computer. I was testing my sense of the natural world I'd grown up in, all that bright sunlight and leafy shade, all those stars and bees. The years of mystery and human complication went into the computer, too: in some ways I would always be answering the parables of my childhood, from Vietnam protests to cultish surveillance, and that's as close as I can get to the truth. You have to have a self in order to lose it – or use it – and I'm sure the work I have done at WikiLeaks bears the ghostly imprint of my younger years. I say ghostly, because that is how it appears. The work is haunted with first principles and early experiences and that is how it goes.

This is the story of a person who came in time to do a piece of work. The work made a difference in the world. But the story did not begin with the work: the work began with the story. This is why I have taken you back to the wilderness of early childhood, for we both – the work and I – began in those perfect glades of unknowing. At the age of sixteen, I sat at my computer and began to leave everything behind. There were desks, old socks, piles of computer disks and half-eaten sandwiches. The computer and I were one: into the night we went in search of newness. The next phase of life, the phase that included code-breaking and hacking, would indeed prove to be the link that made possible the future we had hoped for. Soon I was wandering inside the computer, inside the inner circle of a network in which hundreds of thousands of computers lived in sync with one another, and there I was, trying to train myself to think in the computers' own language. New life was burning within me, and within the others I met as I walked. I'm sure my face glowed blue in the bedroom of our final house, in the middle of the trees, as the lure of a brand new discovery went far into the night. It seemed as if justice itself might live on the other side of a flashing cursor.

4

MY FIRST COMPUTER

The computers back then came with nothing; they had no programs of their own. That's one of the things lost to the new generation of kids coming to their first computer. They are pre-loaded now with all sorts of software and fancy graphics and so on, but when I started you were just one layer above the bare metal. You were typing into this wonderful emptiness, waiting to be populated with minds. The thing was programmed to accept your typing and that was it: as teenagers, we went into that space exactly like explorers, seeking to discover new terrain. Just like in mathematics, where there is the atomic realm, the computer had a space and a set of possible laws that could be discovered gradually. All laws and modes of operation and side-effects were to be freshly discovered. And that is what we did. The excitement was barely containable, in that, within minutes, you could learn to do something on your computer that was infinite. You could train your computer to type the words 'hello there' to infinity, a command that would never end, and for a young person to discover that kind of deep power is at very least thrilling, and, at most, revolutionary.

Your thoughts had to be clear, though. The computer was not going to do your thinking for you: it was the difference between saying 'I want the computer to count' and saying 'This is how you count'. As teenage computer nerds, we got into the business of precise instruction. School didn't teach us that. Our parents didn't teach us that. We discovered it for ourselves while getting to know the life of the computer. There were guys, of course, who just wanted to play games and that was fine. But a few of us were interested in projecting our thoughts into the computer to make it do something new. We began writing codes and we began cracking them, too.

Wherever we went, I had a desk for my computer and a box for my floppy disks. It was heaven. You would look at the stars and get a certain notion of infinity, then at your computer, and think: infinity resides there, too, but much less remotely. A lot of our initial knowledge came from the people who wrote the computer manuals. The better manuals weren't always easy to get hold of, but we'd pass the information around, and a teenage underground began to form, loose groups of us who had gained access to certain knowledge and could exchange it. It soon became clear that the subculture we were involved in wasn't just local, wasn't just Australian: there was a worldwide subculture of people who would take computer programs invented by software companies and modify them, breaking the encryption codes on them so you could then copy them and give them to your friends. It was mainly for the challenge. The guys who wrote the codes and the guys who broke them were in a kind of competition, except the guys who wrote them were in their twenties and working for companies. We were in our bedrooms laughing at the screen.

Those guys were the authorities. And we never met them. They would sometimes leave hidden messages inside the software, hidden under layers of encryption that we would have to get around, and sometimes the program was built in such a way as to attack parts of our computer as we struggled to decrypt the software. Our relationship with our computers was an important element in our own expanding minds. We had learned so much, so quickly, and we knew that we could teach the computer to expand its own complexity based upon our instructions. The competition between us and those initial software manufacturers actually speeded up the process: we may have been enemies, but together we pushed the art forward, which I suppose is what happens in a very good game of chess.

I began writing programs. Much later on, with WikiLeaks, some people would think it was all about politics. But much of what we are doing is locked into the logic of computer intelligence, and locked into what a precise interaction with computer intelligence makes inevitable. In many respects, nothing has changed since the box bedroom. The ultimate limits of computer power are not determined simply by the man who solders components together in the Chinese factory, they are written into the very meaning of what a computer is. It was Alan Turing who observed that any precise instruction that one could write on paper and give to another human being, could potentially be followed by a computer. And we championed that idea. People might get emotional about it, but it is simply what happens when inventions are allowed to fulfil their potential in company with ongoing human imagination.

By cracking codes we were making the code better, and by writing code we were making the codes harder to crack. It was a circular irony and one that became joyful for teenagers inclined in that direction. Every night was like a new adventure.

I began receiving disks in the post from abroad. From America and Sweden and France, where new friends had cracked codes and would send me the stuff, and I would do the same, all of this postage coming for free because we had worked out a system of re-using stamps. It was great to be alive at a point when so much was changing – so much was new – and to feel the rush of progress flitting through your fingers and over the keyboard. I was sixteen and my time had come: I was finding my calling, my skill, my peer group and my passion, all at once. I'm sure we were, at some level, as arrogant as we were insubordinate, but young men need to feel their own power at that age, and we were flying.

I think it's fair to say Australia was considered then to be some kind of provincial backwater. It suffered from a certain cultural cringe, a definite notion that the country existed as a permanent outback to the main currents of European culture and American life. And in a small way – a small way that became a big way – we opposed that. At this time I was living with my family in the suburbs just outside Melbourne, but I was beginning to take my place within an elite group of computer hackers. We felt we were the dead centre of the turning world, no less significant than cutting-edge computer guys in Berlin or San Francisco. Melbourne was prominent on the world computer map from early on, and we were partly responsible for that: we entertained a global notion of how the technology could work, and never for a second did we feel remote or provincial. We felt we could lead the world, which is a nice thing to feel at the bottom of the planet. Ordinarily, Australia is a lagoon in a sea of Englishness; the culture of Britain tended to wash over us, with its big colonial sense of national values. This had been our reality, so when we fought, we had to fight like kings. The hackers' mentality in Melbourne was unashamed in that way. We had no sense of being away from the main currents: we were the main currents. And given that innovation often relies on self-certainty – however temporary, however misplaced – we found ourselves on top of the world. The Levellers of the seventeenth century aimed to turn a backwater into a political frontline: later historians would speak of *A World Turned Upside Down*. It was Christopher Hill who wrote of the possibility of 'masterless men', a population escaping lordship, who would become renegades or outlaws if need be. My former friends in the computer underground would have enjoyed the words of the Leveller called William Erbery: 'Fools are the wisest of men, and mad men the most sober-minded . . . If madness be in the heart of every man . . . then this is the island of Great Bedlam . . . Come, let's all be mad together.'

It was a time of new ideas, energy, engagement. The idea of popular sovereignty over the Internet, of 'teeming freedom' arriving in that arena, was a way off and would still need to be fought for, and hard. I didn't know it until later, but we could have called on Milton, who wrote a kind of saintly justification for civil disobedience and spoke of 'a nation not slow and dull, but of a quick ingenious and piercing spirit, acute to invent, subtle and sinewy in discourse, not beneath the reach of any point the highest human capacity can soar to'.

We were neither so ambitious nor so capable, but we knew we were onto something that the world had never known before. From our own suburban bedrooms, we were seeking and finding a global computer network. 'The whirlwind comes from the North,' wrote one of the Levelling heroes. Well, maybe. But in a modern world turned upside down, we might call it the south, and give Australia its due. In any event, the energy we had was connected, if only unconsciously, to many a great, untold effort to wrest freedom from the arms of invisible power. Some of us might have been deluded enough to think the future would thank us – it wouldn't. There were prisons waiting for such victims of delusion.

The real morning of revelation came not with the computer, but with the modem. When I got that, I knew it was all over. The past. The old style. Australia as it used to be and the world as it once was. Over. I was about sixteen years old when this fresh dawn came in a little box that dialled up really slowly. Before the Internet, the sense of a global subculture in computing worked through bulletin boards. These isolated computer systems would be set up in, say, Germany, and you would dial in and swap messages and software. Suddenly, we were all connected. There was always a problem with the cost of these international calls, of course, but some of our friends became experts at manipulating the phone lines. They were called phreakers. There is all this nonsense about the early computer hackers stealing from banks and so on: most of the hackers I knew were only interested in pulling back some free phone time. That's as rich as they got; but what riches, to spend the night connected to all this overseas expertise. And the sense of discovery was fairly galactic.

Within a few days of getting my modem, I had written a program to tell the modem how to seek out other modems. It scanned around the central business districts of Australia, and later other parts of the world, to discover which of the computers had modems. I knew there would be interesting things on the end of those telephone lines. I just wanted to find out what the numbers could lead you into; it was almost mathematical, seeing how the numbers could be played with. It's not that it was subversive at that stage: it was simply a great reaching out and a great exploration of the world, and you felt you were riding on some brand new wave, the most technologically sophisticated part of industrial civilisation. It's a grand thought, but it was a grand feeling and I can't diminish it. The thing was sophisticated, but we weren't, and to many of us it was like we were kids breaking into quarries or abandoned buildings. We had to see what was in there. We had to feel the rush of getting over the fence and making it inside. It was the thrill of making it into the adult world and being ready to challenge it.

That's how hacking begins. You want to get past a barrier that has been erected to keep you out. Most of them had been erected for commercial reasons, to preserve profit flow, but for us it was a battle of wits, too, and in time we saw that many of those barriers were sinister. They were set up to limit people's freedom, or to control the truth, which I suppose is just another kind of profit flow. We started by breaking the commercial desires of some companies, and the thrill was exorbitant. It was like the first time you beat an adult at chess. I'm amazed when I run into people who don't understand the pleasure in this, for it is the pleasure of creation itself, of understanding something intimately and making it new. Hacking began to seem like a creative endeavour to us: it was a way of getting over the high walls set up to protect power, and making a difference. Keeping people out of the world's computer systems was, for the people who ran them, a matter of control, much as Orwell understood the meaning of state control, and it was only a natural progression for us to go to work on them as part of our youthful attempt to explore the world.

Governments, of course, had computer systems at this time whose sophistication existed in direct proportion to that nation's wealth and military might. For us the most interesting computer network was X.25, through which most countries ran their classified military computer sites. About eight hackers in the world had discovered and shared the access codes: it was just breathtaking to see how governments and corporations were working together across this kind of network. And the *crème de la crème* of the world hacking community was watching them. I was entering my later teenage years, and the Berlin Wall was about to come down and change everything; a great epochal change in the meaning of ideology that played out on the news every night. But we were already changing the world. When the TVs were switched off, when the parents went to bed, a battalion of young computer hackers were going inside those networks, seeking to create a transformation, I would argue, in the relationship between the individual and the state, between information and governance, that would come in time to partner the wall-breakers in their effort to bust the old order.

Every hacker has a handle, and I took the name Mendax, from Horace's *splendide mendax* – nobly untruthful, or perhaps 'delightfully deceptive'. I liked the idea that in hiding behind a false name, lying about who or where I was, a

teenager in Melbourne, I could somehow speak more truth-
fully about my real identity. By now, the computer work was
taking up a great deal of my time. I was beginning to get
the hacker's disease: no sleep, bottomless curiosity, single-
mindedness, and an obsession with precision. Later, when I
became well known, people would enjoy pointing out that
I had Asperger's or else that I was dangling somewhere on
the autistic spectrum. I don't want to spoil anyone's fun, so
let's just say I am – all hackers are, and I would argue all men
are, a little bit autistic. But in my mid- to late teens I could
barely focus on anything that didn't seem to me like a major
breakthrough. Homework was a struggle; ordinary conversation was a chore. In some way I found myself tuning out
the local noise, the local weather, to maintain a sense of a
frequency that was international. We saw a thousand tasks
and became obsessed with exploring those early networks,
the internet before the 'Internet'. There was this American
system called Arpanet, which, early on, Australians could
only connect to if they were part of a university. That's how
we piggybacked onto the system. It was certainly addictive,
projecting your mind across the world in that way, where
every step was unauthorised. First you would have to hack
the university computer system, then hack your way back
out of it. While inside, you would then hack into some
computer system elsewhere in the world – typically, for me
at the time, the Pentagon's 8th Command Group computers. You'd dive down into its computer system, taking it
over, projecting your mind all the way from your untidy
bedroom to the entire system along the halls, and all the
while you're learning to understand that system better than
the people in Washington. It was like being able to teleport
yourself into the interior of the Pentagon in order to walk

around and take charge, like a film in which you got to bark orders at the extras in shirtsleeves sitting at banks of radar screens. Awesome was the word. And we quickly stepped away from the fantasy of it all to see that some bright new element of the future was being played with. Virtual reality – which used to be a mainstay of science fiction and is now a mainstay of life – was born for many of us in those highways we walked solo at night.

It was spatial. It was intellectual. You had to want to connect to the minds of the people who had built the paths. You had to understand the structure of their thinking and the meaning of their work. It was all wonderful preparation for dealing with power later, seeing how it works and what it does to protect its own interests. The weird thing is you didn't especially feel like you were robbing anyone or engaging in any sort of crime or insurrection. You felt you were challenging yourself. People don't get that: they think we were all rapaciously going after riches or engaged in some dark dream to run the world. No. We were trying to understand the scope and capacity of our own minds, and see how the world worked in order to fulfil a commitment, a commitment we all might have, to living in it fully and making it better if possible.

You would bump into your adversaries inside the system. Like meeting strangers on a dark night. I'd say there were maybe fifty people in the world at that time, adversaries and brethren, equally part of an elite group of computer explorers, working at a high level. On a typical night, you would have, say, an Australian computer hacker talking to an Italian computer hacker inside the computer system of a French nuclear complex. As experiences of young adulthood go, it was mindblowing. By day you'd be walking down the street to the supermarket, meeting people you know, people who have no sense of you as anything other than a slacker teenager, and you'd know you had spent last night knee-deep in NASA. At some basic level, you could feel you were taking on the generals, taking on the powerbrokers, and in time some of us came to feel we were in touch with the central thrust of the politics of our countries. It didn't feel sinister; it felt natural. It didn't feel criminal; it felt liberationist. And in the end, we had no sense of entitlement beyond that which came with our expertise. We owned the box. We looked at the Pentagon or Citibank and we said, 'We hacked that. We came to understand that system. Now part of that computer system is ours. We have taken it back for general ownership.'

None of us ever harmed anybody or caused any damage in our night-time forays, but we were never naive enough to think that the authorities would see it that way. By about 1988, the Australian authorities were trying to establish some test cases to justify a new Computer Crimes Bill, and it was clear I had to be careful. I used to hide my floppy disks inside the beehive. I was sure the guys from the Bureau of Criminal Intelligence wouldn't risk getting stung for real as they went about their sting.

There were some totally inspired hackers who were friends of mine: Phoenix, Trax and Prime Suspect. The latter two bonded together with me into a group we called the International Subversives. We were doing nightly raids on the Canadian telecom company, Nortel, on NASA and on the Pentagon. One time, I got the passwords I needed to access the Overseas Telecoms Commission by phoning their office in Perth pretending to be a colleague. As I spoke, I played around me a tape I had made of fake office

noise – photocopiers whirring, keyboards clicking, a hum
of conversation – just to create the right ambience for
my fraud. They came up with the password in seconds. It
sounds playful, and in a way it was, I suppose. But when the
new legislation came in we went from feeling like climb-
ers breaking into a nature reserve to explore, to criminals
facing ten years in jail. Some of my friends had already been
busted, and I knew it was only a matter of time before I got
raided.

In the event, my brother let them in. He was only eleven.
By sheer good fortune I wasn't there. Anyway, the police had
no evidence and the whole raid was a fishing expedition.
There was a lot of fiction doing the rounds about hackers
stealing from Citibank. Bullshit, actually. We were worried
about stealing electricity to run our computers, and stealing
phone calls and postage, but money, no. Far from looking
for commercial gain, we were careful not to destroy anything in our path. If we hacked a system then we repaired
our way back out of it, leaving, oftentimes, a back door to let
ourselves back in again.

They started tapping some of our phones on a 24-hour
basis. It was weird, and the weirdness crept into the charac-
ters of some of those kids. True to say, some of us were weird
anyway, coming from what are now called dysfunctional
families, where addictions had played a part, where disguises
were already part of the picture. That was true enough of me,
and I was probably one of the less obsessive kids. My friend
Trax, for instance, had always been eccentric and seemed
to suffer some kind of anxiety disorder. He hated to travel,
rarely came to the city and once made reference to seeing a
psychiatrist. But I have often found that the most interesting
people are a little unusual, and Trax was both.

Hacking was a way for us to connect with other kids who didn't feel like hostages to normality. We wanted to go our own way and we had an instinct for questioning authority. In my case, I was born into that instinct. We were born into a permissive society, but our generation was perhaps more questioning of what permission meant. We weren't into '60s psychobabble about freedom – neither were my parents, who always felt the hippies were appallingly apolitical – and what we wanted to do was not protest abusive power but unseat it. If we were at all subversive, it was the kind of subversion that worked from the inside. We had the same mindset as the boys who were running the computer systems. We knew the language and had cracked their codes. The question would increasingly become one of following the inevitable, following the logic of what we had discovered and seeing how it held society to account. Around the time of the Australian bicentenary, 1988, there was a new confidence, a new abundance of home computers, a new vibrancy in popular culture, and a sense among my kind that the military–industrial complex of bombing people and buying stuff should be subverted. We grew up fast and made ready for trouble. We were already being targeted by the Bureau.

It is probably right to say I was more political than many of my friends. I had always believed, and still believe, that oppressive forces draw much of their strength from their ability to wield their power in secret. It wasn't long before I realised, from my experience inside the systems, that the 'clandestine' zone might be the right place to confront them. Hacking gave us a start. We knew from the hysteria our fun had created, and from the new government legislation, that we had hit upon something fundamental about how secrets were hidden. Governments were scared: much more scared, it turns out, than they were of people demonstrating in the street or throwing petrol bombs over barricades. The Internet would offer a model of insurrection that baffled corrupt authority with plain science. It said, 'You no longer control how I think of you.'

One Australian headline, of 1990, read: 'When sharing your disc can be as dangerous as sharing a needle.' This manages to get information-sharing to sound like Aids-spreading, which is pretty much the level of attack we've been dealing with ever since. We were Ned Kelly; we were Robin Hood; we were the Mongol hordes: but, in fact, we were young men in our late teens, discovering what made the world tick and then asking why certain clocks were rigged. We had a finger on the pulse of our new technology and, when the opportunity arose, we wished to use our knowledge for justice and decency. But many people didn't want that. Many authorities hated us. It has been the major element in the story of my life – lock him up, keep him quiet.

Only now, twenty years later, can I see how I was running on nervous energy. I thought high pressure was just how it rolled in a young life, never having known an extended period of calm since I was about ten. The sheer size of our trespassing was beginning to make me shudder. We were kids, and finally we were dealing with forces so sinister, and so powerful, it began to dawn on each of us that we would not only be raided but also that we would likely be marked for life. The world was full of Goliaths and we were vulnerable. Time teaches you – or my time has taught me, anyhow – the ways of smearing and avenging that characterise the powerful when they are forced into a corner. You learn to hold your position, correct errors where you can, keep your chin up and never forget that people who fight grand public liars have always been vilified. The wiles of vilification would become almost comic in my case, but, back then, as a teenager not quite ready for handcuffs, it was hard to keep my bottle. After the raid on my mother's house I felt the shadowy forces getting nearer and nearer. I wiped all my disks and burned all my printouts and ran away from the suburbs with my girlfriend to live in a squat in the city. Life on the run had begun again in earnest, and it would never stop.

5

CYPHERPUNK

The International Subversives were different from other hackers. Some hackers were noisy, leaving footprints everywhere. But we were silent and contemplative. We operated like ghosts, haunting the halls of power, passing like ectoplasm through keyholes and under doors. I always felt hacking was like looking at a painting. You see the canvas, you see the achievement, the movement of the paint and the drawing-out of themes. But what you were really looking for, if you were like us, was the flaw. And once you found it, the flaw in the picture, you worked on it until it became larger and took over. At one point, we wanted to take over the world of communications. Can you imagine that, not as a science-fiction trope or a crazy comic-book imagining, but as a real possibility in the mind of a bunch of teenagers? It sounds ridiculous, but we found our own keyholes into the inner workings of vast corporations, and we installed others, until we found we would be able to control their whole system. Turn off 20,000 phone lines in Buenos Aires? No problem. Give New Yorkers free telephone calls for an afternoon with no good reason? Do it.

But the stakes were high. There were many trials for the hackers before my own. The legislation was new and was finding its feet, and we watched those steps with our breath held and our self-esteem high, knowing it would be our turn next. We saw ourselves as a group of young freedom fighters under fire from forces that just didn't get what it was all about. That's how we saw those trials, though to others, to Australians in thrall to American corporations or to secret servicemen crazy at being out-witted, we were the dangerous harbingers of a new kind of white-collar crime. We sniggered at that – through the vanity and confidence of youth, no doubt – thinking collars were meant for dogs, or for those who might take their self-strangulation for granted. But it was getting serious. He wasn't yet my friend, but Phoenix of The Realm was someone I was aware of, another Melbourne hacker chased from the dim light of his bedroom to the harsh light of the courthouse.

Phoenix was arrogant – he had once telephoned a *New York Times* reporter, calling himself 'Dave', to boast about attacks Australian hackers were making on American systems. The reporter wrote about it, putting 'Dave' and the other hackers on the paper's front page. Some hackers were more withdrawn, but Phoenix liked the attention. He ended up getting the wrong sort, facing forty criminal charges in a case that had a shadow of US pressure hanging over it. I went to the court that day and sat anonymously in the public gallery, watching the face of Judge Smith with a rising sense both of public threat and private honour. I thought the case might prove a pivotal day for our brand of explorer, and I wanted to witness it. As it turned out, Phoenix did not get a custodial sentence. I breathed freely, if breathing freely is ever something one can do in an Australian court. As Phoenix left the dock I went down to offer my congratulations.

'Thanks,' he said. 'Do I know you?'

'Sort of,' I said. 'I'm Mendax. I'm about to go through what you did, only worse.'

When you're a hacker, you live above, or beneath, or within, or beyond the scope of your everyday friends. That's not a boast or a value statement: it's just a fact. You live otherwise from the norm, not only using a *nom de plume* or a *nom de guerre*, but a series of masks within masks, until eventually, if you are any good at all, your activity is your identity and your knowledge is your face. After a long time with computers, there's a measure of detachment that makes you homeless within your own home, and you find yourself only really yourself with others like you, people with cartoon names whom you've never met.

Even though most of my hacking friends lived in Melbourne or its suburbs, like me, I usually met them online on bulletin board systems – a bit like chat rooms – such as Electric Dreams or Megaworks. The first BBS I set up myself was called A Cute Paranoia – a further sign of my well-balanced nature – and I invited Trax and Prime Suspect onto it as much as they could manage. I was nineteen in 1990, and had never spoken to those guys, except modem to modem. You build up a picture of the reality of a person without ever really meeting them. It can give in to paranoia, and too much secrecy, and too much alienation, I suppose, and it would be fair to say I thought Trax and Prime Suspect were odd. I wasn't in the least without oddness myself, as people would always be quick to tell me. But I trusted these guys' instincts. My endless travels across the Australian landscape – and education system – made me something of a social outsider, but in Trax I found a kindred spirit. Like me, he came from a poor but intellectual family. Both of his parents were recent immigrants to Australia, still retaining the German accents that had embarrassed Trax as a child. Prime Suspect, on the other hand, came from an upper-middle-class background and on the surface was a studious grammar-school boy bound for university. But Prime Suspect was a damaged young man. The only thing that had saved his parents from an acrimonious divorce battle was his father's death from cancer when Prime Suspect was eight. Widowed and stuck with two young children, his mother had retreated into bitterness and anger. And Prime Suspect in turn had retreated into his bedroom and into his computer.

We were all misfits in our different ways, but our differences equalised in the strange impersonal universe of the hacker. Under our own and each other's tutelage, we had graduated from being funsters to being cryptographers. And in company with a whole international subculture, we had become aware of how cryptography could lead to political change. We were cypherpunks. The movement started around 1992 and was held together by a mailing list, a meeting point for our discussions of computer science, politics, philosophy and mathematics. There were never more than about 1,000 subscribers, but those people laid the foundations of where cryptography was going: they showed the way for all the modern battles over privacy.

We were engaged in establishing a system for the new information age, the Internet age, that would allow individuals, rather than merely corporations, to protect their privacy. We could write code and would use that ability to give people jurisdiction over their rights. The whole movement tapped into a part of my mind, or you could say my soul: I realised through the cypherpunk movement that justice in the future might depend on us working for a balance, via the Internet, of what corporations consider secrets and what individuals consider private. As it used to stand, before we seized the tools, privacy was only a matter of advantage for corporations, banks and governments: but we saw a new frontline, in which people's power could be enhanced with information.

The Internet, as you can see if you look at China today, was always capable of being a zone of selective censorship, and so was every area of computer culture. The cypherpunks get too little credit for breaking the whole thing open and keeping the tools from becoming weapons, exclusively, in the hands of commercial opportunists and political oppressors. The media was so busy warbling about hackers they missed, right under their noses, how the best of them had become cryptographers busy fighting for the freedoms of information that they themselves claimed to be built on. It was a lesson on the moral infirmity of the media: by and large, they took what power was offered to them, and did not, at the dawn of the Internet era, fight to establish freedom of access or freedom from censorship. To this day, they take the technology for granted and miss how it materialised. It was the cypherpunks, or the 'code rebels' as Steven Levy called us, who prevented the new technology from merely becoming a tool used by big business and government agencies to spy on populations, or sell to them. Computers could have come preloaded with commercials. Smartphones could have come embedded with surveillance devices. The Internet could have been repressive in a great number of its facets. Emails could have been generally interceptable and lacking in privacy. But a turf war went on, invisibly to most commentators, a battle that guaranteed certain freedoms. It is the basis of today's understanding – a cypherpunk commonplace – that computer technology can be a major tool in the fight for social change.

At one time, governments wanted to make cryptography illegal, except for themselves in support of their own activities. And this was preparation for how certain governments now view WikiLeaks: they wish to keep control of technology so that it might only serve itself. But this misunderstands the freedoms inscribed into the technology. We fought for it, so that powerful bodies could not merely use data to suit themselves. The whole struggle was about that and still is about that. For some in the libertarian movement, this was essentially about privacy as capitalist freedom, the right to be free of big government, to have your data kept back; but this is my book and I'll tell you what it meant to me.

The cypherpunk ethos allowed me to think about how best to oppose the efforts of oppressive bodies – governments, corporations, surveillance agencies – to extract data from vulnerable individuals. Regimes often rely on having control of the data, and they can hurt people or oppress them or silence them by means of such control. My sense of the cypherpunk ethos was that it could protect people against this: it could turn their knowledge into an unreachable possession of theirs, protecting them in the classic Tom Paine way of securing liberty as a bulwark against harm or aggression. We aimed to turn the tools of oppression into the instruments of liberty and that was a straightforward goal. Eventually, in 1997, this would lead to my developing a new tool called Rubberhose, in which encrypted data can be hidden beneath layers of fake data, such that no single password will ever provide a gateway to a person's sensitive information. The data is essentially unreachable, unless the person to whom the data refers wishes to make an effort to reveal it. It was a way of keeping important information secret not just by encrypting it, but by hiding it, and it was an application of game theory. For the general good, I wished to break the power of interrogators, who could never be sure that the last of the keys had been exhausted. WikiLeaks, I should say, was founded on the notion that the very presence of sources would be infinitely deniable. One day, I imagined, this technology would enable people to speak, even when powerful forces threatened to punish all speakers. The cypherpunks made this possible by arguing, from day one, against all treaties and laws that opposed the right to encrypt.

But I'm getting ahead of myself. Our problems at this time included constitutional issues. At one point, in the early '90s, the US government tried to argue that a floppy disk containing code must be considered a munition. We scarcely knew, as we went about what felt like world-changing business, but on a small scale, that we would be tied up so quickly in freedom-of-speech issues. But we were. Sending certain strips of code or going on a plane with a bit of code tattooed on your arm essentially made you an arms trafficker. Government absurdity has always stalked the effort to make freedoms clear.

I was finding these things out for myself, in Melbourne, in the company of my friends Prime Suspect and Trax. They were the ones who spoke most directly to me in my happy submersion, because they were submerged, too. Prime Suspect said that when he first got his Apple II, at the age of thirteen, he found it to be better company than any of his relatives. Strangely, our bedrooms were more connected to the world than our classrooms, because of one very crucial and amazing thing: the modem. None of us aced our exams or was top of the class. None of us shone in the halls of academe. It just wasn't in our natures. Something in us rebelled against rote-learning and exam-fixation. In short, we felt we had bigger fish to fry and the private means to do it. This lays down another plank in the house of correction for computer hackers: we are arrogant. Compared to policemen, lawyers, army generals and politicians, of course, the computer hacker, you might argue, is a paragon of self-doubt. But we were young and we felt we knew things. That's for sure. We did feel certain and we did feel abundant in our small way. And arrogance in youth might be counted the budding flower of self-defensiveness.

From early on, the International Subversives wanted to attack military systems, and I invented a program called Sycophant that would run through a computer system harvesting passwords. Each night, through the summer of 1991, we wandered through the corridors of the US Airforce 8th Group Command Headquarters in the Pentagon. We tramped through Motorola in Illinois, padded through Panasonic in New Jersey, tiptoed through Xerox in Palo Alto, and swam down into the twilight lakes of the US Naval Undersea Warfare Engineering Station. There would come a day when people would run revolutions out of their Twitter accounts, and it would feel entirely natural and democratic, but, back then, it was new and totally subversive to feel the pulse of history through a flashing cursor. The journey between the two has been a story of our times.

In the book *Underground: Tales of Hacking, Madness and Obsession from the Electronic Frontier*, my friend, the author Suelette Dreyfus, captures perfectly the scale of ambition that was expressed by our new breed of nerd cognoscenti. And our group, the International Subversives, was going further than any of the others in Australia, further than Phoenix and the other members of The Realm. By the time I was twenty we were attempting to enter the Xanadu of computer networks, the US Department of Defense's Network Information Centre (NIC) computer. Under my handle, Mendax, I was working most closely with Prime Suspect. Here's Suelette:

> As both hackers chatted amiably on-line one night, on a Melbourne University computer, Prime Suspect worked quietly in another screen to penetrate ns.nic. ddn.mil, a US Department of Defense system closely linked to NIC. He believed the sister system and NIC might 'trust' each other – a trust he could exploit to get into NIC. And NIC did everything.
>
> NIC assigned domain names – the '.com' or '.net' at the end of an email address – for the entire Internet. NIC also controlled the US military's own internal defence data network, known as MILNET.
>
> NIC also published the communication protocol standards for the Internet. Called RFCs (Request for Comments), these technical specifications allowed one computer on the Internet to talk to another . . . Perhaps most importantly, NIC controlled the reverse look-up service on the Internet. Whenever someone connects

to another site across the Internet, he or she typically types in the site name – say, ariel.unimelb.edu.au at the University of Melbourne. The computer then translates the alphabetical name into a numerical address – the IP address. All the computers on the Internet need this IP address to relay the packets of data onto the final destination computer. NIC decided how Internet computers would translate the alphabetical name into an IP address, and vice versa.

If you controlled NIC, you had phenomenal power on the Internet. You could, for example, simply make Australia disappear. Or you could turn it into Brazil.

We got inside, and the feeling was overwhelming. Some people make the mistake of saying it's like playing God: it's not, because God, if he's God, already has all the answers. We were twenty. The joy was an explorer's joy at breaking through to a new frontier despite all the odds. I created a back door into the system for future adventures. This system was awesome, and I felt almost subdued at the connectivity on offer: for me, and this is relevant to my future work on WikiLeaks, I saw a perfect join between a mathematical truth and a moral necessity. Even in those early days, I saw that breaking through the portals of power was not just a matter of fun. Governments depended on secrecy and patronage networks to deepen their advantages, but it began to appear possible that what street riots, opposition groups, human rights gurus and electoral reform had always struggled to achieve, we could actually begin to bring about with science. We could undermine corruption from its dead centre. Justice would always in the end be about human beings, but there was a new vanguard of experts, criminalised as we were, who had fastened on to the cancer of modern power, who saw how it spread in ways that were still hidden from ordinary human experience.

Our skills made us valuable, and some of us were unable to resist the Faustian pacts we were offered. It amazed the rest of us that some hackers were working for governments – hacking was innately anarchistic – but they were, and I saw it from inside the US Department of Defense network. They were hacking their own machines as target practice, and no doubt hacking computers around the world on behalf of what they understood to be US interests. As treasure hunters with an ethical bias, we entered a labyrinth of power, corruption and lies, always knowing that we would be the ones accused of corruption if we got caught. We were a hardcore unit of three: Prime Suspect, myself and Trax, who was the best phreaker in Australia. He wrote the book on how to control and manipulate telephone exchanges.

We were anarchists, I suppose, by temperament if not by political conviction. We had started off having fun and ended up wanting to change the world. There was a developing understanding that cryptography was a liberating concept and that it would allow individuals to stand up to government, to whole governments, and that it was now possible for people to resist the will of a superpower. Our temperaments were drawn to an Enlightenment sense of liberty and we felt we were part of the way forward for technology. Many mathematicians were involved with the cypherpunks. Timothy May wrote the 'crypto anarchist manifesto' and John Gilmore was another founding member of the group. These guys were pioneers in the IT industry – Gilmore was the fifth employee of Sun Microsystems – and they had both made money and bailed out, to focus on trying to physically realise their liberation ideals with the help of mathematics and cryptography. For instance, they wanted to come up with a new kind of digital currency, a digital coin, something that would replace the Gold Standard, which would make financial transactions cleaner and not traceable by governments. Your credit rating and your credit history would be yours and yours alone. This was the dream of cryptography: to permit individuals to communicate securely and be at liberty. (If you look at the cypherpunk alumni, you see some of them went on to invent watered-down versions of all this, such as PayPal.) If allowed to develop, I foresaw that it would permit small activist groups who were in danger of being surveilled to resist government coercion. That was the hope, anyway. That was the plan and the dream. But many of the brilliant minds of my generation of cypherpunks floated off in the dot com bubble. They became obsessed with stock options and Palm Pilots and lost the urge for real change.

Digging down into our cypherpunk mindsets, we saw that one of the great battles – our Spanish Civil War, if you like – was going to be about how we served in the effort to defend the world against the surveillance of private computer networks. Issues of freedom and the fight against oppression were located there, as surely as they once were in the hills of Catalonia, and we wanted to zip up and go out and fight the good fight against police statehood as best we could. We were idealistic, of course, and young: the usual condition of people wanting to make a difference. We would make mistakes and we would be punished for them. We also might never gain the sense of possibility again that we had among ourselves. That is life's risk, almost life's certainty, though we set out nonetheless.

The issue of privacy would always haunt me. It haunts me now. At WikiLeaks, I would come to seem the arch-proponent of transparency, forever described as the man who thinks all privacy is bad. But it was never my position that all privacy is bad: rather the opposite. We fought, as cypherpunks, to protect people's privacy. What I opposed, and continue to oppose, is the use of secrecy by institutions to protect themselves against the truth of the evil they have done. This is a clear distinction. Even in this book, where I try to tell my story as best I can, there will be moments of privacy, because I owe it to some greater sense of justice, to my children, for example, not to drag them into the limelight. Some people, in love with a category error, will wish to hold me to account on this score, as if the founder of WikiLeaks must, out of some bogus sense of consistency, blow the whistle on every element of his private self.

I will not indulge that fantasy. I will not play that game. Yet I will try to open up about all the matters that truly matter. I say this, because at the time I have reached in this account of my life, I had a child with the woman I was going out with and living with. The child is Daniel. He is a good man, and I have tried to be a capable father to him. We had him young and his mother and I were later in dispute, for a long time, about how he should be cared for, but that is all there is to it. It was a difficult time, there was a custody battle, and no great principles emerge out of it. This is a book about my life as a journalist and as a fighter for freedoms: my children are not part of that story and I won't say much more about them. There is Daniel and there are other children born to people I cared about. Over my career so far, when I speak about the need for truth, I am talking, very often, about the truth in relation to the deaths of thousands of people. Or I am talking about frauds, tortures, corruptions that destroyed people's lives. Despite the wishes of the category error-makers, I will not insult that legacy by suggesting some kind of equivalence between those truths and my own small concerns. I will reveal to you the growth of a mind, and an attitude, a sensibility, and a plan. I will talk to you about criminal charges brought against me. But I will not pour forth on issues that matter only to my family and which can add nothing to your sense of the personal journey towards the work of WikiLeaks. Disclosure is my business, but we don't deal in gossip.

I've got ahead of myself. The cypherpunks' mailing list, and with it the movement, was launched in 1992 and would capture my attention during the middle years of the decade. But let me take you back to 1990. Just before Daniel was born, my girlfriend and I had been living in untraceable accommodation in Fitzroy, a bohemian suburb of Melbourne. Fitzroy had an Italian population and a Greek crowd and lots of students, all of whom felt comfortable being near the university. We began squatting. And many of our political thoughts at the time – thoughts that would lead to bigger questions about ownership of information and so on – were centred around the issue of squatters' rights. We formed a squatters' union. I would put posters on lamp-posts and encourage people to call into our office with information about empty properties. I'd plot them on a map, then go round there and work out how to break in. We kept filing cards of these places, and noted whether they had working gas and electricity, how long they were likely to be empty and stuff like that. My girlfriend and I moved into an Edwardian property and made an issue of the freedom to use these properties and the rights adhering to occupants. I realised I was probably built for struggle because this wasn't the easiest way to live. Conditions of threat suited me and made me work harder. Anyway, we were tossed out of that house but the union worked well, giving homeless people a place to call. The way of organising it was interesting: we behaved like a real estate agency for no profit and for the good of the community. It was a lesson in using free-market means to ridicule free-market ends.

The uncertainty that surrounded our daily life – our home, our gas and electricity connections and such – was mirrored in our night-time activities. Each of us in the International Subversives knew that the police were seeking to make an example of us. The Australian Academic and Research Network were co-operating with the Australian Federal Police in order to try and catch us, and we were able to hack into their various systems to see how close they were getting. Our nemesis in the police even had a name, Sergeant Ken Day, and he seemed to have become obsessed with our activities. To us he was just a name at the time, though we came to know him well after our arrests, which he had worked so hard for. (It is one of the ironies of my life that Ken Day would later become a strong supporter of WikiLeaks in the Australian press.) We were visiting systems and learning from them, but, as hackers, we were also fairly competitive, each wanting to be first. I would work hard to create Trojans, ways of tricking a computer system into letting you inside and believing you are the legitimate user, which encouraged it to give up its secrets to you. All good, clean fun, except it was the kind of fun that made authorities crazy. We were basically turning ourselves into people who had the power of system administrators over many powerful networks.

The net closed in on us with Nortel, the system belonging to the Canadian telecommunications company that ran a network stretching over the globe. It had been one of our greatest explorations. There were more than 11,000 computers in Nortel's network, and we had fought long and hard to gain access to them. From Melbourne, I had commandeered, or hijacked, forty computers housed in Canada, with the intention of bombarding Nortel with guesses as to their passwords. The program I'd designed could throw 40,000 guesses per second. Eventually we got in and it was like walking inside the Sistine Chapel at midnight. You could look at all the expertise, all the evidence of civilisation, and notice their methods, their habits, their corners of liturgy and mystery. We had root control within that system and could have transferred money or sold their commercial secrets. But we did none of those things. Prime Suspect, Trax and myself would have considered that the lowest move. We were above that kind of dirt, wanting simply to master the system and move on.

One night I realised I was being watched. It was 2.30 a.m. and a Nortel system administrator was on to us. I tried for an hour to circumvent his inspections, block his way, all the while deleting the incriminating directory and walking backwards, clearing the path of my footprints. The administrator had been logged on from home, but after a break he appeared at the main Nortel console. He had gone into work. I was now in trouble: you can only obfuscate for so long, and I could no longer block this guy. He had me. Well, he didn't have me right there and then: it was still cat and mouse, but Prime Suspect would unwittingly lead him straight to us the next morning. I made a message appear on the administrator's screen:

I have finally become sentient.

Then, a little later:

> *I have taken control.*
> *For years, I have been struggling in this greyness.*
> *But now I have finally seen the light.*

The administrator kept cool. He began checking all the modem lines. The scene could only play out to his advantage. I typed:

> *It's been nice playing with your system.*

Pause. Nothing. Pause. Like cyber-Pinter. I typed again:

> *We didn't do any damage and we even improved a few things. Please don't call the Australian Federal Police.*

For several years we had been Houdini-like and had invented ways to deepen our own escapological nature. Tracer calls to our modems would go dead in the middle of the effort. We had the Australian phone lines down pat, and no one could reach us. Until 1 October 1991 that was. After that date the Feds managed to trace a line back from Nortel and started tapping Prime Suspect's phone. He led them to Trax, and then to me. The Feds were listening to us, hearing our conversations, watching our moves. They called it Operation Weather. It dawned on us that we were on borrowed time. Trax flipped and went to the police. The police came and dragged Prime Suspect away from a party on 29 October. The game was up. Or, more accurately, the game, for me, was really beginning.

I was alone and sad when they came. My wife and child had just left, and I had come to the end of my rope. My computer disks were strewn around the computer table. The squat was a mess, and I sat on the sofa reading – a vision of things to come – the prison letters of George Jackson, kept in the toughest US prisons at the pleasure of the authorities. I was broken. I was listening, half listening, to a telephone fault signal that was sounding through my stereo speakers. At 11.30 that night there was a knock at the door and a play of shadows outside. The police announced themselves and I thought of all the times I had expected them, all the times I dreamt they were coming. I opened the door and found about a dozen federal officers with battering equipment. A man at the front looked me in the eye as if he always knew we would meet. At that moment it occurred to me that the disks with the Pentagon stuff on them weren't in the beehive. They were on my desk in full view of the cops. 'I'm Ken Day,' the head policeman said. 'I believe you've been expecting me.'

6

THE ACCUSED

I wonder if I knew before the trial that literature could bring clarity. It was during that period that I read Solzhenitsyn's *The First Circle*, and it was more than clarifying and more than revealing: it made me understand the meaning of empathy and it gave me strength. I had been a reader since childhood so I certainly knew about the pleasure of books, but this one, this book, made me see into the heart of my predicament. If a book can make you feel less lonely, then this was the one for me and it came just in time. I suppose I've always forced feeling to give way to action – that was the kind of practical, campaigning childhood I had – but in those years when I was waiting for the court case I'm sure I was close to feeling lost. Where there is lostness, there are sometimes the seeds of new strength. Professor Chelnov, in the novel, is an old mathematician imprisoned seventeen years earlier. When filling in a form and asked for his nationality he puts not 'Russian', but 'Prisoner'. His mind is set upon inventions and he feels he is nothing if not stateless. And that is a kind of empowerment when the state is against you.

The struggle is always to be oneself.

The Federal Police took sixty-three bundles of my belongings away from the house in the Melbourne suburbs. I stood in the street and watched them go. It was dark, a warm October night, the crickets were out, and I felt I was whirling down a chasm.

In the event, it took them until 1994 to come up with some charges. It's worth remembering, as more than an aside, the extent to which the sudden infusion of computers into society had created a legislative and common law vacuum. State prosecutors tried to apply traditional property protection and deception laws to new technological crimes, and often they succeeded. Yet there were a number of high-profile cases where the prosecution of hackers was a farce, cases where the only real crime revealed was the crime of the computer geek having embarrassed someone powerful. In an atmosphere of increased government reliance on computer databases, legislation rushed towards the absurd criminalisation of a plethora of computer use. What we saw with computer science was how quickly it allowed for a society of information-sharers, and this sharing, this society, exists in a greater condition of democracy and freedom than the traditional worlds of publishing and broadcasting. Freedom of information – and freedom *from* information – were quickly on the table, but the legislation has always struggled to understand what it might be asking the law to deal with and recognise. Given that ownership in the digital sense is not at all like ownership in the old physical sense of owning a watch, the legal world has failed to see what's in front of it. You don't steal information. You simply create a platform for it when it finds its way into the public realm. If I have a look at your watch, I'm not mugging you, I just want to know the time. Even by the mid-1990s, and even today, the legal establishment are none the wiser on how to consider the legal implications of our life with computers. That's why it took our Australian case so long to come to court.

Eventually, the trial came together in 1996. And all the while the struggle, indeed, was to be oneself – to go on and do the work you knew you could do and play your part. Opponents past and present have the same essential weakness about them: first they want to use you, then they want to be you, then they want to snuff you out. It's a pattern that stretches in my life from toytown Feds to hacks at the *Guardian*: the old human pattern of someone needing something from someone else, getting it, denying they got it from them, then resenting the person for having been in a special position to give them what they needed, which is usually, by the way, an aspect of self-hatred on the asker's part for having needed any help at all. Usually it ends with these people enumerating one's personal faults, a shocking, ungrateful, unmanly effort, to be filed under despicable in my book. You'll meet more of these people in due course, but I've been meeting them all my life.

The long wait for an arrest and a trial was one I wanted to use, and I was keen to see how I could discover more and more useful applications for the knowledge I had. Trax and I teamed up to form a computer security company and bought a massive mainframe computer from La Trobe University. It was quite funny to meet an old friend: this computer, the size of four fridges, one I'd hacked into years before. The security work basically involved me being paid to hack into the systems of large companies, at their behest, just to see how secure they were. They never were very secure and the work was boring. But it allowed me to continue with my own investigations and get back on my feet. I knew it wouldn't work out for me in the long run because I'm not sufficiently interested in money and not at all interested in legitimacy.

I am interested in what I can do to further the cause of justice. In 1993 part of that involved helping the police to break an Internet paedophile ring. I helped them to understand what these men were passing around on the Internet and how they were doing it. I could see how these people moved around on the Net in ways the police could not, because they didn't have the expertise. I could lead them to an understanding of who these people were. I wasn't coerced into this, and did it less to help the police, in fact, than because I was concerned about protecting children.

But the raid took something out of me, for a time. The old nomadic strain took hold and has never gone. I suppose to a large extent I was unhappy. More than unhappy: I was stressed beyond anything I'd ever known. That rebellious climate that had always surrounded me travelled inwards, and for a while I lived outdoors and felt anguished. If I want to be comical about it, and encourage my critics, I would say it was my period in the wilderness. The only bit of Jesus worth having is the bit where he percolates his rebellion, and he does that over forty days while eating berries, facing down the temptations of the Devil and preparing to do the do. Like Milton, I believe the Devil quite often has the best lines, so, for that reason, and more obvious ones, I won't be aligning myself with the God-child. Let's just say I was upset and felt abandoned as I wandered in the Dandenong Ranges National Park. I must have been exhausted as well, yet filled with a notion that significant achievements lay up ahead if only I could reach that point. In the Sherbrooke Forest the temperatures could be extreme: freezing at night, and in the day the mosquitoes ravaged me. I drank water from the creek and otherwise just picked up provisions from town. I wanted to be alone and contemplate my position. I never saw a computer. I was out of communication.

I felt I could be a good father to my son but not a good mother. I was good at teaching, structuring, protecting, even at the bedtime stories, but I was hopeless at the other bits, the more mundane and less heroic parts of parenting. Eventually, I came to be looking after my son. That brought me back into focus, and so, over time, did my old friend, communications. At the time, people could only run email through the university system, and, back in Melbourne, I got involved in setting up a non-profit network and lobbying for deregulation of the Internet. It was a platform for setting up Suburbia Public Access Network, one of the first Internet Service Providers in Australia. We were 'the free speech ISP', and we made a point of hosting material others wouldn't. You don't get any thanks for that, but we fought for connectivity in the country and it came in the end. I continued to write code, most of which I released for free, culminating in Rubberhose.

Many of the early cryptographers, these inspired brainiacs at Stanford or MIT who wanted to live in a world of pure maths and blue-sky thinking, were concerned about how to protect privacy. Everyone with a computer now takes it for granted, but the facts of authentication and key protection were established by guys working hard with little thanks: they knew that electronic mail and digital signatures and so on would depend on privacy, or else the Internet would become an enemy of free speech. Without security, people's computer lives would be too easily monitored, controlled and abused. So this was the great issue and it was a matter, at that stage, of mathematics, the basis of cryptography.

As things got established with the Internet, I began to flow more naturally in that direction and I felt very strongly, as I still do, that you have to fight to organise and maintain freedom of intelligence. I wrote a posting in March 1996 appending an online advert for something called the Emailers Profit Centre, a 'Multi-Level Marketing' project that aimed to sell millions of email addresses to commercial companies. 'Who wants to take this site down first?' I wrote to fellow cypherpunks. This was the kind of challenge we were facing back then: how to stop the Net from simply becoming a vast tool for giant companies and governments to exploit people. Or for the security state to keep an eye on us. I loathe these security types, the types who point out that 'Everything which is not explicitly permitted is denied.' Who do they think they are, or, more to the point, who do they think we are? They are security fascists who would mobilise technology to secure their brutal vision. They are types whose idea of Nirvana is to maintain a cyberspace status quo in which the laws of physics have been rewritten so it is not possible for you to shift your chair without written authority. No longer a case simply of Big Brother watching you, but of Big Brother controlling your fingers, the movement of your mind, and keeping you from finding the world and its information on your own terms. Big Brother is home. He is installed in the item you just dragged home from the Apple Store.

That was the threat, and we applied ourselves to it, quite frankly, while everyone else was still trying to work out how to spell email. As I say, it's taken tremendously for granted by everyone: people who send a hundred emails a day and never worry, kids who live on Facebook, but these things had to be invented, and the governments at the time were reluctant to allow ordinary Internet users to encrypt freely. Governments, especially the US government, wanted a back door into the system. They were working for a military understanding of surveillance, and the early Internet, the early forms of electronic mail, presented issues they wanted control over. But the cryptographers stuck with it and now we have an Internet relatively free of government interference, unless you happen to live in China.

I was moving towards this – the dissolving of my hacker instincts into something more mathematical, more purposeful – when the hacking case finally came to court in 1996. My two friends in the International Subversives, Prime Suspect and Trax, had suffered differently since the raid. For Prime Suspect it was the short joy of Ecstasy and the long misery of coming down, ending in paranoia and depression, and the slow unravelling, with the help of a counsellor, of his relationship with his mother and of his feelings about the death of his father. For Trax, it was panic attacks. His downward spiral had started well before the raid, and led to it, indeed. He was in a car crash that left him constantly fearful. In her book *Underground* – which I had helped research in the intervening years – Suelette reports that Trax at this point was reduced to fully-fledged agoraphobia. That was about the size of it. The police raid brought us all low. We all vanished for a time into a private hell, all in our early twenties, badly marked for too little reason, it seemed. The charges were shuffled around. There was a terrible kind of ignorant glee going on within the press at the time. They didn't know what the offences meant and they had built up a ridiculous picture of the threat posed by these teenage boys. In reality, ours was just a grubby little case of too much obsession and too much curiosity and not enough care; but it was turned into something of epic, state-threatening proportions by a bunch of lunatic prosecutors and media slags who should have known better.

I wrote something on the cypherpunk mailing list in January 1996 that captures my disgust at the time. My comments related to the felling of Kevin Mitnick, an American hacker, characterised in a book written by his capturer, Tsutomu Shimura, as 'America's Most Wanted Outlaw'. 'This makes me ill,' I wrote. 'Tsutomu, when Mitnick croaks, will you dig up his grave and rent his hands out as ashtrays? The man who murdered one of the last notorious American gunslingers went on not long after to produce and act in a strange show which described just How He Did It. Some years later, he himself was murdered by a disgusted member of the audience.'

People were feasting on us and on our naivety, but the fact was that, by the time of the trial, the old hacking scene was dead. The Internet had made it too easy and many of the new breed were too brazen about what they did. It had become part of the pop and film culture, and some of us were already thinking about other ways in which secrets could be accessed or revealed.

The other two wanted to plead guilty but I didn't want to collaborate, so to speak, in my own criminalisation. By the trial date, I faced thirty-one charges; Prime Suspect, twenty-six; and Trax, six. Part of our crime was to have written articles for our own International Subversives magazine, which had a circulation of three – the three of us.

Stress breeds stress, of course. And by the time of the committal hearing in Melbourne Magistrates' Court my mind was blown apart, not least by the news that Prime Suspect had turned Crown Witness against me. As I've found again and again to my cost, you don't get far in this world by over-relying on loyalty. People are loyal until it seems more opportune not to be. I'm sorry if that's cynical, but experience brings its own slow wisdom. Prime Suspect signed the papers, though he didn't colour the picture as menacingly as he could have done. When I saw him across the courtroom I stared at him. He looked impassive. He was frightened, he was young, but it was a look that I would come to know: the look of betrayal, organised on the face to look like a high-minded interest in the truth. Nevertheless, it brings a focus to your life, the moment when a judge says, 'The prisoner shall now rise', and the only person standing is you. I once said true belief begins at that point. In my line of work, true belief begins with that and with the jackboot at the door.

Prime Suspect, having pleaded guilty, was heard some time before me. There was no custodial sentence, a $5,000 good behaviour bond, and an order to pay reparations to the Australian National University to the tune of $2,100. The judge made the point that no special leniency had been afforded Prime Suspect as thanks for his co-operation. That was a sad moment: both of us realising that he had crossed the divide for nothing, wrecked our friendship and compromised our dignity without benefit. Court seems long, but it is never as long as memory: I have never spoken to him again. In some ways, my ethics must be simple-minded, but I am not a politician: I couldn't abuse a private or a working friendship for a public gain. I just couldn't. And for someone who was part of a group called the Subversives to ally himself with the pieties of the law in times of strife, well, I felt very sorry. Trax did similarly well and would have done so without coughing up: the judge in his case ordered that no conviction be recorded against him.

My case presented itself first to the Supreme Court – almost as a point of order, or as a case study, to help define the terms of the trial – and this allowed us to seek an understanding of what the charges meant. What exactly did it mean to accuse someone of gaining access to a computer? If there was commercial data on the system that was not read by the intruder, does he still stand accused of theft? If a crook breaks into a house and steals that day's newspaper, is he then liable to stand trial for the theft of the Matisse that was hanging over the sitting-room fireplace? The Supreme Court, however, wanted to make a point to the County Courts that they should not send matters to them except in extreme circumstances. This was a shame, as it would prove a missed opportunity when it came to future computer crimes cases. The law failed its own benchmark of intellectual curiosity that day, and everybody suffered, not least Australia itself, which even today fails to spot the difference between a child molester and a person interested in using computers to secure our liberties.

In the end, I was tried before a judge who knew little of the case. He made it clear he would have preferred a custodial sentence, but, following a code of parity, he gave me a similar sentence to that enjoyed by Prime Suspect. My good behaviour bond was ten times greater and I had less time to pay the $2,100 reparation. I was tarred as a criminal, and I minded that, of course; but there was some relief that I wouldn't, this time, be going to jail. Nobody would be opening champagne, and I had a working life to rebuild, but the case taught me how vulnerable hackers would be in the future. I walked into that court already a different person from the boy who had hacked into Nortel, and my dander was up, as they say, not to follow the logic of the court, which was primitive in my view, but to follow the logic of mathematics and exploration, and go further into the realms of justice. I wanted to discover how computer science could influence the ethics of the modern world. That was my plan, and I rebuilt myself for the purpose. In the meantime, Nortel and other victims of my so-called hacking crimes began using the cryptography software I'd invented during my late-night walks through their system.

No victory comes without a shadow of defeat. And some decades of your life, weirdly, can come out of the wash looking defeated. Some people say that being young is a victory in itself, but I doubt that. I was tired and nervous in my twenties in a way that I never am now. What I might observe is the strain of trying to push things forward. There's an invitation in front of me to a party we threw in North Melbourne at Easter, 1996, organised by the group of us involved in setting up that early ISP, suburbia.net. Just looking at the invitation gives me an indication of who I was at the time. I was excitable and committed, but no doubt overbearing and a pain in the arse. Having set out the logistics of the party on the invitation, there follows a little questionnaire.

Q: who's invited?
A: you. A cross-social strata of individuals, occupations and ages. It will be an eclectic evening.
Q: no, I mean who will really be there?
A: now is not the time for potentially dichotomatic simplifications of character, but what the heck . . .

• *Suburbia users:*
From magistrates and politicians to convicted com-
puter hackers. We have as users private investigators,
writers, programmers, QCs, record producers, musi-
cians, film directors, journalists, policemen, intelli-
gence agents, chess champions, members of obscure
religious sects, netball umpires, many, many types
of scientists and engineers, security experts, doctors,
accountants, bartenders, choral conductors . . .

I hope you like netball umpires. I'm not sure what their
role was intended to be in the coming revolution. Anyhow,
the 'invitation' goes on to suggest our reliable associates
were to be found among fans of the rock group St Etienne,
and fans of the writing of Philip K. Dick and Nabokov.
There was no entry fee, though people could bring hardware and cables as a donation. Dress code: '1930s incog-
nito is just fine'.

I can't recall if the party quite lived up to my rhetoric. But
all of my life at the time was there, in the invitation, if not
at the event. Among these rather soulful wilderness years,
I also learned to hate religion. I say hate, but I'm enough of
a child of Aquarius not to want to hate anything. Let us say
I learned in the period before going to university – my next
move, to study Mathematics and Physics at Melbourne –
the extent to which organised religion was probably a kind
of evil. I would come to understand my dislike of religion
to be a crucial part of my confidence. Take that as you
will. I'm sure it's true of many of us. I once ended up at a
backpackers' place filled with dozens of Christians from the
Australian University Christian Convergence. Most were
young women, and I turned, somewhat disgracefully, into a

sort of Chesterton's Hardy, the village atheist, while they tried
to convert me with the rise and fall of their bosoms. One of
the devout was the lovely daughter of a Newcastle minister.
At some point in my unintended wooing of her, she looked
up, fluttered her eyelids and said, 'Oh, you know so much!
I hardly know anything!'

'That is why you believe in God,' I explained. This
conversational brutality appeared to take her breath away.
It seemed I was exactly what she secretly longed for: a man
willing to openly disagree with her father. A man, in other
words, willing to be man enough, strong enough, the
romance-writers might say (and I felt she'd read them), not
to creep in supplication before her father's God.

This, I'll call the funny side of religion. The less funny
side I found to be manifest amongst the Scientologists, the
brain-burp of the late L. Ron Hubbard, which rakes in millions a year and is the acme of occultist thinking. As usual
with such cults, they have found it advisable to keep their
more wacko beliefs and practices out of the new recruits'
faces until the recruits are sufficiently wacko themselves,
which can take years as the fresh blood works its way through
the costly 'levels'. The whole Scientology system breeds
subservience and secrecy, the two things I was born to run
from. I'm sure I have had my moments of bad judgement,
but none of them can ever compete with the constant jet of
nonsense coming from the Church of Scientology. I may be
wrong, of course, and the earth is, in reality, the destroyed
prison colony of aliens from outer space, but I'm not convinced. In our defence of the Internet, it became clear, years
ago, that Scientology was among the great enemies of the
freedom it might make possible. The Internet is, by its true
nature, a censorship-free zone. Not good for those in the

Hubbard cupboard, who see censorship, concealment and revelation (for a fee) as the very reason for their existence.

The church has fostered a large network of manipulation. It has used legal processes and illegal harassment to pursue newspapers, ex-members and many others, even while it remains subject to an FBI investigation itself. Sinisterly, the church considers its religious teachings to be copyrighted trade secrets. Later, WikiLeaks blew the whistle on them by publishing a collection of these nonsense teachings, complete with 'Copyright 1966, by L. Ron Hubbard, All Rights Reserved' emblazoned on each page: 'The state of Clear is terrific. We have waited on this state for a very long time. When an individual goes Clear, he goes over a bump.' If you'll forgive the pun, confronting these nutters brought me clarity. The fight against the church is far more than the Net versus a bunch of wackos with too much money. It is about the corporate suppression of the Internet and free speech. It is about intellectual property and the meaning of personal expression and the principle of unfettered access. The year of my Australian trial I wrote about all this, and of how the precedents set by the Church of Scientology today would prove to be useful weapons for corporate tyranny tomorrow. I'd always been an activist in my bones, but back then all my time, when not with my son, was spent building what you might call global platforms for local protest. We demonstrated outside the Church of Scientology, for instance, on Flinders Street, handing out leaflets while also opposing, on mailing lists and message boards, their every effort to suppress free speech.

It was a journey from the local to the global and back again. My favourite kind of journey.

7

THE MATHEMATICAL ROAD
TO THE FUTURE

Towards the end of 1998 I wrote an email to what had become an international band of merry men and women. I was taking off from Melbourne – 'the planet's most liveable city' – to throw myself into the wider world of snow, ice, slush and imploding Communism. I don't know how other people meet colleagues, but my approach has always been a little, say, existential. You like someone's face or the fact they loved a book that you read and liked, too. Maybe they set up a group or opposed some fetid old council or just rambled late one night in a nice way. I wasn't yet the head of an organisation, but, even when I was, my methods have remained the same. Keep moving on, keep trusting people. 'If anyone feels like getting together for beer, vodka, Siberian bear steak, or just a good yarn, please let me know,' I wrote in the round-robin email.

28 Oct 98 San Francisco
 5 Nov 98 London
 6 Nov 98 Frankfurt/Berlin

  9 Nov 98 Poland/Slovenia/Eastern Europe
15 Nov 98 Helsinki
16 Nov 98 St Petersburg
20 Nov 98 Moscow
25 Nov 98 Irkutsk
29 Nov 98 Ulan Bator
  3 Dec 98 Beijing

The itinerary was ambitious, but it worked out. As I met, stayed with, drank and ate with like-minded young people across Europe and Asia, I felt at every turn I was seeing a new world. It was a world running at its own heels, not sure quite how it would turn out or how it would express its beliefs or share its technology, but it opened my eyes all the same.

Some people have a talent for friendship. It might be one of the things that marks out leadership. I used to have it, but I'm not so sure nowadays. After I'd been back in Melbourne a while, I started making plans to attend the University of Melbourne, to study maths and physics. I met a great guy there called Daniel Mathews, who was bright, with a kind of electric flair for fresh thinking and political judgement. I met some people who shared my political instincts, and of course my friends and colleagues understood the power of the Internet, but Dan was the only person I met who shared both of my great passions. He really understood the opportunity that new technology offered to activists. He once wrote a long poem called 'If You Saw', which I posted on my blog, liking the nice, idealistic sweep of the lines:

The ordinary people, not –ese and not –ism,
They stood there and shrugged – I'm just a human! –

And spilled over borders, and greeted their neighbours,
And played with their children, and looked to the future,
And cared not for great things, but just to continue.

Nobody should be immune from the hope embedded in those lines. I was living in eastern Melbourne at the time, with my son, who went to Box Hill High School, and I was burying myself in maths problems. There had already been a coming together, in my mind, between activism and technology, and I had founded a fledgling organisation called leaks.org in 1999. Like many a fledgling, it was starved of nourishment and didn't go anywhere, but it grew in my head and so did the name. But, as I was saying, the future seemed to lie for me in new friends and new kinds of problems. There was something beautiful in the truth revealed by maths – something perfect and just, and I grew experienced in the study of that, not just the problems themselves but the entire moral scope of quantum mechanics.

I finally started at university in 2003. It felt overdue, like something I had been working towards for a long time. Melbourne University is the second oldest in Australia, an avowedly secular institution run by the state. The campus is in Parkville, a leafy part of town with many Victorian t erraces, and I always had a sense of contentment coming to study there. I had always been pretty good at maths, and enjoyed the history of it and the practical side, making my own machines and so on when I was a boy. By the time I came belatedly to study maths at Melbourne, I was probably to some extent jaded with cryptography and by what the best cryptographers were doing to make money in the Internet boom. My experience with hacking had made the universe seem harder to understand, not easier, and I suppose I wanted to retreat into the realm of pure thinking.

At first, the university felt like a sheltered workshop for mental outpatients. Everything was so tame, and the days were so structured, and everyone was absorbed in a way that made it seem like the real world had somehow been filtered out. It was nobody's fault, of course, but it was hard for me to connect with my fellow students, given the fifteen-year age gap with most of them and everything that I had been through in my twenties. After all the ups and downs I'd suffered – the hurly-burly of the underground and the media attention round the trial – it felt weird suddenly to have become this passive student. But I was determined to master quantum mechanics and pure maths. I wanted very much to learn everything I could from them and suspected they would push me forward. In no time at all I was immersed in the whole history and traditions of physics, Nils Bohr and Heisenberg and Feynman, and I was keen to become a figure in the Mathematics Society, if not in the university.

I remember, during one period, going to the University of New South Wales to do some advanced maths courses. It was a good time, and I had got back in touch with my real father – I'll write more about that in a minute – and was riding on my bike every day to the university. One day, as I was turning a corner on my bike, a truck suddenly appeared and swiped me into the gutter. I smashed my arm in six places. I was picked up and taken to hospital, where they put my arm in plaster. They also gave me Tramadol, which had a strange and interesting effect. It's a synthetic opiate, and, though it didn't interfere with the clarity of my thought, it removed all negative emotion, including every experience of what you might call psychological pain. So, during a conversation, for instance, I would experience all the positive parts of the conversation but not the negative parts. I went to a class and was aware that my heart rate was up. And all my calibrations were off: the way I placed my foot down to take a step was off, and so was my social sense, my notion of how much attention to give a person who was speaking in a way that wasn't accurate, for instance.

This was the way my mind was going at the time. My study of quantum mechanics was causing me to question the measures of pain and pleasure in my life, and how they could be balanced, or what would happen if I had more of one than the other. The broken arm was important for me – it was an analogy, almost a parable, of how to go about making and sustaining a change. That probably sounds odd. What I mean is that it made me think about the way in which single discrete events could have far-reaching consequences. When my arm broke it had to be healed – remade, in some way. I started to think about how I could begin to heal the injustices I saw around me – how one could remake the world through a political act. In this way I was arriving at a philosophy of change and I believe it influenced everything I later did. I knew you couldn't test these things in the cloistered economic unreality of the university in the long run, but the process began, for me, from that period of study in which I deepened my experience of cause and effect.

Yet, my capacity for finding things intolerable was always in evidence. Too much in evidence, perhaps. But what can you do? There was a research project in the department to study sand, because the Americans were dealing with sand as part of their adventures in the Middle East. Some woman came to give us a talk about how beautiful it had been to take part in the testing of military hardware and assisting with the flying of the cargo planes that bombed retreating Iraqi troops in the first Gulf War and created all that carnage. I thought, 'Why are we sitting here listening to this mass murderer?' I began to see how the universities were being used by people interested in military profiteering. You could see it if you went to conferences, the whole thing being underwritten by the Australian Defense Science and Technology Organisation. Everything was coming together in my head during this period: the clarity of mind that quantum mechanics forced upon me, my ideas about cause and effect, my horror at military outrages and my increasing insights into Western foreign policy. It was becoming obvious to me, during those years of studying at university, that we needed mechanisms – brand new ways – to take the fruits of science and implement them for the common good. Not for the service of particular agencies, but for truth itself. I loved studying physics, but my hatred for institutionalism only grew. I could see how spineless many of the scientists were, how willing to accept a sponsor's logo, no matter how vile or how murderous or how anti-intellectual, and I suppose I must count that part of my university education.

I once represented my university at the Australian National Physics Competition. At the prize ceremony, the head of Physics at the Australian National University motioned to us and said, 'You are the cream of Australian physics.' I looked around and thought to myself, 'Christ Almighty, I hope he's wrong.' But I had a certainty, a covert certainty in that company, that my interest in quantum mechanics could do more than make the chancellor blush with pride. I shared the view with a handful of computer scientists around the world that quantum mechanics offered a methodology for understanding justice.

Let me explain. Quantum mechanics is not merely a description of how the small parts of the world operate – and operate together to create very large parts of our experience, the whole observable universe – it also constitutes a systematised way of thinking about physical phenomena. If you study it properly, it will train you how to think clearly. You might remember that my early experiments with computers made me realise the difference between saying 'I want the computer to count' and 'This is how you count.' Studying quantum mechanics was a bit like that. It taught me how to ask questions about the world in such a way that I left every option on the table, not prejudicing the outcome. You've probably seen TV journalists asking soft questions to politicians with whom they – or the boss of their network – are sympathetic. You know, like 'Have you always been motivated by a desire to serve your country?' or 'Can you explain how your spending cuts will help our economy?' Quantum mechanics doesn't involve questions like that. It teaches you to ask questions that might actually produce a useful answer, and over time it will enable you to organise your thoughts about the natural world. It shows you how to prove things through experiment, and how to take nothing for granted, no hypothesis, until it has been exposed to every test of cause and effect. After the end of the Crypto Wars, and my trial, I had decided that I had some unfinished business in this area. As I said, I wanted to try and pierce the fabric of reality, and, when it came to social action, take the skin off all our assumptions and see what was underneath. Advanced mathematics and quantum mechanics allowed for that.

To get to the truth, you have to look at your behaviour in how you set up the experiment and see how much the outcome has been affected by what you did and how you did it. You have to find a true measure. You have to look at how things are constructed – and how you yourself have constructed your way of looking – so as to get some insight. Now, the more I looked at this feature of quantum mechanics, the more I saw that it might constitute the thing I had long been looking for: a theory of change, a theory of human-initiated change in the world. That's the beginning of quantum mechanics. I had a handle on the subjective element, which is part of the thinking behind the book you are holding. By laying out my own life, I can show you how it was we did what we did.

I began to think of information as matter, and started to examine how it flows through people and through society, and how the availability of new information brings about change. Let us imagine there is a pipeline that allows a flow of material towards what provides for a state of justice. You can look at who contributed to the flow and come to an estimation of what it was that helped constitute the state of justice. Of course I'm not talking about an actual, physical pipeline, I'm talking about all the different ways in which people communicate. But just imagine for a moment that we are talking about a real pipeline. In order to examine the way that information moves around the world you would have to be interested in the whole pipeline: who makes the pipeline, who pays for it, who maintains it, and whether it is blocked anywhere or whether the flow is hindered. Then what if we map that pipeline onto the Fourth Estate, onto the media, and how it helps or hinders that flow of information? We are interested in what it is that contributes to a state of just actions. What do we see? How can we introduce ethical reforms into the system to enhance justice?

We want to remove blockages, but we also want to increase the number of observers who are contributing towards the good of this flow. If material is suppressed, we must see it as a blockage and allow the maximum number to observe the suppression and alleviate the problem. That way, we get to justice.

So it occurred to me that the Internet is a reconfigurable system of pipes that can connect these observations and these people who can take actions, leading to an increased likelihood of virtue. In the future, I felt, there would be a new way of providing an optimal flow between observers and actors. And that seemed to me to be a new way forward for societies: to make their media answerable to its observers, to make agencies watchable, and to break the hold on information maintained by governments and their collaborating Fourth Estates. There would have to be an alternative gathering process, a gathering process that would combine new information with the information you already know about the world. It would mean contextualising it for all these different actors. We would require a way that kept the actors honest, which is why WikiLeaks – which would grow out of this yoking of quantum mechanics to journalistic ethics – would require the involvement of the mainstream press in the effort to publish material that led to a greater state of justice. In this way, the flow of information would not be a matter for single journalists alone, or for individual media organisations, but for societies working together.

At the time I was still at university, but everything had led to this, and there was some way to go. It's important to write it down, because later hysteria and blaming and mistakes – including mistakes on my part – would obfuscate the basic philosophy of change I was aiming for. Later on, it would always baffle me, when I was too much in the public eye, how people wouldn't want to handle the ideas being generated. They wouldn't have a clue about the issues at stake or the methods being deployed. They would just want to write about my hair or my girlfriends. This has been happening to me, as you know, on an international scale now, and I don't suppose I've helped the situation one bit. But I didn't invent the media's smallness: I merely got tangled up in it and tried to turn it towards something important. But turning the media's attention towards, say, justice, or the real issues of cause and effect in modern history – well, even the so-called 'good papers' are only interested for a couple of headlines and then they're back to how weird you are. It's the most morally offensive way of living you can imagine, to pretend to be interested in life, and committed to the truth about it, but actually you are not interested in complexity at all. And worse: you are cynical about the possibility of your readers' interest in it. I'll save my Jeremiad until later. But my experience at university told me how complex were the relations between the search for truth and the possibility of justice. It took me, a former hacker, directly into the world that produced WikiLeaks.

There are a few recurring themes in my life, and in the telling of it, too. I already mentioned reading Solzhenitsyn's *Cancer Ward* in Wandsworth. At one point in the story Kostoglotv is discussing the value of university with a fellow patient: 'Remember, education doesn't make you smarter . . . of course you should study. Study! Only remember for your own sake, it's not the same as intelligence.'

However much I learned from studying quantum mechanics, I learned almost as much from my more frivolous-seeming activities. I've always loved to exercise my mind in unusual ways, and this instinct was served during this period by my starting the Melbourne University Mathematics and Statistics Society Puzzle Hunt. For the first-ever prize hunt, in 2004, we challenged contestants to solve a wacky scenario based around the Australian election and the death of the then Prime Minister. 'Who hit Howard?' our promotional material asked. 'John Howard seems to have been vaporised while giving a secret speech at Melbourne University. Who was behind such a dastardly act and why? What, if anything, does it have to do with grave robberies in marginal electorates, temperature swings and strange night-time goings on under Melbourne University Private?' There was a serious point to all this silliness, though. As I said at the time, when I spoke to the university newspaper, 'It's about thinking clearly and deeply to try to solve a problem.' In the end a team of statisticians, computer programmers and a musician dug up the $200 prize buried under a garden gnome in the System Garden of the Parkville campus. I know, all this hardly puts me up there with the great hedonists of the age, the great druggists, sexualists and rock and rollers of the period, but, despite what they say in the papers, intellectual playfulness has always been more my thing.

I shared such intellectual adventures with my son. I wanted to protect him from some of the real harshness of the adult world and yet I could see he had good humour. Many parents are, I suppose, frightened of what their children might learn, but I wanted Daniel to follow his own organic growth. By then he would be spending half his time with his mother, and he was great with words, better than I was. There's always frivolity if you have a child. The pressure of adult life can knock the frivolity out of you, just like a queer storm can blow the wind out of your sails, but I loved the fact that my son was such an optimistic creature. We would go out exploring abandoned buildings together, and, at Christmas one time, we gathered Barbie dolls and toy dragons and blew them up with some home-made explosives and liquid nitrogen.

Clever children, because they pick things up quickly, then very quickly become themselves. So they start to deviate from the average. You can see how their inquisitiveness begins to make individuals of them, because they are looking for unusual things in their environment, things that their peers wouldn't even begin to notice. So much of what I'm telling you now is about the children, but also about myself: even today, I constantly want to find the unexpected thing in a room or in a person. Jean Renoir once said that in every imaginable situation there's the perfect shot: it could be through a glass or from behind someone's head. The job is to find it. That's my instinct, anyhow, and it's an instinct I love in other people.

I'm sure I felt I was in preparation for something. Not to play a giant personal part – that wasn't the intention – but to bring the experience I was gathering, and the expertise I had gained, into forming an organisation that might itself guarantee the pursuit of justice in public affairs, despite the aura of complacency that so often surrounds them. You could say, without too much sentiment, I hope, that the stars were coming into alignment for that organisation. I began to feel the pulse of them, the possibility and the stars, during a trip to see a total solar eclipse in the Australian desert at the end of 2002. We were physicists, and the tradition of skywatching in that discipline remains a thrilling part of the game. We worked out that the eclipse would be at its best over a 7.5-kilometre track for thirty-eight seconds, and that we'd want to be at the centre of that track for the duration.

A team of us, about twelve cars in all, headed off for this three-and-a-half-day drive to find a little patch of desert. In the event, we would have to be so precise in our predictions that we'd be standing on only one piece of ground, no more than half a kilometre long, and for this I laid out a great deal of expenditure and came near to exhaustion. But the philosophical impact was very great on me at the time: I finally realised that if you believe something is true, and you weigh and measure the possibilities well, and you carry on with good faith, then your prediction will come good. I had put myself into the project entirely and trusted our powers in conjunction with the intellectual traditions we had studied. And it was the right thing to do.

Stick with me. Behind the setting up of WikiLeaks was not only the experience of a life, and the lives of others, but also an experience of thinking my way towards clarity about human rights. There is no way to give you an honest and good book without going into those ideas. I have tried to show you the extent to which it grew out of my personal history, but a great deal of it, too, came from thinking hard about what to do. I'm told by industry-watchers that thinking is no great aphrodisiac when it comes to celebrity memoirs: then so be it, let us agree to let this book fail as a celebrity memoir. The work of WikiLeaks that would become so famous was born, and continues to be born, out of a passion for new ideas about how global society might go about protecting freedom. It is also born from the application of a scientific frame of mind to the issue of rights.

What are rights, anyway? Rights are freedoms of action that are known to be enforceable. A right therefore implies an equal responsibility. I don't mean this in the way that right-wing journalists mean it when they say that a petty thief has forfeited his rights because he didn't meet his responsibilities. I mean that if we recognise that somebody possesses a right, we must also recognise our own responsibility to protect that right. As I write these words, children are dying of starvation. I may proclaim the right of every child to freedom from hunger but if I stand by while they starve, my words are worthless. And yet some rights go unrealised, unenforced. An oppressive state squeezes dissidents, tries to make them small, to lock them up, to isolate them – all in an attempt to diminish their right to speak until they are alone, chatting to themselves in an empty room. And to return, therefore, to our goal of justice with a seemingly banal but truly fundamental observation: we cannot realise the basic rights that underpin justice in a world of concealment, secrecy and lies. It is the right to know that draws forth the right to speak. And, taken together, we can call these two rights the right to communicate knowledge.

We should remember that the decision about which rights will be enforced, and which shall be ignored, is always a matter of politics. To put it baldly: I have a single goal, not a very original one but a definite goal to my life, which is to help in the creation of a more just society to live in. I am not for transparency all round, or even democracy all round, but I am for justice, and the contribution we are making is to argue the case for new inevitabilities when it comes to justice and technology. I believe we have an innate yearning for justice. We have an innate aversion to censorship. And the Web can speak to that.

We have a responsibility to knowledge. We have a duty to information. That is why we love our libraries. But, in the digital age, we might also understand that, finally, we have a responsibility to use our technology to stand against those who would prevent knowledge or information from appearing in the public record. We cannot trust newspapers alone, as they have proved again and again to be both censors and partisans. We cannot trust broadcasters, who show, in most cases, that the value of advertising is more compelling to them than news values. Publishing in the computer age therefore becomes about performing the task that the systems allow and facing down the ingrained, self-protecting habits of the old publishing way. As our work has shown and our ongoing collaborations attest, we are not against the old media. We just forged a position that allowed us to do better publishing on the modern scene than they could do. We work with them because we do not wish to be rivals: we wish to pool resources, but they, as we will see in forthcoming chapters, struggle with the notion of their own legitimacy in the computer age, and with the machinations of their own egos. That is fine. But civilisation, if I may suggest so, is moving on without them. They are dying.

I grew towards WikiLeaks by trying to establish in my mind a science of journalistic honesty. What would keep us honest? I had established infinite deniability of sources when I was a hacker and activist. And now I wondered if this could help people place stories in the public domain? Could a new method of publishing sustain a new way of localising power? It was inevitable, once the heat was on, that the old media institutions would shy from these questions, rush into their habitual dugouts and prepare to denounce me. But none of that matters. The more important issue is to do with how institutions adapt to the new expectations put upon them. When clever young people trust their social media more than they trust their elders, how will institutions prove their virtue? Our fathers took them for granted, but our knowledge, in detail, of how human institutions actually behave across the world in the modern era is very poor.

And that won't stick any more. People relate to each other, countries relate to each other, ideas relate very differently now that the technology keeps the globe in touch with itself. That's it, really. All the old hiding places are open to exposure, and the institutions can bark, the military can weep, the *New York Times* can ride its pious high horse, but it won't change the fact that people want answers now to questions they once didn't even know were questions. And they know where to look. They know how to talk to each other about the fact that certain public bodies are keeping secrets. As WikiLeaks began to look possible, I started to believe, myself, that the old security state was no longer feasible. It is not an emotional position; it is just a fact of modern life. The game is up.

But what if I have it wrong? What if justice isn't really the most important goal and I overestimated its chances of ever being wholly achieved? Then we will have the pleasure, if only a small one, of knowing that week by week we helped achieve some modest goals for justice. We are not an ideology and we are not fastened to some kind of historical imperative: we are publishers who tried to respond honestly to what was happening. Part of setting up the organisation was to do with inspiring people – journalists, broadcasters, activists, readers, viewers, ordinary punters – to expect better behaviour from their institutions and from themselves. That little dream would stand behind everything we would set out to do.

But there's one guarantee in journalism: if you make it your business to point out a vast sickness, it won't be long before they're accusing you of being in the throes of some sickness yourself. I would come to say 'J'accuse', and, like all Dreyfusards, I would in quick time find myself characterised as a child-frightening weirdo with questionable hygiene and a horrible record in the treatment of colleagues and lovers. But that was all to come. As I left the University of Melbourne in 2006, it looked like the night sky and my own past gave a guide to how to proceed.

I had one or two certainties. Just one or two. They were to do with how we generated our history and our stories and our justice. George Orwell caught it best, when he wrote, in his novel *Nineteen Eighty-Four*, that he who controls the present controls the past, and he who controls the past controls the future. Orwell was talking about the power of governments to manipulate the people by propaganda, but, increasingly, I foresaw that by using our technology to understand why certain material was kept out of the public domain, and then devoting ourselves as publishers to making that material public, we could subvert the meaning of Orwell's words and turn them into a message of hope. Who would control the future? All of us. The digital era could begin to answer Orwell's point. The message, in fact, was the medium. And we were the messengers. The Net would work for the cause of revelation no matter what. And our job was to work as editors and context-makers, as well as protectors of sources. But could it actually work? Was there a way to make such a thing reliable and how could it be funded and how would we deal with the flak? Because one thing was certain and for sure: the messengers would be the first to be shot.

It was a US president, Theodore Roosevelt, who pointed to a crucial truth about good governance. 'Behind the ostensible government sits an invisible government,' he wrote, 'owing no allegiance and acknowledging no responsibility to the people. To destroy this invisible government, to befoul this unholy alliance between corrupt business and corrupt politics is the first task of statesmanship.' Out of all my youthful experience came a certainty about how to do this. It was a certainty in my imagination, at least, and I was now ready to move and make it a progressive reality.

Authoritarian power knows how to strengthen itself through conspiracy, but it came to seem natural to me, logical indeed, that resistance would grow in direction proportion to how much people understood the conspiracy. I am not talking about conspiracy in the sense of secret, one-off cover-ups, the ramblings of tinfoil-hat-wearing weirdos. I am talking about systemic conspiracy, the habitual *modus operandi* for governments who prefer to do everything in secret. Information would set us free. And computer science, as a form of maths, would be our aid in revealing political relationships. Conspirators trust and depend on other conspirators – I have called these dependencies 'patronage networks' – and when we stop being hysterical about conspiring parties in society, and become instead rational, we can begin to oppose actions they commit together that they could never commit alone.

And what does a conspiracy compute? It computes the next action of the conspiracy. By the time I was ready to found WikiLeaks, the biggest question for me had become, 'How can we reduce the power of a conspiracy?' And the answer seemed within our grasp: to chase their secrets into the open air. I did not invent opposition to these forces: I merely saw that they bred their own opposition, and then tagged them to our new technology. Our job is to stop conspiratorial power from thinking and acting efficiently. And the way to do this, on a global scale, is to open up those conspiracies to the people. We might remember the soothsayer's advice to Julius Caesar – 'Security gives way to conspiracy' – and add a coda of our own: 'And conspiracy gives way to the people's power to know it and break its power.'

I should also say something about the role of the technology in all this. The Internet by itself does not give you freedom. The Internet is simply a way to make publishing cheap and, within the limits of local censorship, international. But it does not give you any extra freedom. If you want freedom in the age of the Internet, you still have to fight for it yourself. Some people have referred to the transformation of Egypt in 2011 as the 'Twitter Revolution', as if Mubarak was toppled by a flash mob in Silicon Valley. There's a reason for the popularity of this fiction, and that is that it serves the American perception of itself in the world as intrinsically benign. It also serves the American tendency to see any form of popular yearning for freedom and democracy as inherently American in character. Thus Hillary Clinton's rhetoric switched in a second from 'Mubarak's a great guy and he should stay' to 'Isn't it great what the Egyptian people have done, and isn't it great how the United States did it for them?' I will never know how she managed to keep a straight face when she proclaimed, on 15 February 2011, that Internet freedom was to be at the heart of American foreign policy on the very same day her government went to court to force Twitter to give up the account information of three members of WikiLeaks staff.

The fight against oppressive regimes begins, and will end, always, with the fight for information and communication. Egypt was not the Twitter Revolution, any more than the French Revolution was the revolution of the printing press and the political pamphlet; but what they both represent are revolutions of the people sharing ideas and information using the technology available to them, and expressing themselves in the public space. My friend John Pilger got it right when he said that it is not WikiLeaks the United States government is afraid of, and it is not Julian Assange that they are afraid of. What does it matter what I know? What does it matter what WikiLeaks knows? It matters not at all. What matters is what you know. This is all about *you*.

Back in Melbourne, in 2006, I'm glad to say some of the old hacking spirit remained. A bunch of us were living on a house at 177 Grattan Street, right next to a busy road, and the general chaos in the house was only made worse, I'm sure, by our mathematical adventures and nocturnal habits. In the flurry of working things out, I had scrawled algebra and diagrams first on a number of light boards, then on the walls and on the windows, on the tables and over anything flat, and sometimes the noise of traffic outside would become too much for concentration. There were traffic lights outside. One day, in the old style, we hacked into the city traffic system and changed the lights to be on permanent green. That put an end to the revving for a while, though not for long enough.

It was around this time I began to think about my biological father. I had no view of him when I was a child. I had a view of my stepfather as a good father and was loyal to him in that way. I called him Dad. My actual father wasn't mentioned much, neither pejoratively or otherwise, and I suppose that was just tactful of my mother, given Brett's commitment to us. There had been no visitation and that was standard in Australia at the time; the idea was that you didn't contaminate the dynamics of the new family with regular and possibly resentful incursions from the old. My childhood was pretty much without stress and I didn't think about him all that often.

But something happens to boys in puberty. You have this sudden spike in self-awareness and hopefully in intelligence. You're suddenly embracing the world and rejecting parts of it, too. In quick time I was a father myself, and I had taught myself with books. The books had become special to me, all that Dostoevsky, Koestler, Kafka, and I think I realised at the time that I wasn't getting that interest from a mysterious source. It took me years to discover that it was probably coming from my father. During those years, it seemed an unnecessary emotional complication, the idea of seeking out my father, but, nonetheless, I felt his presence in me. By the time I was completing university, I saw that a significant part of who I was, whoever I was, had come from this invisible person who might have helped me.

After a little correspondence, we spoke on the phone. And then I went up to Sydney to see him. It was odd. They came to the airport to meet me – my father, his partner and a son. I had brought my bike with me, which my father decided to ride back to their house in New Town, while we went ahead in the car. The partner was curious: a film producer, clearly besotted with him but in some way unconventional. My father had, at some point around thirty-five, decided to retrain as an actor. I don't know if the experience was an opening-up of things, or a closing-down, but it was poignant all the same to be in the house and see him. And I had a weird experience there. In the evening I walked around the house looking at his bookshelves. I found myself getting sort of angry as I did so, because there, on shelf after shelf, were the exact same books as those I had bought and read myself. I suddenly realised I had started from the bottom of myself, on the first rung, and built myself up via many trials and tribulations, when, all the time, if I had only known him, I might just have picked his books down from the shelf.

Maybe the feeling was acute because of the work I had embarked on, the investigations of cause and effect, the attempt to find a scientific basis for understanding the relationship between individuals and authority. Anyway, the feeling was powerful. It galvanised me, somehow. I suddenly knew there was this genetic connection between us, an intellectual temper as much as anything, and that I had missed out by not having him to refer to or learn from. I was struck during that visit by a sense that I had done too much on my own. Perhaps, if I'd known him, I would have built faster. It wasn't about love; it was about rapport. He had a kind of cultivated graciousness that made you warm to him and I found it easy to talk to him, even though he could sometimes be aloof. We still have that ability to talk to each other very easily, having this instant access to one another's mental make-up. I never had a mentor. On reflection, that might always have been a problem for me. I was forced to make myself up as I went along and was happy to be a mentor to other people. It's odd, that. It leaves you always having to play the part of the strong one.

I always knew I was different, but meeting him made me feel less so. It would probably be fair to say that I'm not good at making people feel relaxed. I was born arguing.

And there is always so much to fix and so little time. My father was also a yoga teacher, and I once went with him to an early morning yoga class, after which everybody met in a café for breakfast. People were happy and drinking their orange juice or whatever and somehow I started a debate about maternity care. You could feel the agitation, but I had fixed upon this intellectual problem and continued making my point, while, one by one, people started peeling away from the table. I didn't know these people from the yoga class especially well and eventually I saw I'd emptied the table. When most people sit down, they look for commonality, but I don't, I look for difference. But these people had paid their $25 to feel relaxed and they ended up drinking juice with this guy trying to get an unruly debate doing. It's just part of the story. Being relaxed was not relaxing to me. I know my faults.

I saw my father was the same. But maybe I did better not to be surrounded by his books and his patronage. I had to fend for myself and find my own ground, not being able to rely on the established power network of my father and all he stood for. As he and my mother would once have avowed in their '60s heyday: the personal is political. And maybe my avoidance of him all those years was part of my politics. I wanted to find a fresh way to be in the world, and, by then, in 2006, I wanted the world to be free of the taint of patronage, the conspiracy of mutually assured benefits that make the world tick and eventually cause it to explode.

8

THE BIRTH OF WIKILEAKS

And so the rubber hits the road. I happen to have seen many institutions from the inside, either by going out to greet them or by hacking their systems and walking through their portals in the night. But in 2006 that exploration came to an end and I wanted to tackle those institutions and those governments, wherever they led their dark lives. I'm not an original political thinker, never claimed to be, but I know the technology and I understand the structures of government; and I was ready to throw the latter, where possible, into a bath of acid and boil them down to the bone. It occurred to me: we can just live our lives complacently, worrying about the mortgage or whether we're famous enough or rich enough or truly loved, or we can look at the bones of our world and test if they are good and true.

When you get stuck into most institutions, you see they float on power and patronage and defend themselves with marketing. That seems to me just a basic truth about the world, though one, I've learned, that most organisations

will go to the wall denying. Whether it's the government of
Kenya or the Bank Julius Baer, they work for themselves, and
they build a clever network of people who can gain by them,
and prop them up, while ordinary people are cast into a state
of disadvantage. Since my teens, really, I'd been exposed to
patronage networks, and I understood their incentives. Any
person or organisation that stood against them would be
murdered, either in the courts, or by intelligence agents, or
in the press. I was ready for them. I had honed the technology and the method of using cryptography to protect
sources to a point that I wouldn't even know them myself.
We had the activist experience and the will to disempower.
We didn't have offices, but we had our laptops and our passports. We had servers in different countries. We knew that
we would be the most secure platform for whistleblowers
the world had ever known. We had the gumption. We had
the philosophy. Game on. I registered WikiLeaks.org on
4 October 2006. I guess I knew that my ordinary life, if I'd
ever had one, would never be the same again.

I had a number of helpers or exemplars, you might say,
such as the New York architect John Young, who founded
cryptome.org in 1996. Not everything on Cryptome is a
leaked document, but Young does make it his mission to
publish material that governments and corporations would
rather keep hidden. They've been attacked by Microsoft
and, like WikiLeaks, had a run-in with PayPal. Cryptome
is on the right side in the battle over information, but they
don't have protection mechanisms for the people giving
material to them, and I knew that would be required. Young
was treading on the right domain, but he wasn't ready to be
a publisher of last resort, which is what I envisaged, using
the complex system of deniability I had by then refined for

WikiLeaks. It was all happening quickly and I wanted to make sure the curating and archiving were excellent. Most of the work to set these things up was being done by me at various locations around the world, with the help of some old cypherpunks. My old friend Daniel Mathews from the maths department – more of a traditional leftist, a Chomskyist, I suppose – also helped me at that time. In fact, Dan helped me to put together the founding documents for WikiLeaks, and, later on, wrote an analysis of the first thing we ever leaked.

My job at that point was to create alliances. I was trying to build up an advisory board and tap into future sources of data. At that stage the board was more about giving ourselves some credibility and building contacts that could be useful later; it didn't actually sit anywhere and it didn't really do any advising. Still, I made contact with important, inspiring people such as Daniel Ellsberg, and he agreed to be involved and has stayed loyal throughout. A British mathematician called Ben Laurie also came on board. His father, Peter Laurie, wrote an influential '60s book, *Beneath the City Streets*, about underground nuclear bunkers and government facilities in Britain, and perhaps Ben saw something of his father's work in ours. I tried to build contacts with Chinese activists as well. Because we were predominantly Western ourselves, and subject to Western jurisdictions, I tried to give birth to WikiLeaks not as an anti-Western organisation – which wasn't difficult, because it's not anti-Western, it's pro-information – but I knew we'd turn our attention to the likes of America eventually. At first, the corruption in African countries seemed the obvious place to start. Our philosophy was, from the beginning, fundamentally anti-bastard, and, coarse as that seems, it's also got a certain honesty.

Before the launch, the finance for registering
domain names and so on came from me. Everybody
else contributed their time for free. From the start, we
knew we would face legal challenges and I was keen to
register as much as possible in San Francisco, knowing
that the civil liberties movement there would prove to be
significant fire-power on our behalf once we got into trouble. After that, it was just a case of emailing everybody we
could think of and waiting for the responses.

Our first leaked document, which we published on 28
December 2006, seemed to come from the Union of Islamic
Courts in Somalia, though, as we explained at the time, it
was of mysterious provenance, coming to us via a Chinese
source, and we couldn't be sure that it was genuine. Following years of violence in Somalia, which had already seen the
secession of around two-thirds of the country, the Union
had begun to establish some kind of order out of the chaos.
People began to feel safer in Mogadishu and ordinary citizens became more confident that they would be protected
from everyday violence and the frequent systematic looting
by warlords. Our leaked document purported to be a letter
from a military commander, an inflammatory instruction
in which he referred to the 'Islamic Republic of Somalia', a
form of words rarely used by the Union. 'As you are all aware',
the commander wrote, 'the so-called Transitional Government formed for Somalia is hunting the Somali religious
leaders and the Muslims in general. They have influenced
the International Community to believe that the Somali
religious leaders are Al-Qaeda.' Intercepted email traffic
that was passed to us along with this document seemed
to imply that Somali ministers, including the minister for
petroleum, were preparing to meet with Chinese officials.

It appeared to reveal something that people should have known about the Somali attitude to China and the Chinese attitude to Africa.

This situation in Somalia was getting no real attention in the West at the time, and here, in two small documents, one could begin to see how complex the situation was. The Union really was trying to make a difference: under them, the garbage was collected in Mogadishu for the first time in eleven years. But, whatever they did, the US were unthinkingly opposed to them through their strongest regional ally Ethiopia, seeing any kind of politicisation of Islam in East Africa as somehow linked to the 1998 bombing of the US embassy in Nairobi. Just after we prepared the leaks, Ethiopia invaded Somalia, with US assistance. We continued to follow the situation, offering analysis, comment and other leaked information where we could. Even if the document was a fake, perhaps prepared by Chinese sources, it still raised important questions and showed how the disclosure of secret documents could enhance our understanding of complex political situations. It seemed like a good first move for a young website like WikiLeaks.

We're so used to the pieties of the Western media – to say nothing of the rampant censorship in vast portions of the East – that we forget how many countries have a great hunger among their people for free publishing and for the exposure of abuses. We got a quick response from many areas of the world, not all reliable, not all helpful, but people were tuning in to what we were doing. From the start, of course, being a whistleblowing website, as they call us, certain people were keen to blow the whistle on us and that hasn't changed. My response was, 'Fair enough. We should eat our own dog food and see how it tastes.' We were a group of committed, idealistic people who were trying to get something done. We could take what flak was on offer, but our basic position was strong and ethical, and I couldn't see what rubbish could be thrown at us. I suppose I hadn't prepared myself for the personal smears, or, to any great degree, the smearing of the whole organisation by people who decided to hate us. Some mad individuals thought we were working for the CIA.

But we pressed on. I tried to bring in friends, but friendship, in my experience, will only buy you about nine hours of free labour. And there was an unbelievable amount of work. I had worked through the ideas over many years, but the programming and the logistics had to be done quickly and effectively. I was going from Kenya to Tanzania to Cairo, building the site all the way, and that's when I really began to live out of a small rucksack. I must say I had never been one for belongings. I didn't have many clothes. I ate whatever was going. I spent or gave away whatever money I had almost instantly. It was galling, watching so many of the bright computer nerds of my generation become millionaires, not because I wanted the money but because I could've used their help. But during these itinerant years that began WikiLeaks, I realised, quite gradually, that I had need of very little material stuff at all. I had a bag of socks and underwear, and a bigger bag of laptops and cables.

I came through Paris and London looking for more help. I often got volunteers for short bursts, but they'd burn out, understandably, or want something that paid in cash or glory. At one point I was shut up in a room in Paris on my own for two months while Nicolas Sarkozy was going about getting himself elected as president. It was spring 2007. I felt completely crushed, knowing WikiLeaks could be great, but that I was just ailing under the sheer volume of work required to make it happen. I was the only one doing the work, and it was hard to remember, on those Paris nights with the sound of laughter in the street below, that the site might actually do something good in the end. I had a girl-friend who would come round. She just brought food and I stayed at the computer. She spoke Russian, and would sometimes lend a hand with that, but it was a lonely time. Obsessional. I just couldn't see how to leave the computer.

Sometimes, I'd imagine I heard a squawk outside and think it must be one of the tropical birds from Magnetic Island. Or I'd feel for a second that sugar ants were running over the desk and across the floor. It got strangely warm as the days and weeks flowed on, with me trying to ensure that the submissions system for WikiLeaks would be totally right. Although I already had a large cache of material, we began attracting new stuff right away, and much of that new stuff came with a promise from me that we'd publish it. So I prioritised the new stuff, while also doing the final tinker-ing with the system, working out how people would email each other, and establishing how, say, the Kenyans would be able to get secure interaction. It was like setting up a branch office of the CIA. It was inevitable that WikiLeaks would, like any new business, have to grow organically: even more so, in our case, because it wasn't like a normal company where you had the financing and a business model under which the whole thing would be run by advertising or by fresh injections of venture capital. It wasn't like that. I was constantly searching for voluntary labour and having these online meetings that I'd scheduled. Once or twice, quite comically (though not at the time), I turned out to be the only person at those online meetings. And of course the

whole thing was right on the border of schizophrenia: I'd
be there, tapping away, being the Chair and the Secretary
and bringing the next thing on the agenda and calling the
vote. Mad. But I felt I had to go on as if the whole thing were
possible, and that way it would really happen. In the same
spirit of self-reinforcement, I would sometimes decide that
a particular piece of work – writing an important press
release, say – would demand that I wore clothing that suited
the gravity of the occasion. Imagine me sitting in a hot poky
flat in Paris, unshaven, typing away, but wearing exactly the
right sort of jacket. I know.

Daniel Mathews stayed on board as long as he could but
he started to burn out with the lack of rewards. By this time
he had moved to Stanford, where he was completing his
PhD and teaching at the same time. It wasn't even, at that
point, as if we were getting a lot of positive feedback from
the community. There's wasn't any sense of us gaining an
uplift in our popular reputation on the back of all the hard
work: the volunteers must have asked themselves, as they
probably still do, what was in it for them and at the time
I had no answer to that. I was just intent on doing it and
I hoped other people would find a deep source of motivation in the work itself. It all got pretty difficult at several
moments. It wasn't human, the amount of work in front
of us in 2007, the intensity, the pressure. I went to Africa
during that time and came back to Paris with good connections, but I wasn't feeling well. After a while it turned into a
fever and there was a sudden spike in my temperature. As
you'll have gathered, I'm a bit of a know-all – one of those
vices that can quite often be turned into a virtue – so of
course I've read a few medical textbooks and I'm extremely
sceptical of doctors. The fever was bad, but I felt certain it

would burn itself out in a few days. After ten days or so of sweating and suffering, it wasn't getting any better.

I had malaria. Spending time in a French hospital can make you understand why there was, and always will be, a need in that country for revolution. A short visit, even, can make you see why Flaubert hated the bourgeoisie and why the '60s radicals wanted to burn down the Sorbonne. Not that I came out of it very well, either. The nurse who was looking after me had the demeanour of a natural bully. She tried to put paracetamol in my arm. I said I wasn't in pain and didn't need it. She said they gave it to all the patients, no matter what. I said no. She tried to stick it in during the night and I refused and she tried again, so I ripped it out and said if she kept it up I would walk out of the hospital. I know, I know, who would go to war with a nurse? But, I'm telling you, these nurses are fascistic, and I was ill with fever so I was a bit off my head anyway. And this old man who was sharing the room with me was cheering me on, saying the nurses were always trying to push you around. He loved this display of resistance to the nursing staff. They just couldn't deal with me because I wouldn't take paracetamol. And when I later got a stomach cramp they wouldn't bring a doctor, because I'd refused the stuff. The whole system is rigged to punish people who have different ideas of how things should be done.

I don't have the gene that helps you to help yourself. And that lack would cause trouble for me all the way down the line. But I can't make too many apologies for that: I was, and always will be, more concerned with the wars going on around the world than with making things easier for myself. It soon became clear that WikiLeaks would have a crucial role in throwing some true light onto these wars when, in the autumn and winter of 2007, we received a number of documents that had come from deep inside the US military. In November we published this incredible database that revealed all the military equipment that has been registered by the US Army for use in Iraq, about 150,000 records. I made an analysis of the material and saw that what it amounted to was what is called 'the order of battle', the whole pyramidal planning system, detailing each unit, their name and everything they had; not expendables like bullets, but fixed-down stuff like Persian rugs and computers. I took the complete list and wrote a computer program to analyse it: looking at a military supply site and getting the prices, we were able to get a sense of both the giant costs and which units had been the best-funded. About half of all equipment purchases had been focused on dealing with insurgents' improvised explosive devices, most commonly called roadside bombs or IEDs. Most of this money was being spent on 'warlock' machines, which are very sophisticated jammers of radio signals. The total money spent on evading IEDs – on detectors, jammers, robot defusers, extra armour and so on – amounted to about $13 billion. Even if you adjust the figure for inflation, that's more than the entire cost of the Manhattan Project, and something I believe the world has a right to know.

It was like setting up scaffolding for lots of new and deeper stories about what was actually happening in Iraq and Afghanistan. Reporters, generally, were taking too much for granted; no one was asking where the money was going and how the command structure worked.

New material began flooding towards us and I could see the change it might bring about. We were going to crack the world open and let it flower into something new. Yet we found early on what the struggles were going to be, and one of the biggest, one of the most persistent, was to do with journalists' apathy. You could open up all these new lines of enquiry, these new routes to justice, and they would just shrug and say they didn't have the time to work through the material. It was frustrating. But I now see it as an important factor in the way we see the world through the media. The journalists don't just report: their assumptions and their apathy have a part to play in making the picture that comes down to us. And we saw ourselves as journalists from the start. Better ones.

In the Internet Age, when so many people are driven into knowledge by their search engines, I knew the material would filter down anyhow. Even some military personnel themselves began visiting our site, to see what kind of replacement parts they might need for their vehicles. Irony of ironies: some NATO military contractor would appear in a chatroom saying can you help me find a wheel for my armoured vehicle. But the media sat back. I suppose we weren't yet an authoritative source, and we couldn't offer exclusivity – a thing that controls the whole universe of motivation in the media. Worst of all, the material we revealed was complex. But we had built a system that would alter the basic rules of journalism. With powerful organisations, such as the British Army, for instance, the Fourth Estate is used to looking at uniformed individuals and waiting for briefings, the journalist situating himself in a position of deference to an unregulated body of power. We forget there is real skin under those uniforms, and that is what we wanted to reveal, the naked truth under the disguises of power.

We had set off on a mission of grand witnessing. Computer technology was watchful, indeed, and was coupled, in our minds, with a burgeoning psychology of decency. I wrote a blog post at the time, trying to describe our motivations and our task. I wrote:

> *Every time we witness an injustice and do not act, we train our character to be passive in its presence and thereby lose all ability to defend ourselves and those we love. In a modern economy it is impossible to seal oneself off from injustice . . . If we can only live once, then let it be a daring adventure that draws on all our powers. Try as I may I cannot escape the sound of suffering. Perhaps as an old man I will take great comfort in pottering around in a lab and gently talking to students in the summer evening and will accept suffering with insouciance. But not now. Men in their prime, if they have convictions, are tasked to act on them.*

Reality is an aspect of property. It must be seized. And investigative journalism is the noble art of seizing reality back from the powerful. By the time WikiLeaks was up and running and making headlines, much of this had been forgotten, or had not occurred to a new generation of journalists or readers. We made it our task to revivify the art of observation. With all due modesty, I think we became the first intelligence agency of the people. And those early, heady days, only four years ago in real time, but a different era to us, were filled with a sense that we would spill over borders and prejudices, including our own, and get better by the month. We still had a lot to learn. But the principles of good journalism in service of better governance would remain undiluted from those days to these.

The African experience was filtered through this period, but I want to relate that experience in the next chapter. The day before leaking the equipment list for Iraq, we hit a home run by publishing the manual for Guantánamo Bay. It's an incredible modern document, something that one can imagine being read in hundreds of years' time by people who want to understand the ideological struggles of our period. Not just ideological struggles, either, but mental ones. Its classification was low, so clearly the authorities never expected this manual to be read by anyone outside the prison camp, and isn't that part of the problem with secret documents? They are often written by people with a heavy bias, an almost fetishistic hatred, and with a deep wish to inculcate that bias in their colleagues. The Guantánamo manuals cover all the main aspects of how detainees are brought to the installation, how they are to be kept, and what should happen to them. It reads like something taken in dictation for Attila the Hun or Vlad the Impaler: relentlessly cruel, dehumanising, paranoid, dramatic and excessive, it would make even the sleepiest tax-payer wonder what fundamental weakness, what fatal need, was being addressed by this manual and this crazy detention centre, all paid for in tax dollars.

The manual relates how records should be faked to hide prisoners from the Red Cross. It states that all prisoners will be placed in maximum security for their first month after arrival, to soften them up for interrogation. 'The two week period following Phase 1 will continue the process of isolating the detainee and fostering dependence on the interrogator.' It outlines the whole aggressive mindset of the Quick Response Force (QRF), the unit on permanent standby in case of 'a disturbance in the Detention Facility'. How the

prisoners could ever cause any kind of dangerous disturbance given the conditions they were held in was a mystery,
but the 'QRF soldiers will don riot control gear consisting
of: face shields attached to the Kevlar, non-ballistic shin
guards, a shield, and a baton'. The manual shows how fear
at the highest level can inform brutality: these prisoners
were not treated like normal opponents or normal men,
they were to be handled like Hollywood supervillains who
posed, as they lived and breathed, the most extraordinary
security risk ever encountered. They must be kept like
demons and patrolled by dogs. One detainee was forced
to wear women's underwear on his head. Psychological
torture was rampant. And the manual made it clear that
disorientation and humiliation were understood to be part
of common practice. The insecurity present in all of this is
truly staggering; it tells you about America under Bush, a
place that appeared willing to suspend all its constitutional
decencies in the effort to annihilate the phantoms of danger.
These techniques, as later reported in the *Washington Post*,
informed the way things were done at Abu Ghraib. Cruelty
and hatred live inside individuals, but when I talk about
'injustice' I am making an observation about a political and
social system. The torture techniques used at Abu Ghraib
were not invented by a few working-class American military policemen and women who were later conveniently
scapegoated. They were part of the system and the moral
responsibility starts at the top.

We released this manual without fanfare and with little
introduction. It didn't need anything – at first glance you
saw how explosive it was. Nothing happened for a week
and then we got a letter from Southern Command, who are
responsible for Guantánamo, asking us to remove it. That

was good news: it proved the publication's authenticity. We ignored it. Then *Wired* magazine picked up the story and later the *New York Times* and the *Washington Post*. It was the way I'd always expected word to get out, bubbling up from blogs and smaller press and into the mainstream. At first, when the heat came, it didn't come directly to me. I was called Investigations Editor, and there wasn't yet the habit, which has now become a contagion, of linking every WikiLeaks utterance to me. At the time I think I knew that my past, as a convicted hacker, wouldn't necessarily help the cause we'd undertaken, and I wanted to keep my position dark as far as possible. But the rules of showbusiness, and, it must be said, the wiles of treachery, made it predictable that I should become the Bond villain and the designated bogeyman.

As the press coverage increased, Lieutenant Colonel Edward M. Bush III, who was the public affairs spokesman for Guantánamo, responded to our leak by saying it was no longer like that. The manual related how things had been under Geoffrey Miller. So we then leaked the 2004 manual so that people could compare the two. What they found was that the second manual was, if anything, worse. They revealed how the prison would perform these show-trial rituals, and how, when a visiting dignitary came to call, the prisoners had to turn their heads away. That kind of thing. Oh, and where was Miller posted after Guantánamo? Abu Ghraib.

We wanted people to have an opportunity to understand exactly what was going on under our noses, and that it stank. We were able to describe how the renditions actually happened and we printed the floor plan of the aircraft that carried the detainees to the island. The detainees somehow

required goggles, helmets and hoods, and had to be chained
to the floor. Why did the US authorities imagine these men
had superhero powers? What deep well of fantasy did that
tap into?

WikiLeaks was gathering momentum. The Guantánamo
leak, and the accompanying press coverage, brought us more
sensitive material. The US Army's report into the Battle of
Fallujah was marked classified for twenty-five years. But we
posted it as soon as it was handed to us in December 2007.
On 31 March 2004, four Americans working for the private
security firm Blackwater were kidnapped by Iraqi insurgents who beat them, burned them, and hung their bodies
off a bridge. The following attack by US troops was reactive, and the report made it clear that there had not been
enough planning beforehand, not enough understanding of
the political landscape or preparing of the media. Growing civilian casualties led to pressure on the US from the
Iraqi Governing Council and a unilateral ceasefire was
announced on 9 April. The WikiLeaks documents made
it clear the fighting did not cease, however – 'the ceasefire
was a bit of a misnomer' – and also revealed that the whole
operation had been mounted more as a media-pleasing
exercise than anything else.

Our leaked document made it clear that the attack was
ordered at the behest of Donald Rumsfeld, who resented
the way Fallujah had become a 'symbol of resistance'. There
were many civilians in the area and these facts were ignored
by the US military. A journalist from Al Jazeera who was
known to me, Ahmed Mansour, was in the city during the
final assault, and he and his colleague were attempting to
tell the truth about the battle and the methods being used.
According to our leaked report, 'approximately 150 air

strikes destroyed 75 buildings, including two mosques', and the operation 'stirred up a hornets' nest across the Al Anbar Province'. As part of the ceasefire agreement, the US insisted that the Al Jazeera journalists be removed from the city. As our leaked document put it, 'Al Jazeera was claiming that up to 600 Iraqi civilians had been killed by the US offensive. Images of dead children were being displayed repeatedly on televisions around the world.' The report-writers lamented the fact that there were no embedded Western reporters in the area to present the views of 'military authorities'.

In November the US attacked Fallujah again. It was later to become famous as the bloodiest battle of the war. The Americans had used white phosphorous as part of their campaign, and while this was perhaps not illegal it was deemed highly controversial at the very least. Indeed, Saddam Hussein's deployment of white phosphorous against his own people in 1991 was counted a war crime and used as part of the justification for the Allied invasion of 2003. In between the original attack on Fallujah and this second one, the scandal of Abu Ghraib broke in the world's press – or, as the writer of the report preferred to see it, ignoring American responsibility for this scandal, 'the insurgents got lucky'.

The work never stopped. I sent the leaked Fallujah document to 3,000 people and waited for the levees to break. Nothing. That was one of the most baffling of all the situations we've got into. Just no response. People had been writing about Fallujah for the previous three years; they never had a document from inside the mind of the US military like this one, and yet they didn't jump on it. I must say, I wasn't just baffled at my journalistic colleagues at that point, I was ashamed of them. The shallowness exhibited by those correspondents is actually mindblowing, if you think about it, and you are left, or I was left at the time, wondering if the mainstream of Western journalism wasn't just made up of – there's no other word – wankers.

But, for the long term, there was a lesson. It would become part of my thinking when it came to the Afghan War Logs. What were the unfakeable metrics in modern journalism? They were sales, hits, take-up and exclusivity. And I had to learn how to use these metrics to get the stories out.

9

THE WORLD THAT CAME IN FROM THE COLD

Not long before the incidents I've just been writing about, I made a point of going to Africa and testing my ground. It was early days for WikiLeaks and I felt I had to travel in order to broaden, if you like, the mind of the project. I knew that the World Social Forum would be happening in Nairobi in January 2007, and a Melbourne friend, Matt Smith, was willing to finance some of the journey and come with me. The forum sprang up as an alternative to the World Economic Forum. As it was happening in Kenya, I knew it would attract many NGOs and connected participants, which made it the ideal place to give the first full-blown talk about WikiLeaks. I hoped at the time that it would attract volunteers and contacts. We had published a few of our early things, but the big initial leaks – Guantánamo and Fallujah – were to come. I'm sure I felt that opening my stall in Africa would set the tone for us, making it plain from the start that we

were a global organisation, not a Western one, with eyes
everywhere.

I immediately felt a connection with Africa. The air was
different, and during the great period of labour to set things
up, I needed a change of atmosphere, as well as the tonic
sense of expansiveness that seemed to travel on the wind.
Isak Dinesen caught the perfect breeze I'm talking about in
Out of Africa. 'In the middle of the day the air was alive over
the land,' she writes, 'like a flame burning; it scintillated,
waved and shone like running water, mirrored and doubled
all objects . . . Up in this high air you breathed easily, drawing a vital assurance and lightness of heart. In the highlands
you woke up in the morning and thought: Here I am, where
I ought to be.'

After buying our $50 visas, Matt and I drove in from
the airport and watched the giraffes loping in the distance.
They say human beings initially came out of the Rift Valley
in Kenya, and so, at some level, coming to Kenya is always
a returning to Kenya: you are coming back to what your
biology expects, to a certain right degree of light and
humidity and temperature. Maybe that is why people often
remark how at home they feel. Isak Dinesen said it, but we
all say it when we're in Kenya. And the people are friendly.
For someone like me, who has always been on the road,
there was this sense of generosity and general satisfaction
that this was the place to be. The rates of crime and the
incidence of Aids, of course, are very high, but if I felt at
all tense on our way to Kisumu and the Commonwealth
Games Stadium, it was because I felt so sure that this visit
would be crucial to the development of WikiLeaks.

'Think global, act local' had long been an article of faith
among the left-wingers that predominantly made up the

crowd at the World Social Forum, but I preferred to see things slightly differently. When the world only extended to your surrounding villages, hills and mountains, and beyond them was only legend, saving the world was approachable and a natural activity to all of independent character. But in the modern world, one needs only a minimum of education and a little access to the media to realise how vast the world is. And this fact is demoralising. It is impossible to envisage your actions making any significant difference. To interact meaningfully with the world, one either has to constrain one's imagination – to artificially shrink the world – or try in some way to really engage with the world as you perceive it now, information overload and all. I was becoming convinced that this second option was the only way to achieve real change, and coming to Africa was in a way an attempt to test that out, to see whether WikiLeaks could be an organisation that 'thought globally and acted globally'.

Nairobi was quite wild, in a way. We were staying in tents, three tents, as it happens, one built inside the other to avoid mosquitoes (fat chance), and we quickly found ourselves helping to organise the recording, translation and archiving of the events at the forum. At one point I moved into the president's suite at the stadium. It was thought to be a good centre from which to co-ordinate things. A large desk, cheap Georgian furniture everywhere, and paintings of former president Daniel Arap Moi looking down from the sun-bleached walls. The corridors were lined with female security officers bearing wooden truncheons. On one of the days there was a commotion in the corridor and suddenly, out of nowhere, a crowd of Kenyan Communist Party members came bustling down the hall, pressing the guards and everyone else to the walls as they entered our

makeshift office. They were accompanied by a large press
pack carrying notebooks and video cameras. A large black
woman threw herself on the desk, stood up, and began
ranting first in Swahili and then in English, demanding that
the World Social Forum's entrance fees must be reduced to
allow greater access for people from the Kabira slums. She
gave this loud press conference from the top of the desk and
then vanished, taking the crowd with her. 'Yes,' I thought,
'now here is a country I can work with.'

After twenty-four years of misrule, Daniel Arap Moi was
finally removed from power at the Kenyan election of 2002.
His replacement, Mwai Kibaki of the Rainbow Coalition,
was elected chiefly on an anti-corruption platform, but by
the time we arrived it wasn't looking so cool. Despite the
new regime having gained support and momentum out of
the movement for constitutional reform, we found that they
were little better than Moi and were carrying out a whole
new rash of injustices and oppressions. Kibaki himself,
in fact, wasn't quite the new broom that was hoped for: a
scion of the old regime, he developed an alarming capacity for suppressing free speech. The offices of the Kenyan
newspaper *The Standard* had been raided by the police six
months before we arrived and the editorial staff had been
incarcerated for half a day. The *Standard* had managed to
capture this brutality on their security cameras, and, excit-
ingly from our perspective, were able to report it in full.
But an atmosphere of intimidation lingered, and it became
clear that the press existed there in a state of threat, which
encouraged us to think we might help them.

A company called Kroll Associates, who did private
investigative work into businesses and assets, looking at
accounts and security systems, were commissioned by the

Kibaki regime to find out what had happened to the money embezzled by former president Moi. It looked like Kibaki wanted some of this money but also, clearly, he wanted to use this information to blackmail Moi into compliance with the new dispensation. (Moi was still a powerful figure on the scene.) The report revealed that up to £1 billion had been channelled abroad by Moi, his sons and their associates through a litany of companies and banks. The report was explosive in that it names the banks in Zurich and London, and gives details of further properties and commercial interests in America and Kenya. The staff at Kroll didn't pull any punches. These extracts concern a Moi associate, accused of being one of the biggest money-launderers in Geneva:

> Katri devised an elaborate system. Rather than send corrupt money straight to banks overseas, he would use local banks in Kenya, such as Trans National Bank, owned by the Mois, Biwott and Kulei, to send vast sums through Nostro accounts – the bank's Forex accounts overseas – and then several months/ years later would send the money on and split it between several banks such as UBP . . . Katri has gone underground since 2001, when a Swiss investigation was launched into his dealings in Kenya. It is understood that he lives in Monte Carlo. Katri has also been connected to the Halliburton scandal in Nigeria through Jeffrey Tessler who he helped to set up an account at UBP five years ago. Tessler, an unscrupulous lawyer from north London, was getting commissions somehow connected to the bribes paid out by Halliburton, and new evidence implies he is still receiving commissions.

Even major global institutions such as Barclays and HSBC were named, and while there was no suggestion that they themselves had done anything illegal, the report showed

that no part of the international financial system was free
from the taint of stolen, dirty money. Looking at the report,
you could also see exactly how such money had been routed
through other jurisdictions, wearing a new disguise at each
stage, often but not always ending up in international tax
havens. This was exactly the kind of corruption WikiLeaks
was set up to reveal. And upending tax havens would be a
future hobby of ours.

I got hold of this document and later, after leaving Africa,
it became an important new posting for us. We fed it to Xan
Rice of the *Guardian*, who ran it as a front-page story on 31
August 2007, headlined 'The Looting of Kenya'. The coverage was good but was not much picked up by other papers
in Britain. The reaction in Kenya itself was giant: they took
their lead from the *Guardian*, though they were more cau-
tious in the way they presented the story. The Kibaki regime's
denials were prominent, though we felt satisfied, knowing
the secret was not only out but that the long-term effects
were sizeable. It was clear that Kibaki, who had been supported by Moi – perhaps as a result of the leverage Kibaki
had gained by commissioning the report in the first place –
was now on the back foot and that was a gain for justice. A
former UK High Commissioner to Kenya had a clear view
of it when he said that the report had enough in it 'to blow
not just the Mois but most of the Kenyan establishment out
of the water'.

From our point of view, the leak supported the idea
that oppressed media organisations could suddenly be
freed when a story that mattered to them – and which they
couldn't reveal on their own – was given legitimacy and the
oxygen of international exposure first. WikiLeaks was the
publisher of last resort, but also an untouchable platform:

we had proved it, and established a *modus operandi* for the future.

We had other business in Kenya, culminating in a document we published in November 2008 detailing cases where, in seeking to confront a criminal organisation known as the Mungiki, the Kenyan police had ignored any kind of consideration of the basic principles of evidence, due process or justice, and had engaged in the extra-judicial murders of hundreds of people. We published this information in the form of a heart-rending report called 'The Cry of Blood', containing the stories of some of the disappeared – 'a 26-year-old mechanic', 'a farm help in Kanunga', 'a taxi driver in Eastleigh', 'a hawker in Baba Dogo' – and photographs of some of the victims and the places their bodies had been dumped. Police had sometimes demanded large sums of money from family members to spare the lives of arrested men.

This was a huge, shocking story, and two of the human rights activists who had helped us, Oscar Kungara and Paul Ulu, were later followed by the police and shot dead in the street in central Nairobi. We made this front-page material on WikiLeaks and made the point that the possible murder of at least 349 people by an out-of-control police force was implied by the material we were seeing. Our commentary made it clear that this was comparable to what happened in Chile under Pinochet. And this was not happening in the Congo, or in neighbouring Sudan: Kenya is a place with significant business development and a sophisticated relationship with the West.

We kept at it, kept publishing stuff that the African papers were too frightened to publish, and eventually Philip Alston, an Australian who was the UN Special Reporter on

Extra-Judicial Killings, came to Nairobi for a week to document what had happened and what had been revealed. The
issue was now out and has never really gone away since. We
had worked on it non-stop while fighting to breathe life into
WikiLeaks. Kenya was a massive test case. We gave it everything we had and our work began to change the picture. We
wanted to do better and do more, but were happy when,
after all that, we won the Amnesty International Reporting
Award for our coverage of the country.

But things are never easy for more than a minute at a
time. The thing about WikiLeaks, right from the start, is
that we were subject to hostile fire from the left as much as
the right. You think you have natural allies, but, when you're
dealing with material this sensitive, and with journalists
under such economic pressure in a culture of distrust, you
find that everywhere you turn there are people waving their
finger at you. That's fine, so far as it goes, and it must come
with the territory, but it's vexing to find yourself in conflict
with people you thought were on the same side. During the
Kenyan campaign, we came across a very important book
by Michaela Wrong called *It's Our Turn to Eat*. The book
gave a detailed insight into the ways of Kenyan corruption
and was banned there, or banned in the sense that no one
would distribute it and no bookseller would stock it. And so,
seeking to expose the immorality of the ban and ensure that
Kenyans could gain access to the text despite the actions of
their government, we outwitted the censor by leaking on
the site a typeset PDF of the book. What we failed to outwit,
however, or in any way foresee, was the author's sense of
copyright. Michaela Wrong erupted. She felt that we were
robbing her not only of her royalties, but also, in some way,
of the credit to which she felt she was her due.

I think I made the point that such a book, such an excellent book, might originally have been her baby, but it was now out there in the world, and had captured the attention and imagination of the people of Kenya – it was now bigger than her alone. I eventually saw her argument in terms of how our posting of it might eat into Western sales, so I put her in touch with our friend Mwalimu Mati, who had been involved in so much of our work in Kenya, suggesting that he could buy the rights to distribute the book in Kenya in paper and electronic form. But the author was slighted and remained so. We were trying to create deterrents and reforms in Kenya, and these people, these smart people, were attacking us for not respecting democracy by insulting copyright law. I found the whole thing baffling, but another early lesson in the complications of political commitment. People have their different priorities, for sure, and it would be a mistake to assume that people who were critical of the authorities were immune from criticism of each other. The left has always been provincial in that way, and I wrongly imagined the issues were much bigger in all our minds. But you can't predict what's going to ail people: one person's bigness is another person's smallness, and it was obvious already that we were being characterised as mavericks who stepped on people's toes. I'm sure we could have been more sensitive to that, but the issues seemed to me too pressing for social or professional niceties, and I guess I wrongly assumed Ms Wrong would be pleased to know her book was so appreciated. Maybe I was over-zealous, but you get like that when the stakes are so high and the conditions so desperate.

We had to learn to deal with resistance. Another person we had admired, a transparency activist called Steven Aftergood, head of the Federation of American Scientists Secrecy

Project and someone I had originally hoped to recruit to our advisory board, also came after us from our own side. When it came to government corruption, we imagined we could begin to become the people's silent advocate in the room. But often we found the prosecution side included people we thought we might have counted on for guidance, for support, for encouragement, or just for tolerance. Aftergood attacked our editorial judgement, feeling some of our targets were undeserving or unworthy of scrutiny – the Church of Scientology, for instance, or the operating manual for the US military's guided bombs – while other work of ours he felt to be 'irresponsible'.

It was never my intention to be responsible in the sense that Aftergood understands the word. We are not of a party or a state; our remit is neither national nor corporate, and we hold no candle for one grouping over another. Unlike too many media organisations, we are not *parti pris*. We will shine a light into any murky corner. When Aftergood spoke of responsibility, he was invoking a misnomer: what he really meant, though he couldn't see it, was that we should take on trust the idea that some secrets have to be kept secret just because a powerful and interested party said so. He knows too much about the self-serving nature of modern government to imagine that we could ever take such a thing on trust. And neither should he. The fact was our organisation was taking a tough new stand. Invading people's privacy, as he put it at the time, was no great crime in my book, not when the potential crimes of the people whose privacy we were invading were evidently so great and so covered up. Aftergood disliked some of the same things we did, but he wasn't willing to shake them down. He was timid. And, like so many, he was probably dismayed at the way our relentless working methods put the softly-softly approach that he favoured in the shade.

To our emerging critics, we were primitive. But in my mind, we were not primitive enough. You have to get over your own need for reassurance and resist the comfort zone of knowing you're only doing what others have done or are doing around you. Innovation can't work with that. We would certainly make mistakes, but even our mistakes would be honest if we resisted the temptation to shy away from danger. To me, a great number of those working for liberal causes are not only shy but borderline collusive. They want change to happen nicely, and it won't. They want decency to come about without anybody suffering or being embarrassed, and it won't. And most of all they want to give many of the enemies of open government the benefit of the doubt, and I don't. It's not just a difference of approach, it's a complete schism in our respective philosophy. You can't go about disclosure in the hope that it won't spoil anybody's dinner.

My travels in Africa also took me to Cairo. An American contact we had made in Kenya invited us to share the place she was staying in, a house that belonged to a former Miss Egypt. It was a grand house, and there were several paintings of Miss Egypt on the walls, so it was an amusingly surreal place to stay. However, it was right next to the American embassy – there was a van full of soldiers permanently stationed near our front door – and I thought it might be easier to keep a low profile if I moved somewhere else. Together with a Korean girl I had also met in Kenya, I moved into an apartment near the Nile. It was an enormous, tall building and we were almost on the top floor; sometimes when the Cairo smog wasn't too bad we could see the Great Pyramids through the windows.

It was easy to sense the tension under the surface in Egypt. There were always lots of police on the streets and there was an air of controlled confrontation, particularly in the centre and near to government buildings. But the great changes we have seen recently were still four years away, and like many people I didn't see them coming. Cairo had an influence on me in more emotional ways, I suppose. Being in that teeming metropolis of the rapidly developing world validated my sense that, to have a true impact, WikiLeaks would have to be an organisation with global reach.

I soon felt a great affection for Cairo. I enjoyed the bustle and the activity of the streets, the cafés, the Shisha in the evening. On the roof of an apartment building near me a family kept a tiny city farm. Every morning the daughter would feed and water a few sheep, while her brother released his flock of pigeons from their cages to search the city for scraps. He had trained them to follow a huge chequered flag, and I used to love to watch him waving this flag against the sky like some Grand Prix starter, while the call to prayer rose from mosque to citadel and the sun lit the haze into a furnace.

By Christmas 2007, we had a number of successes – or *succès de scandale* – under our belts. Fallujah and Guantánamo had brought too little attention, given the size of the leaks, and we continued to add to the Kenyan revelations. I attended the 24th Chaos Communication Congress in Berlin, which allowed me to meet some of the people I'd been chatting to or otherwise dealing with online. Among these was an excitable fan of our work called Daniel Domscheit-Berg, a systems company employee who soon proved useful for some tasks. From the beginning, Daniel Schmitt, as he was referred to then, was a curious asset. He couldn't write code, but he could prove dutiful to the needs of the growing organisation. We couldn't have guessed then how ambitious or how reckless he would become. But need is blind when it comes to volunteers, and we badly required as much help as we could get.

The Chaos Computer Club, which organised the convention in Berlin right at the end of 2007, is famous for good reasons and bad ones. They are a hackers' organisation, founded in 1981 to campaign for technological progress, openness, freedom of information and free public access to technology. They quickly grew from their origins in Berlin and they are now a powerful, cross-border organisation that keeps a close eye on how information technology is being used and abused in contemporary societies. They have protested against French nuclear testing and against the use of biometric data in passports, but others of the group, led by Karl Koch, were arrested for cyber-espionage activities in the late '80s, including taking material from corporate and government computers in the US and feeding it to the KGB.

That wasn't our bag. We admired the brainpower in the group and supported its broad efforts to question how information was used, but WikiLeaks never saw itself as an organisation that would campaign for one ideology against another, or for one nation against others. Inside the organisation, we are a broad church and our enemies are, in each case, and everywhere, the enemies of truth. We accepted no piety when it came to the work of security services and governments (a fact that would bring us much hostility when it came to altering the documents we leaked); we simply felt it was for history to judge what was in the 'public interest' and what was not. We would use our best editorial judgement, but it was not for us to do as most media organisations do, and act as censors on behalf of governments and commercial interests. We would reveal what we judged should never have been made covert: others would take it further. And almost always our efforts would lead us into a lion's den of self-interest.

Talking about the lion's roar? Look at the case of Switzerland's Bank Julius Baer, who – even in times of banking crisis – were subject to allegations of malfeasance thanks to our having taken custody of important revelations about them in January 2008. Julius Baer is the largest Swiss bank and it has trusts in the Cayman Islands. We were given evidence that those trusts were used for asset-hiding and tax minimisation, arguably tax avoidance, and it seemed entirely in the public interest that we revealed what these people were doing and to what extent they were doing it. Right on publication, we received legal notice from a lawyer who wouldn't even reveal who his client was, but the potential litigant was Julius Baer. The legal firm, Ludley & Sanger, are a Hollywood outfit representing the likes of Celine Dion and Arnold Schwarzenegger, who specialise in keeping things out of print. They're very aggressive and they came on hard. They made various threats and were going on about banking law and secrecy law in the Cayman Islands and in Switzerland, proper baloney, but our own lawyer told us these people were too powerful to mess with, too connected, too rich, that they would stop at nothing and the whole thing was too murky. I said we would certainly go ahead and publish and stand by the publication: I had established certain principles against censorship and would not fold. We had made promises that if sources gave us good material we would publish it, and we were uncensorable: that's what our technology dictated, and that's what our ethic dictated, too, as a matter of fact. It didn't mean, 'We are uncensorable, except in cases where a very rich person appears to scare us off.' I knew that, tactically, this might be a very difficult (and potentially ruinous) first fight, but we had established a principle and that was that.

Like everything else, it was a giant lesson delivered in real time. We were being brutally squeezed by a relentless patronage network, in this case two branches of that network, Julius Baer and the American lawyers, the former protecting a mint and the latter making a mint, and determined to protect these things at all cost, even in the face of our vulnerability and our chutzpah. They immediately brought a case against us in San Francisco, as a result of which the judge repealed our domain name, WikiLeaks. org, and demanded to know who had registered it and from what address. The company, Dinadot, immediately rolled over and closed the site. But we had set a trap for our opponents by registering in San Francisco, the cultural centre of gravity for the cypherpunks and the Californian instinct for non-conformity and free speech. They could have sued us in Switzerland or London, but by going through with San Francisco they immediately faced the wrath of the ACLU, the Committee of the Freedom of the Press and many other organisations. When we went back to court we had twenty-two organisations and a battalion of lawyers fighting for us, with favourable coverage in the *New York Times* and CBS giving out our domain number (since the name was banned) in order to reach us ('Free speech has a number'). We had set up other ways of accessing our site, anyway, via secret links and mirror sites, which we knew would come in useful. You've got to remember, we established ourselves knowing we would, early and late, be dealing with the Chinese and their throwing-up of firewalls.

We won the case completely against Julius Baer and it was seen as being a crucial win, not only for us but for First Amendment campaigners all over the place. The bank were just about to launch themselves in America before the court case, and afterwards they held off. It was an important victory because it showed how WikiLeaks would stand up to just about anyone and not be immediately crushed by those who could pay for the kind of lawyers who facilitate such crushing. The sub-prime thing was riding high and the British mortgage lender Northern Rock had already gone under. It was looking like a bad time for a private bank to be suing the arse off a not-for-profit whistleblowing team.

The real tragedy of this incident was that it finally saw the end of Daniel Mathews' involvement with WikiLeaks. Dan's name was on quite a few bits of paperwork, and Julius Baer were looking for anybody and everybody they could prosecute. He was sitting in his office at Stanford one afternoon, marking his students' homework, when some bloke walked in with a huge stack of paper and slapped it down on the desk. He told me afterwards that his first thought was that it was the biggest homework assignment he'd ever seen, but, no, it was a subpoena. Dan found this quite scary and afterwards elected to focus on his academic career. He's now a visiting assistant professor at another American university – but he's definitely one of the good guys and I will always value his support and his friendship.

The guy who brought us the material on Julius Baer, Rudolf Elmer, wished to be outed, and he was fined €7,500. He then said he wanted to call a press conference at which he could be seen handing over to me two CDs full of data about the bank. We did the press conference, and it seems it might bring him further trouble, but who's to say what was on the CDs? You can't prosecute a person for handing another person a couple of blank CDs, unless you can prove there was something on them. Deniability is not just a word, it's a way of life and a programme for us. We had faced big threats before, not least from the Church of Scientology. And we always seek to reward our torturers with further revelations.

Lawyers often behave like thieves, especially the good ones. And legal action has proved a blunt instrument with which to dissect WikiLeaks. We are designed like the many-headed Hydra: you cut off one of our heads and another one pops up elsewhere. This only reflects the irrepressible nature of people's appetite for the truth, and my own liking for a scrap. There would be court cases that seemed to me terribly sinister, the kind one would relish neither fighting nor winning – one can never relish losing – but the majority of those who sought legal injunction against the activities of WikiLeaks can best be understood with reference to King Canute. He ordered the waves to go back and they ignored him, wetting his feet.

Occasionally, though, you see how legal action has simply scared a good moral cause out of its wits at the first post. Late in 2008, we became aware that eight *Guardian* and *Observer* stories on Nadhmi Auchi, an Iraqi-British billionaire whose bank, BNP Paribas, was the sole financial institution receiving billions in 'oil-for-food' programme money during the regime of Saddam Hussein, had been pulled from their website. Auchi has been the subject of a 2004 Pentagon Inspector General's report into mobile telecommunication licences. And before that, in 2003, he had been extradited from the UK to France and convicted over multi-million-dollar kickbacks on Kuwaiti government asset sales. Martin Bright, a reporter on the *New Statesman*, had, in 2008, drawn attention to the fact that the *Guardian/Observer* had bowed to legal pressure from Auchi: '[They had] been forced to pull down six articles about Nadhmi Auchi, the Iraqi businessman convicted of fraud in France in 2003. Auchi has been on the warpath since his name was connected with Tony Rezko, the Illinois fundraiser currently on trial in America, who was one of Barack Obama's earliest backers. In the UK, the *Times* has been pursuing the story with impressive tenacity.' When Bright first posted these words, he was able to name the six articles censored by Auchi's legal efforts and removed from the online archive of the *Guardian/Observer*. Then, in a bizarre twist straight out of Kafka, Bright's *New Statesman* blog was itself subject to the interference of Auchi's long legal arm, and he was forced to remove the names of the censored articles and amend his own piece. The story is one of those that points up the baroque nature of journalistic fearfulness. When WikiLeaks reported the whole thing and the *New Statesman* tried to link to our coverage, they received a letter from legal firm Carter-Ruck.

By the end of 2008 we were drowning in leaked documents from all over the world. Every day brought new material, much of it requiring further research and commentary by us before publication. Had we been a single newspaper or a single broadcaster, we would've had the busiest investigations team in the world, turning out exclusive stories hand over fist. But WikiLeaks didn't see itself in the role of proprietor, or commercial engine, even though, I have to admit, commercial motives are often the only real metric with which to measure what a piece of information is worth. We didn't want to make money, but we wanted to deal with media organisations that could fasten our stories to a bank of journalists and a distribution network, and those organisations understood their work in commercial terms to do with tight deadlines and exclusivity. At this period, we were trying to learn to work with that while also keeping the website true to itself.

All sorts of stories were bursting over the dam: late in 2008 we released the membership list of the British National Party. This is a neo-fascist organisation that believes in a white-only Britain; yet their members included police officers, serving soldiers and government employees; people who have a moral and professional obligation to serve all British people equally, regardless of race. Then, in December, we put out a private report authored by the South African Competition Commission, which told of cartel behaviour in the big South African banks. The most important sections had been redacted, supposedly to protect commercially sensitive data, but we published the report in full. Here's an example of a 'commercially sensitive' sentence: 'It is evident that Absa failed to pass on these unit cost savings to any significant extent to its customers by way of price reductions, choosing instead to retain most of these savings as profits.' Two months later, we came out with 6,700 reports written in private for US Congressmen, which gave a detailed picture of their preoccupations and sources of information. These reports are not classified, but they are only made available to Congressmen, who choose only to release some of them when it serves their own political purposes, not when the information is embarrassing or damaging to the government but important to the public. By publishing them we wanted to give American voters the opportunity to measure the actions of their elected representatives against the information with which they had been provided. We were releasing the reports on the basis of public interest, not political calculation. We posted the private emails of Sarah Palin in an attempt to highlight the fact that she was conducting political business via a private email address, arguably in order to avoid having to comply with rules about retaining copies of messages on the public record. Throughout this time we were attending conferences on journalism and free speech around the world to seed our ideas and recruit support.

I had become a full-time spare-room guy. I didn't own a car or a house. I didn't see my family much. I didn't have money and I had one pair of shoes. It was all perfectly reasonable and not an issue. I had some books and a razor and a couple of laptops. Friends would cut my hair, often while I worked, and, thankfully, when it came to equipment and costs, there always appeared to be someone willing to put their credit card where their passion was. WikiLeaks has been hand-to-mouth from day one, and maybe it has to be: it works from principle not profit, and the work, frankly, is obsessional, and was from the moment we saw how much people wanted to reveal.

I felt 2009 was going to be the start of a big few years. We were getting better at what we did, and the world was sitting up now and listening. We were refining our methods, pissing off bigger and more fearsome giants, and I began to think it would be great to find a haven from which to work. Surely, the world must possess a place that wanted to be an island of free speech, a world of anti-censorship within the larger world. For a time it appeared the *coup de grâce* would be to establish such a base in Africa, but it was too complicated there and, in a purely practical sense, too hot to store the servers. What about Sweden, Iceland, Ireland, or some other brand new Xanadu of the truth? I couldn't live out of a rucksack for ever – or maybe I would, or should, because the organisation depended on a hierarchy of nothingness in order to work. In the same vein, at the beginning of this seismic period, I was already becoming my own ghost, an author in charge, but barely, of my own fiction, as the world got busy trying to turn me into something I was not.

10

ICELAND

The history of journalism is the history of leaks. Only in fiction is it the case that everything that happens is witnessed, in some sense, by the author. In journalism, the witness is often absent, and we rely on reports of the truth that use witness statements as part of the picture. In many cases, good journalism will rely on an absent witness, who, either on or off the record, will leak what they know. We forget that everyday journalism relies on the leak to an extraordinary degree. 'According to documents seen by the *Washington Post.*' 'According to an unnamed senior official speaking yesterday.' 'Sources close to the subject say.' 'Information received by the *Daily Telegraph* suggests.' The truth does not always come as a single spy, but it often comes inadvertently, or covertly, or via a blind source, and this has always been the case. We gather what we see, but also we gather what has been seen by people beyond the range of our own eyes.

With a trusted colleague, Rop Gonggrijp – founder of one of the first ISPs in the Netherlands and organiser of a long-running hacking conference in Amsterdam – I took up an invitation to attend the Hack in the Box Conference in Malaysia in October 2009. A lot of those gathered there were politically-minded and had been involved in the local reform movement. The government of Mahathir, leader of the Barisan Nasional, had been subject to strong opposition and calls for reform, spearheaded by Anwar Ibrahim of the People's Justice Party. Ibrahim had previously, as finance minister, steered Malaysia out of financial crisis and was named 'Asian of the Year' by *Newsweek* in 1998. But by the time we arrived in Kuala Lumpur, things had long since changed for Ibrahim. After criticising the prime minister, he had served six years in prison for 'corruption' and was constantly smeared with sex allegations. When he got out of prison, he spent time advising the World Bank and served as a professor at St Anthony's College, Oxford, and at Johns Hopkins, among other institutions, before returning to Malaysia and winning a landslide election to parliament in 2008.

The speech I gave at the Hack in the Box Conference focused on the history of unauthorised disclosure in the media. This, as I say, seems to me to be the backbone of journalism. It always surprises me when critics remark that WikiLeaks doesn't serve the interests of journalism because, whatever you might say about us, much of our work is, in some very obvious way, quite traditionalist. We aim to bring things into the light which certain powers would rather remain in the dark. That could have stood as a rubric of the *Times* of London during the Crimea. It was the silent motto of the *Washington Post* during Watergate. Coupled with this, I had always argued that WikiLeaks should be an organisation that partnered the established media, not one that either replaced it or shunned it. At the Malaysian conference, I made the point that, in the future, there might be a 'WikiLeaks button' that could be placed on the websites of major news organisations, to be used by people who had information. We would take on the burden of protecting the source and dealing with legal issues – our specialities, if you like – while the news organisation went about preparing stories and commentary around the leak. This was always our central idea, and though our organisation would be distracted by much hysteria over the coming two years, we return to this, notwithstanding that other organisations based on our work would claim the idea is new. OpenLeaks. org now uses this idea as a way of slamming the set-up of WikiLeaks, an unfortunate playground game that does no good to anybody. But let us be clear, I laid out the idea for co-operation with the media in Malaysia in 2009.

It was interesting to see how these subcultures work in modern life. Where the hacking scene in Europe or Australia is made up of middle-class or working-class kids, in Asia, typically, the people involved in this kind of work were part of some societal elite. But Malaysia's reforming groups are interested in advancement, wishing to increase the country's linguistic and ethnic diversity and break down the rigid racialisation of Malaysian politics. Just before we arrived, something new seemed to be happening: support for the old regime was waning. In the election of 2008 they gained less than the two-thirds majority required by law to amend the constitution, the first time this had happened since 1969. A number of by-elections throughout 2009 would, it was understood, act as a weather vane for the future of the country, including one around the time of our visit, in Bagan Pinang, ninety kilometres south of Kuala

Lumpur. After the conference, in our WikiLeaks capacity, we toured to speak in different venues and meet with politicians. One of the few ethnic Indian MPs in the mainly Chinese-Malaysian Democratic Action Party took us to a former rubber plantation, where we met three generations of Indian workers who had been born, educated and employed on the same land. They showed us pamphlets that had been distributed by representatives of the governing party, along with money intended as a vote-buying bribe. Despite this obvious evidence of the corruption endemic in the political system and the unwillingness of the governing party to bring about change in their lives, these people were not morose, not fatalistic, not beaten.

I met with Anwar Ibrahim, and quickly Rop and I found ourselves immersed in Malaysian political dynamics. It was head-spinning how quickly the sand was moving under everybody's feet – a foretaste, you might say, of what would be happening in Cairo and Tunisia and Libya within two years, but we'll come to that. Ibrahim seemed to have his finger on the pulse of change, but needed support and information and publicity advice. WikiLeaks had helped to publicise a very sensitive document about the death of a Mongolian woman, Altantuya Shaariibuu, who had been killed in an explosion near Kuala Lumpur in 2006. The document made allegations of extraordinary seriousness surrounding her death.

The document itself was a statutory declaration signed by Raja Petra, the editor of a campaigning online news site, *Malaysia Today*.

Petra had been so under threat from the authorities – evading two arrest warrants – that the website had had to move its service to Singapore and the USA. Meanwhile, the subject of Shaariibuu's murder had become so incendiary that it could scarcely be mentioned in Malaysia. If it was mentioned at a political rally, the riot squad were immediately sent in. I often want to tell this to people who feel that a single document can't make a difference.

I told Ibrahim that this leak was a powerful lever. The reaction to it revealed an incredible weak spot in the government: they feared reform more than they knew how to resist it. The reform movement was being reactive in its press campaigns and our advice was to get off the back foot. They had to get ahead of the government's media line – the government had the stronger voice but the weaker heart – and we fed them material. By the way, Ibrahim was obviously representing a big, secular call for change. His party was being backed by the Americans, which should close the mouths of people who imagine WikiLeaks automatically takes up causes opposed to America. Like some of the Middle Eastern uprisings to come, this was a clean fight, and America was backing the right horse (without having groomed the favourite, which they did for years with Mubarak). Ibrahim was also likeable, having spent the six years he was locked up in prison reading Shakespeare. You can probably trust a man's sense of human nature if he has spent every day for that long studying Othello and Julius Caesar. We spent our time running ideas past the opposition reformers and writing some papers. It was dangerous work. One night, coming out of the headquarters and walking down a dark side-street, a place filled with shops and cafés, a man jumped out and flashed his card at me. At first, I thought he was a hawker. Turns out he was secret police. He asked me for ID, and I said I'd get it from the car, and on the way got a message to my friends from the opposition. I told him I was a journalist and wouldn't say anything more to him. The opposition guys were round in no time, pulling me away from the agent.

In the end the governing party held on to their seat in Bagan Pinang, but the mood among Malaysia's opposition was that this was just one minor battle, part of a long war that the Barisan Nasional were bound to lose. Our friends at *Malaysia Today* were certainly taking the long view rather than worrying about one by-election: 'Ever since the epic 12th general elections, which saw a realignment of the political landscape, the average Malaysian, normally apathetic to politics due to the boring regularity of BN's sweeping victories, has started to take an interest in elections, especially the next general election.'

We were doing so many kinds of work, and on so few resources, that I began to think of ways to steady the organisation and give it a home. A home is not an easy thing to contemplate when it comes to WikiLeaks: we have active servers operating at secret locations all over the world; we have a network of staff and contacts, most of them wishing to remain nameless, who are never to be found in the same place at the same time. WikiLeaks was different from any other kind of media organisation: we were never going to have a reception desk and a coffee machine, never mind a research department and annual holidays. People imagine I live out of a rucksack because I'm some kind of weirdo. Well, they're right, I am some kind of weirdo, but I'm also forced into a stressful, peripatetic lifestyle by the nature of the work and the facts of the organisation. We have moved around to avoid legal constraints and find stations to work from. Believe me, I feel there's nothing nicer than a set of clean towels and a dining table covered with nice food and surrounded by friends. I love a coffee machine. But it just wasn't likely to happen in a dependable way if we were doing our jobs properly and getting so far up the noses of the powerful that we became hunted. The only hope was that we might find a place, somewhere, sometime, that was disinclined to hunt people working for justice.

To my way of thinking, there was a connection between one side of our work and another, between busting companies who hid money or assets and going after governments who hid people away in places like Guantánamo. Both of these sets of perpetrators were criminals, often sanctioned by the authorities, who were hiding money or people outside the rule of law, usually in a secret jurisdiction. We could exhaust ourselves, and do, revealing evidence of what these people do; but, at some point, we might wish to see that the whole operation, the whole jurisdiction, is intrinsically corrupt. This would mean saying that the Cayman Islands, for example, must be subject to a wholesale inquiry into its offshore banking activities, and it might mean examining Guantánamo Bay as a haven allowing for the wholesale abuse of human rights as civil society understands them.

And what if you reversed this way of thinking? What if you decided there could be anti-secrecy havens in the world? In every country we had worked in, we had become aware of people and organisations living under legal or physical threat from the powerful. Whether it was Raja Petra, the editor in Malaysia, who had to flee from the authorities, or the American Home Owners Association, which was forced to move its operations onto an ISP in Sweden as a result of legal suits brought against it by property developers, or reform groups out of Russia, or great swathes of individuals targeted by the litigation-wielding malice of the Scientologists – all of them could find peace, or a fair hearing, in a haven devoted to transparency and fair play. In my understanding, a new kind of refugee had emerged in the modern world: a person, or a group, on the run from rich or powerful authorities bent on destroying them for telling the truth. We know from the work of Amnesty or PEN that these people are often writers and publishers, but they can be civil rights groups, lawyers, freethinkers, or just the ordinary people next door. I began to feel strongly that a haven not of secrecy but of openness would answer the call.

Such a place would also serve as a journalism haven, a place where sources could be protected as part of the law of the land. Free press legislation would be deeply embedded in such a place. Internet freedoms would be part of the modern ether and liberty from prosecution would be standard. I began to have a vision of this haven: a politically independent zone, a place where one could stop running, where whistleblowers might be considered heroes not public enemies, where legal advice would be free and plentiful and Internet access universal. It sounded like Nirvana to me, until I began to realise it might actually be called Iceland.

In the summer of 2009 we were leaked a copy of the Kaupthing Bank Large Loan Book. This was a document revealing every loan over €45 million made by the Icelandic bank. Kaupthing was the largest of Iceland's banks and had suffered a massive decline in the 2008 financial meltdown, eventually becoming insolvent. The bank's motto was 'Think Beyond', and, it appeared, many of the borrowers had taken that motto to heart. Many were insiders, and even though the loans were for enormous sums, many were unsecured. Kaupthing loaned €791.2 million to Exista hf., the company that owned Kaupthing itself. According to the document we leaked, 'the bulk of the loans [to Exista hf.] are unsecured and with no covenants'. Money was lent to the fourth-largest shareholder in Kaupthing, in order that he could buy even more shares in Kaupthing, and the only collateral that he had to provide was those same shares in Kaupthing! A tiny number of individuals were enriching themselves with these loans, money that only ever existed on paper, and the people of Iceland would have to pick up the tab. Two brothers, Ágúst and Lýður Guðmundsson, and companies owned by them, received loans totalling ISK300 billion, which was equivalent to €1.6 billion. Robert Tchenguiz, a member of the board of Exista hf., received loans of ISK330 billion. It won't surprise you to learn that a number of individuals have been arrested, in Iceland and abroad, following the collapse of the Icelandic banking system.

Within twenty-four hours of releasing the document, WikiLeaks was on the receiving end of a legal threat from Kaupthing's lawyers. It stated that we, and our source, could face one year in prison under the Icelandic Banking Secrecy Law. RUV, the Icelandic equivalent of the BBC, was set to go ahead with a leading item on that night's *Seven O'Clock News* about our leak. And at 6.55 p.m., like a scene in some Hollywood movie, an injunction was slapped down on the RUV news desk. A last-minute injunction had never been served on RUV during its entire history. The newsreader was very cool. They'd just lost their lead item, so he explained that they wouldn't be bringing the viewer all the news tonight, but that a large loan book from Kaupthing Bank had been the subject of a leak. He said the report had been compiled only three weeks before the bank collapsed. We can't bring you that story, he said, but here's an organisation that can. At which point they just filled the screen with the WikiLeaks logo and let it sit there for several minutes to fill up the time they had scheduled for the now injuncted story.

Overnight, the people of Iceland came over to WikiLeaks. They got the story from us and did what I always would consider appropriate: they took the stimulus of our story and became investigative reporters themselves, filling out the details and checking them subjectively. We had helped the country see some of the corruption that had led to the collapse of their own economy and they valued the opportunity. We are often called arrogant, or I am often called arrogant, and I suppose I must be – you might have to be arrogant in order to resist the persistent slings and arrows chucked at you, even on those occasions when you don't deserve them. But there are actually few occasions in this work that allow for smugness. No sooner have you revealed a bit of corruption, hammered a bank or dished on a dictator than the whole weight of power comes down on you. But Iceland was a rare moment when smugness could break out: people hated the idea of these corrupt bankers and people wanted to pelt them with eggs. It was argued in the press that Icelandic people had historically been too passive, that they had no history of rebellion, and that perhaps the time had come to stand up to 'cronyism and nepotism' as never before.

I was invited to Iceland to address a conference on Digital Freedom in December 2009, and began in earnest to think of how it might be encouraged to become the openness haven the world so badly needed. It had some pretty perfect conditions: it was ripe for change, having just come out of such a devastating banking crisis; it had an educated workforce; it had the most Internet-connected population

in the Western world; it was equidistant between Europe
and the United States; it had the cheapest power in all of
Europe (geothermal and hydropower, completely green),
which is an important consideration when you're running
huge banks of computers; and it was cold, which would be
good for the air-conditioning required to keep the servers
happy. It also had a fairly good free-speech tradition and,
just before the banking bubble burst, was rated equal first
with Luxembourg and Norway on Reporters Sans Frontières' Press Freedom Index. Iceland also appealed to my
sense of humour: like a bizarre parody of a tax haven, it was
far from the Caribbean, an icy island in the North Atlantic.
I mentioned to the conference that all of these things made
it possible that Iceland could be the world's greatest openness haven and a natural home for publishers.

I was at the conference with Daniel Domscheit-Berg
and a number of people from the Iceland Digital Freedom
Society. A group of parliamentarians turned up, including a woman called Birgitta Jónsdóttir, who was smart and
friendly. She seemed immediately part of the spirit of our
group and was interested in the idea of the openness haven.
She had been elected to parliament in early 2008, and
immediately on meeting her I spotted her for a potential
ally. She could work for our idea of a safe haven through
parliament and help us develop it in the current climate.
She was a long-term activist, a poet involved with music,
about forty-two, and from a famous family of Icelandic
troubadours.

The seed had been planted and it grew in the minds of
the conference attendees and other supporters in Iceland.
The end of 2009 was a busy time for me, and I returned to
Berlin to speak once more at the Chaos Communication

Congress on 27 December, but I was keen to return to Iceland as soon as possible. By 5 January 2010, we were back again, still filled with the idea that we could help create this haven. There were about thirteen of us working on this – Rop Gonggrijp, Jacob Applebaum, Daniel Domscheit-Berg, Smári McCarthy, Kristinn Hrafnsson, Birgitta, and other journalists, activists and academics who offered us their advice and expertise online from the UK, Netherlands, Belgium, Germany, Hong Kong and the United States. The work meant preparing a legislative request, working from a place called the Ideas House, a sort of start-up incubator for people with ideas but no money. We worked all sorts of hours, researching, lobbying and making the thing ready so that there was a good chance it could enter into law. Birgitta Jonsdottir worked hard to drive the voting numbers to get the haven idea through parliament, and we did special presentations to some of the more conservative members. Such a landmark development was perhaps more complex than I had originally imagined, requiring that at least thirteen major pieces of Icelandic law be changed, but the Icelandic parliament has now voted to task the civil service with preparing this legislation, a process which is continuing now. I guess there was an issue with Icelandic dignity after the financial meltdown. Their eye was understandably focused on local shocks and many believed the main benefit of the openness haven would be that it would, in future, hold bankers to account, as well as other corrupt Icelandic forces. Down the line, I hope, they will see that transparency could be a real growth industry for Iceland. Strangely, though, for all our lobbying, the journalists were the main opposition: they feared that the new legislation would somehow throw attention away from their own plight, as journalists facing cuts. That was short-sighted, in my view, but you can forgive people for feeling they can't always afford to be idealistic.

The idea of Iceland as a freedom jurisdiction is beautiful. It will raise the country's reputation and a general sense of self-worth. I wonder if Iceland doesn't need something like a prize for freedom of expression, which might do for that little country what the Nobel does for Sweden. The fact that they had the prize, and a society that knew how to live up to the prize, would prove exemplary, and bring the country into focus on the international scene. We worked hard with the parliamentary lawyers and the drafters. I was thinking about the transit towards justice it could bring, this move into scientific journalism, allowing every aspect along the pipeline towards truth to be observed and protected. The effect all over the world would be to have a new high standard to hold up, a standard that said that people could not be prosecuted for seeking to tell the truth. It could be disputed, it could be argued over, but no one would be criminalised for essentially disclosing the truth. I hope it all comes together before too long.

Another issue appeared in spring 2010 that seemed, in the moment, even more pressing. In late 2008 the Icelandic banking system had disintegrated, as the reckless lending of all of Iceland's major banks finally caught up with them. Landsbanki went under in October, threatening €6 billion worth of savings deposited in the bank via their 'Icesave' online accounts by people in the UK and Netherlands. The response of the Icelandic state was that it was not their responsibility, representatives of a tiny and now bankrupt nation, to pay the foreign debts of utterly reckless, private sector banks. The response of the British and Dutch was ruthless. The British chancellor, Alistair Darling, used the provisions of the Anti-terrorism, Crime and Security Act to freeze the UK assets of Landsbanki, and the assets of the Central Bank of Iceland and the Government of Iceland that related to Landsbanki. Although these laws were supposed to function in order to keep funds out of the hands of terrorists, they were being used against the government of another European power. It was shocking. There was a great deal of backroom diplomacy on the part of the British – real strong-arm stuff – and the instincts of empire really emerged in them. When it comes to such things, where there is a consuming public passion for the issue, as there is in the banking debacle, the British could use naked power to get their own way. And they did. They stated publicly that they would campaign against Iceland's entry into the EU unless they got their money and that they would leverage the IMF to refuse to give Iceland any loans. The Icelandic parliament attempted to draw up a repayment plan, but, under pressure from public opinion, the president refused to sign it through, triggering a public referendum under the Icelandic constitution. While some members of the Icelandic political establishment frantically tried to find a deal that would satisfy the British, we began to leak documents such as the UK–Netherlands' 'final offer' and the Icelandic counter-proposal. I also spoke at a rally in Reykjavik, and our efforts in general were devoted to providing the Icelandic public with the information they needed to make an informed decision. In the end, about 95 per cent of the voting population voted against succumbing to British pressure, a historic moment in Iceland as the country was experiencing its first referendum since 1944. Our ability to act strategically in the face of a dynamic story is part of our importance, forcing those in power to confront the truth

at a point where events are developing. We eventually published several cables showing the UK had been lobbying an
organisation called the Paris Club – a creditor cartel of the
major Western creditor nations – to refuse to give Iceland
any further assistance.

We would have some deep and final business with Iceland during 2010, but that momentous year of 2009 – the
year we had hoped to found the world's first openness
haven there – ended with a curious reminder of how much
WikiLeaks had become woven into the fabric of Icelandic
self-consciousness. There was a party at the US embassy in
Reykjavik. They always invited the political elite to these
parties, and I crashed it under the guise of being Birgitta's
plus-one. (I was on my own: she didn't come at all.) I was
feeling perky that night: I had managed to secure a series
of documents that revealed the rather shady behaviour of
Landsbanki in Russia in the 1990s and 2000s. Three people
had died during the transactions described in the dossier,
and senior officials in Putin's government seemed to be have
been involved in registering some of the various companies
that had been created. I felt we were getting closer and closer
to the point where we could force real openness on this
mighty issue of the relationship between money and government. One of the first people I met there was the former
CEO of the Kaupthing Bank – the one that had threated
to imprison me for a year for revealing their loan book.
That didn't go particularly well. Then I spoke to the *chargé
d'affaire*, who was surrounded by three of those goons who
seemed to have come direct from Central Casting. Looking
at them, you had to wonder precisely what they had done
in El Salvador to end up marooned in Iceland, where they
spent the day monitoring the Chinese embassy. I showed

some of the Russian Landsbanki documents to people I met there – why not? Openness is openness, right? – and you could see their eyes widen and their diplomatic hands reach out as if to snatch the documents away. It's amazing how stodgy those people are and how little they know about the world they're paid to interact with. Some months later, I released a cable sent by that same Charges d'Affaires I'd been chatting to and they went nuts, thinking that I'd some- how acquired it at the party.

The experience of developing the haven taught us a great deal about how to advance the WikiLeaks ethos into public policy. We did that not for reasons of ambition, as people say, but because it is the natural extension of speaking truth to power. Eventually, it would be nice to find common ground for the project and give it the apparatus of free states to support it. The Internet, in a sense, is a nation, but a nation of the imagination, where one is free to enter and leave without a passport. But it has its primitive aspects. While one is free to post on the Internet, one is not able to be protected by it: on a bad day, the Internet is the biggest sur- veillance tool in the world. It encourages a free press, but it offers the same encouragement to those who hate press freedom. That is the irony of the new technology, and one that we aimed to circumvent, giving our ideas of justice a legislative support network on terra firma. We learned much and met many people, including the aforementioned Kristinn Hrafnsson, an Icelandic journalist and activist who is now an important staff member at WikiLeaks.

It had been a tonic to walk in Reykjavik and see people smile and wave and call themselves supporters, but I was tired that season, feeling I'd already travelled over so much territory, so many big stories and so many changes that enhanced progress but threatened life and limb. I began to feel drained as the legislation dragged on. It was just a parliamentary ill-chance, like many others, but I felt it personally as a quiet condemnation to a life on the lam. In some very obvious way, I have been escaping from some dark pursuer since I was a child and my mother took us across country to escape from her stalker. In Iceland, you could barely tell the difference between night and day, which, I realised, had been my regular position since I was thirteen. I was still up all night with a computer, and escaping by day to some new set of possibilities. But my battery goes low shortly before it magically shows itself fully charged.

A video had been sent to our drop-box. It showed grainy images of some men walking down a street in Iraq. Two of them are journalists. In a minute they will all be dead, shot to pieces from a US helicopter gunship. I watched it again and again, knowing we were about to enter into the full public glare of something new.

11

COLLATERAL MURDER

After a brief time on the road, including a trip to Oslo to speak at a conference, we came back to Iceland in March 2010 and rented a house. The people we rented from thought we were there to watch the volcanoes: that was our cover, and it explained why we had so many computers and so much video equipment. But the real reason was the Baghdad video. We had decided this was our most important leak to date, and the video would have to be analysed, understood and made ready for presentation. I wanted the whole world to see this video. It was that important, not only for an understanding of war in general, but for an ethical comprehension of what the war in Iraq had become, and how it impacted on daily lives.

The main house we rented became a den. It was full of coffee cups and computer wires and chocolate, the debris of strung-out lives. A profile writer from the *New Yorker* came round and he caught pretty well the chaos and the sleeplessness. I barely left my computer for weeks. I had my hair cut while sitting at my terminal, working against the clock to edit the video so all the static noise, the crackle, was at a minimum, and the final version was as clear as possible. People fluttered in and out of the room, full of exclamations, ideas, tears. None of the crazy schedules and lunges across continents familiar from our previous work could stand comparison with the preparation of the 'Collateral Murder' video. I think my reputation for workaholism and infrequent bathing must have started there; it was unavoidable, with the amount we had to do, and the sense that this leak, above all, would change the public's perception of a dreadful war and play a part in bringing that horrible invasion to an end.

The video has now had more than eleven million viewings on YouTube, as well as many more millions on television. It is a famous document of our times. But when I first saw the footage, it wasn't at all clear what was going on; the images were jagged and the sequence lacked drama and impact, though what it depicted, eventually, was truly devastating. I did careful research as I went along, finding out who the people in the video were, when it was shot, from which angles, and how it had all come together to tell the story of this multiple murder in broad daylight. We broke the film into three parts, to better understand the sequence of events. The work was slow, but sobering and mesmerising. When all was said and done, the video, without doubt, showed twelve men – two of them Reuters journalists, going about their business – being shot to ribbons by 35mm cannon-fire from a US Apache helicopter. It took me some time to work out who was involved in the initial massacre, and then to see that the two men who survived the initial attack, only to be taken out individually, were the men from Reuters. It was my colleague Ingi Ragnar Ingason who noticed, on closer inspection, that the van that comes to pick up one of the wounded men and is blown apart in a further round of cannon-fire, contained two children. The footage later shows US ground troops carrying the wounded children away.

We had a full team working on it. Kristinn Hrafnsson took charge of research, finding out what had happened to the children in the video. Birgitta was there throughout, giving advice and acting as a sounding-board for what appeared. Ingi was editor, which involved shedding away a lot of the flak and immaterial stuff on the rough cut, and Gudmundur Gudmudsson worked with the sound. We had Rop Gonggrijp as executive producer, covering expenses and making it possible, and Smári McCarthy organising the web-based material. Daniel Domscheit-Berg, unknown even to himself, perhaps, had begun to marginalise himself from this working group by undermining our efforts. It's inevitable, I suppose, in a group of people who are essentially volunteers, that questions of ambition and motivation will go askew. Domscheit-Berg couldn't see the wood for the trees and became tremendously obnoxious. We were involved in something very large and very scary, and his ill-will was exhausting.

One of the things that drove us was the knowledge of how inaccurate the contemporary press reports of the incident had been. It was an example of history being manipulated for political purposes. It was even suggested in some reports that the van had been shelled by insurgents, but the video shows very clearly the order being given and the massacre occurring. Others suggested that there was a fire-fight and that the Reuters journalists had been caught in the crossfire. All lies. We appended a quote from

George Orwell – 'Political language is designed to make lies sound truthful and murder respectable, and to give the appearance of solidity to pure wind' – in order to show how political language had been used to justify a reckless incidence of murder. There was no other word for it, and although we knew it would be controversial, the decision to call the video 'Collateral Murder' was simply loyal to the evidence.

The storm that blew up about that title was depressing and surprising, even given what I knew about the attitude of much of the Western media to the official US government line. So puffed up are they with a sense of their own importance that, on seeing the video, the first debate they wanted to have was about our title, not about the contents. Much of the press think pairing the truth with the official lie is 'balance', and mistake a solemn delivery to camera for serious engagement with moral imperatives. Paul Krugman once joked that if one party declared that the earth was flat, the headlines would read 'Views Differ on Shape of Planet'. Our 'edited' version showed the first eleven minutes completely unedited, to set the scene. We put it up on the website collateralmurder.net *right next to* the full 40-minute version. Dear CNN, what exactly is your problem? Perhaps we should have called it 'Collateral Cover Up' and had done with it.

I must have seen the video hundreds of times, but, on each occasion, my blood ran cold when I saw those children coming under attack. Unchecked power is such an evil thing and I came to feel a large moral responsibility for exposing the bastards who did this. In a sense, the bastards were the US military, but also those elements of the media who had seen fit to join them in covering the thing up. The

young men in the helicopter may be victims, too; victims
of a brutal military culture gone out of control, and you
can hear the eagerness in their voices to make a 'kill'. It was
certainly the case that one of the soon-to-be victims was
carrying an RPG (a rocket-propelled grenade), but in their
eagerness to build a threatening picture the forces in the
helicopter mistook the Reuters photographer's camera for
a second one. The rush to judgement is obscene, especially
if you listen to the frantic, beseeching voice of the gunman,
failing to understand why there would be any reason to
show caution in such a situation. 'Come on, buddy, all you
gotta do is pick up a weapon' one of them says of a guy
on the ground. 'Gimme something.' And so we go from a
situation of low enemy threat to a massacre in a matter of
minutes. The video gives a massive insight into the merci-
less need for 'contact' that a war fosters in its participants. It
looks and sounds like a computer game, and that's because
the morality of the attacking soldiers has been framed that
way. They behave as if they are shooting at digital bogey-
men.

We decided to unveil the leaked video at a press conference in Washington on 5 April 2010. That gave us ten more
days to get Kristinn and Ingi to Baghdad, to find the families of the victims. Sometimes, in the late hours, I would go
outside the house for a breath in the cold night air, taking in
that fresh scent of sulphur that fills the air in Iceland, and I
would wonder how on earth we were going to pull it together in time. There were many campaigns and many miles,
and now, many years, between me and the teenage boy who
used to stay up all night tramping through the computer
systems of corporations across the globe. With the bite of
the air, and the Washington deadline snapping at our heels,

it seemed at the same time as if everything had changed and nothing had. At the last minute, Kristinn managed to pull some favour with the Icelandic Ministry of Foreign Affairs and suddenly they were off to Baghdad. A fixer they met through the local Reuters office got them into Al Amin, the area of the city run by the Mahdi Army where the atrocity took place. The very day before I set off for Washington the news came back from Iraq: Ingi and Kristinn had found the children and also the widower of a woman killed when the helicopter unleashed Hellfire missiles into a block of flats directly after the attack on the men in the street.

By the skin of our teeth, we got to America and down to the Washington Press Club. It was mid-morning and the room was packed. We played the video and it had an immediate impact. A number of people in the audience were crying. You could see this was no ordinary revelation; the people in there were hardened, but they couldn't fail to respond to these hidden images of war's sanctioned brutalism. However, when it came to questions, well, as usual they were disappointing. A lot of people who cover world affairs from Washington are basically stupid. They often know absolutely nothing about the subjects or the cultures they are reporting on; there's this kind of too-cool-for-school mentality among the older ones, imagining there's nothing they haven't seen before. These people are pretty desperate and they should be ashamed, most probably, of how much complacency and ignorance they have brought into the world. But that's that. Everyone's so frightened of the national press corps in America that pulling the rug from underneath their sorry, negligent arses hardly seems an option. They don't listen and they would be insulted to have to question their own categories. I'm not going to

sugar-coat this: the video moved those people, but hardly
one of them knew how to follow his gut and add his voice
to the chorus of natural outrage that decency demanded.
The nightly news was immoral. They had Wolf Blitzer on
CNN talking to some female anchor, with her saying war
was dangerous and that's it. They showed the first part of
the video and then blotted out the film once the bullets
were fired, out of respect to the families. Nice touch. Shame
about the Iraqi families. Fox News, of course, made it sound
like the US military were owed an apology.

We would come and go with the American media over
the coming year, especially, of course, with the *New York
Times*, but it was difficult then and now to avoid the notion
that a great many of them see themselves as holding a torch
for what they perceive to be the American national interest.
They want to put a curse on other people's suffering, as if
they had no right to expect sympathy in dangerous times.
They will manipulate their own role so as always to seem
pious and basically true to the flag. I don't dislike America. I
dislike what the present crop of political and media elite are
doing to insult its best principles, its fine Constitution, and
it will be our aim, as it is with other nations who behave as
they do at their worst, to bust them.

Within a day of showing the 'Collateral Murder' video in
Washington the backlash could be heard at all levels. And
the attacks did not just come from the Pentagon. They came
from people in the gutters of San Antonio to the former
dreamers in the White House. Left- and right-wing commentators set out to crucify us for showing the world a video,
a piece of military footage that might have made any self-
respecting nation simply sad at the horrors capable of being
enacted under its flag. There was no humility, no apology,

no explanation even; just the rage of those who imagine that anybody who reveals the truth of such situations must be an enemy of the state. Such a poor and primitive response to journalistic truth, and shameful to the founding principles they pretend to cross the world to protect. Of course, they accused us of doctoring the video. Of editing it maliciously. Of erasing gunmen from the tape and making it seem worse than it was. It became surreal the way people would express with certainty all this nonsense. In fact, it was a military video given to us. All the angles were theirs, and the basic production values were theirs, and the acts committed were theirs, and I cannot imagine how they sleep at night while denying it.

There are certain traits that serve you badly in this work: being thin-skinned, certainly, self-pitying, absolutely, and I have probably had to fight hard not to succumb to these. I have a strong sense of self-command, but it vexes me when the world won't listen, and I can only hope to get better when it comes to managing my mistakes. We're a young organisation, and the work we've done has thrown us into the spotlight very quickly. Personally, I've had to learn on the job and take pride in the effort. If we're a people's bureau of investigation, then it's the people we have to keep in mind, while the reaction from left and right will often be hostile. Publishing the Baghdad video was the right thing to do and was not only consistent with our sense of what we were set up to do, but the acme of our moral stance. Millions of people in Iraq and Afghanistan have been living with these aerial attacks and we judged it imperative that people get an insight into how they could go wrong. There will always be people lining up to say, 'This is just war, no battle zone is a playground, innocent people get killed,' and all that, but people should not be forced or coerced into taking these judgements on trust. They should see the evidence for themselves. There had been a cover-up, and, whether coming from a four-star general or a presenter on Fox News, the call to hide such truths from the population is dastardly. War is always a manipulation, but it serves the people amongst whom the war is being fought very badly, and does nothing for long-term peace, when the people conducting those wars are so willing to prosecute them in a flurry of bad faith. We called the US on that, as we would call any nation, and we did so not to make our lives easier – it begins a ghastly period of public renown for me – but to pursue an ideal of openness and accountability without which no true democracy can function. The fact that the US military refused to open a public investigation is shaming to the notion of moral responsibility. But the video, like the pictures from Abu Ghraib, was a crucial piece of the reality jigsaw in that conflict. And the picture presented by these things would bring the war to an end.

We had already published the classified 'Rules of Engagement for Iraq' in 2008, and we collected those documents and posted them on the collateralmurder.net website we had created to host the video, and encouraged people to read them as well as watch the video. The rules show that the behaviour of those in *Crazy Horse*, the Apache helicopter that swooped so eagerly to end the lives of twelve men and injure two children, was not permissible, under those same rules. 'Permission to engage' was hotly sought by those young men, and just as hotly granted, but the military later mangled the chronology in order to present a rationale for firing. They said it came down to the fact that the cameraman from Reuters, Noor Aldin, crouched at the corner and lifted his camera to take a picture, and they took the camera to be an RPG. But if you watch the video, you see that permission to engage is asked for and granted before that, as they are ambling down the street, and the requesting voice is agitated. The whole thing was out of whack, and there wasn't a single broadcaster or print journalist in America who wanted to ask the simple question 'Why?' In a theatre of war of that sort, why is it the case that young men are trigger-happy? What is it in the culture of the Iraq conflict in particular that made pilots so keen to jump over rules of engagement and ordinary human rules of decency and carefulness to murder the innocent? TV show after TV show went out, all fronted by those blank-eyed immoralists, not one of whom chose to contradict the military opinion they'd marshalled for the viewing audience. Not one of them was willing to be a journalist.

We would later find out, over the Afghan logs, just how close American editors are to official government truth. They act pious and make a reckless bid for the high ground, pretending it's all to do with responsibility and propriety and balance, but in fact they are compromising their journalistic independence at every other turn. We will come to that. In the meantime, the editors and their correspondents in the US did nothing during this crucial moment that would compromise their popularity at the annual White House Correspondents' Dinner. They drank their cocktails with the guys on the Hill, while the mothers and wives were still weeping in Iraq. A general blindness to the true actions of the military that day was instantly endemic, as if America's inherent good could not really be questioned. But the video questions it in real time and via their own cameras. The journalists and the government spokesmen merrily entered a revolving door, and pushed each other into a clear space, but anyone who has watched 'Collateral Murder' with an open mind will know what it says.

The snap view of people who don't understand our work – who don't want to understand our work – is that we might endanger lives. But the great thrust of our work is to save lives. By making a contribution, in the public interest, to the ending of wars, by supplying journalists with the means to keep a check on the excesses of power, we aim to limit the hunger for killings, skirmishes and invasions, as well as to limit the effectiveness of the lies that support them. With the banks, our work forced their practices into the open and made a marked difference in their sense of public accountability. And so it has been with military bodies as far apart as Kenya and the Pentagon. These actors depend on covert operations to prosecute violent incursions: and we are the spanner in their works, fighting all the time to expose the lies, end the conspiracy, hold up human rights and save lives.

As an example of this I give you Iran. For some time now, neoconservative elements in Washington, along with their Israeli allies, have been keen to instigate a war with Iran. This is not a mysterious matter. It has been well documented and well sourced by Seymour Hersh and others. Given that many military conflicts begin as border disputes, we kept an eye on the traffic of information there, and noticed that the British and the US military were literally sailing very close to the wind in the Gulf of Persia. Iranian military captured some British navy personnel and an approach was made by the Iranian navy to US vessels in their waters. We saw this early and I contacted Eric Schmitt of the *New York Times* to draw his attention to how this matter was included in a document on the rules of engagement we had leaked.

'In a section on crossing international borders,' wrote Schmitt, in what turned out to be an important article for the *New York Times*, 'the document said the permission of the American Defense Secretary was required before American forces could cross into or fly over Iranian or Syrian territory. Such actions, the document suggested, would probably also require the approval of President George W. Bush. But the document said there were cases in which such approval was not required: when American forces were in hot pursuit of former members of Saddam's government or terrorists.'

The Iranian government then responded: 'The US forces in Iraq have no right to chase any suspect into Iranian territory. Any entrance to the Iranian soil by any US military force to trail suspects would be against international laws and could be legally pursuable.' It stressed that Iran would 'give proper response to any move in this connection in order to defend its security and national sovereignty'. If you look at the next set of the 'Rules of Engagement' published after this exchange, you will see that the officials changed them to make this kind of dispute less likely. That's an example of a little document contributing to a change in policy, a change that potentially makes a vast difference to an ongoing chain of events. I'm not saying we stopped a war with Iran, saving countless lives, but I am saying we set out in that direction and achieved a smaller goal. There has not been a war with Iran, and that is partly because covert operations in that region have been interrupted and dangerous incursions along those borders have been prevented; and we were instrumental in that. We don't want the credit; we merely want the outcome. But it's appropriate to note that no news organisation in the world, no TV station baying for our blood, would ever focus on this aspect of what we do every day.

The Iraq video set the tone for many, especially among the US establishment, who wished to see us a certain way. It was obvious to us, and perhaps to a whole generation of people, that they were railing against the technology as much as against WikiLeaks. We couldn't help them with that: we are not a public relations firm – and don't do well in that area – but our work has been various and consistent and without partisan interests or state sponsorship, and that is how it will always be. We published the video and woke up infamous, though we take no pleasure in infamy. Rather, we find it odd to exist in a world where attempts to advance justice and the freedom of the press can cause one to be regarded as an enemy. Still, we left Washington with a sense of having done our work. No more than that. Neither triumphalism nor sense of defeat, for both were possible, given first the impact of the video and the scorn it had brought down on us.

We were galvanised, though. It was a pleasure to get to Berkeley in California, where we may no longer see students pushing flowers down military gun barrels but there is always a sense of change, or of progress, moving over the Bay. I was reminded of childhood days in the warm atmosphere of gentle protest there and felt we had a good audience – not a captive one but a free one – when Birgitta and Gavin MacFadyen of the Centre for Investigative Journalism joined me in speaking about developments in the freedom of the press. We went from there, soon after, to the Oslo Peace Forum, where I felt an uplifting sense of clarity after the video. 'Our goal is to have a just civilisation,' I said, 'and the message is transparency.' Given the flak we were taking, and were about to take, I knew it was important to underscore our commitment as existing outside of ideology. 'We are neither left nor right,' I said, and I meant it. It would cause a certain amount of wailing on either side, but we are not consistent with the old categories, and have never felt pressed to curry favour with a party. History teaches us of cover-ups and brutalities on both sides, no less in China or Russia or Libya than in France, Britain and America. But some of those cultures couldn't believe they could be subject to scrutiny. Some day, it will be understood why those cultures felt so immune from legal investigation.

I would not see America again. It was made clear to me that the Pentagon were trying to determine my whereabouts, and I had to cancel several appearances in the States. The reasons for this may already have been set in train by a narrow and paranoid understanding of our work, but then, on 26 May 2010, a serving soldier in Iraq, Private Bradley Manning, was arrested on suspicion of supplying secret information. Our deniability structures, invented all those years ago back in Australia, made it impossible to know if Manning was the source for any of our material. Our servers do not supply that kind of information, even to me. But I was certain of one thing: if he had supplied such information, then he was a hero of democracy and justice who had taken a role in saving lives. I went to sleep that night hoping the free world would be kind to him.

12

ALL THE EDITOR'S MEN

Vanity in a newspaper man is like perfume on a whore: they use it to fend off a dark whiff of themselves. I say that as an editor who loves what journalists can do. But I would be failing to give a true account of things in this book if I did not bear witness – sore witness at times – to the way senior journalists from the English-speaking world have serially loved WikiLeaks and then mugged us, almost without missing a beat, and then justified their actions with articles and books that must make them ridiculous in their own eyes. I bear them no deep resentment, but only mourn, as they must, the failing light of their principles in this last attempt to shine.

Everybody who likes a cause likes the *Guardian*, and I am no different, finding the paper to be a beacon sometimes, especially since it increased its global presence online. After the events of 9/11, the *Guardian* was the only truthful news-paper available in America, and I think I always admired its attempt to see the world, rather than just to see itself in the world, which is a trait you can't take for granted. The

Guardian had gone after corrupt politicians and reported the horror of war with a consistency that won't diminish as a result of their infamous venality over me. The *Guardian* is basically twelve angry men, and they function well and morally to the same extent that they sometimes behave self-ishly and appallingly. There is no mystery there, and I have always been happy to see what they can achieve on a good day. They seemed a natural ally, but, as Shakespeare tells it, there is nothing in nature to match an ally's fierce intent.

There was a hullabaloo when we came into partner-ship in 2010 over the Afghan war logs, but we had actually worked together before, in 2007, when I supplied them with a leak about the corruption of Daniel Arap Moi in Kenya. It ran as a front-page story at the end of August and begin-ning of September of that year and had a massive effect in Nairobi, where newspapers suddenly felt able to write about what was happening under their noses. After the arrest of Private Manning, it became obvious that, even with no evi-dence of a connection between us, the US authorities were acting as if there were, and they had me under surveillance. Under those conditions, I realised it wasn't safe for me to be at home in Australia, where I was visiting. The priority for me, quite honestly, was not my own safety – I recognised, even then, that forces would always be after me, and they would trap me in some way or another before long. My concern was for the work that WikiLeaks had been focus-ing on: we had a number of large releases being prepared, and I was afraid we were approaching a 'publish or perish' situation. We have always had a mechanism at WikiLeaks that ensures that if we are unable to continue, then all the material will be released at once. But I wanted to avoid that: the cache of documents we hold is so large and so deserving of individual assessment and discrete publication that I wanted to feed the material out with due carefulness.

It was obvious I had to come back to Europe, so I arranged to be invited to give a talk on censorship at the European Parliament, and I travelled there via Hong Kong, avoiding Singapore or Thailand, where there would have been a greater willingness to respond to US calls to have me seized. (I've found it's always wise to travel on a political invitation, guaranteeing a fuss if you don't reach your destination.) There were a number of MPs there, as well as friends from Iceland, talking about the Iceland Modern Media Initiative, the movement behind our attempt to found an openness haven. I spoke about the increasing business of newspapers removing material from online archives, responding to gag orders, and so on. And I bumped into the *Guardian*'s man in Brussels, an affable sort who was receptive to what I was saying. I told him there were a number of upcoming publications that might be of interest to the paper. He went off, and I soon heard from a special investigations reporter on the paper, who said he wished to come from London to meet and discuss the proposal.

We had always envisaged the material we had on Afghanistan and Iraq being divulged through several established publications. That seemed the right way. It wasn't about single documents and single stories, but a whole slew of stories and hundreds of thousands of documents. We judged it would have the necessary impact only if they were published in an ambitious way, by people who could attach their own researchers and journalists to make sense of the material. We never pretended to understand, or even be in a position to read, every document in these massive caches, which is why we needed the newspapers. We couldn't deal with it ourselves: we were talking about 90,000 Afghan war logs and 400,00 Iraq documents. Traditionally, we had analysed leaked documents ourselves and written the appropriate commentary with them, before feeding the whole thing to a single journalist or broadcaster. But this was different, and I spoke to the *Guardian*'s investigations guy about how to honour the material, and the source, and put together a package that would serve it and truly get it out there, as we'd promised. By that stage, I had already spoken to a reporter at the *New York Times* and was in contact with journalists at *Der Spiegel*.

I spoke to him for about six hours. He seemed professional and nervy and a little tired, but so did I, no doubt, and we seemed to agree on the importance of the documents and that it would be a smart move to involve the other news organisations. I wasn't grandiose about my participation, simply highly protective of the material, and experienced, for that matter, in dealing with these kinds of sources and this kind of surveillance. The later suggestion that I was simply a source myself was just ludicrous: I was the architect of the plan, and for the good reason that I was the only one of the group who knew how the material was stored and how it could be disseminated. I also planned the leak from beginning to end, so as protect it and enhance it, and, though it might offend the famous vanity of my erstwhile collaborators, they could take it or leave it. I wasn't asking them for money and I wasn't asking them for glory: WikiLeaks should be credited in order to advance its work, but they would have to go all-in with the plan to make it work, so readers could check the accuracy of the stories against the raw material. Of course, each partner behaved at the time as if this were a no-brainer. Only later, when

they'd got what they wanted, would they unpick the relationship in such a way as to enlarge themselves and reduce
us, an old-style government trick I should have seen
coming.

The *Guardian*'s investigations reporter said he would
speak to the paper's editor, Alan Rusbridger, who would
speak, in turn, to Bill Keller, the editor of the *New York
Times*. I then wrote a code on a napkin and passed it to the
reporter in a bar. The idea was that he would be able to use
this to gain access to an encrypted version of the material
sent to him through an open channel. He now had the key
and we set up a fake correspondence, saying something like
'It was nice to meet you but sorry the deal didn't work out.'
This would throw any surveillance off the scent, making out
that there would be no subsequent transfer of the Afghan
material. The reporter himself didn't care about exclusivity,
but was aware, understandably, that his bosses would. We
agreed that we would control the embargo date and ensure,
for legal reasons as well as the commercial ones they would
have in mind, that the material would come out at the same
time. We also agreed that each paper would have editorial
control over its own content. Television might be brought
in at the last minute but not before, as the nature of television production would make it impossible to keep the
impending leak secret. We had no dispute over this: it was
my plan and I laid it out, and he nodded it through with
contained excitement. The reporter deserves credit for how
he managed things at that point: he acted like an activist,
which was close to his roots, and strategised about how to
give the material its best platforms.

I was seeking to set up a WikiLeaks production unit
for this massive project in Stockholm. That was proving

difficult – after 'Collateral Murder', the level of heat on me as the main public face of WikiLeaks was intense, and some personnel shied away – but the investigations guy and I met in Stockholm and continued to talk over the plan. At this point another *Guardian* reporter came into the picture. I'd met him before, in Oslo, I think, where he had seen the Baghdad video in a rough form and had wanted to buy it for his paper. We were being too heavily monitored then, so nothing came of it, but it probably fed into my notion that the *Guardian* would be a natural collaborator when the time came. Suddenly, this reporter – a news guy – took a role on behalf of the *Guardian*, the Afghan material was transferred to him and he proceeded to share it with the *New York Times*, as agreed by myself and his colleague.

You've got to imagine this stuff in its raw form. There were around 90,000 discrete entries in the Afghanistan field logs (we eventually released about 75,000), and they had been made on the spot, after every skirmish or battle or IED explosion. They were full of acronyms and army-speak. One entry, picked entirely at random, begins: '(M) KAF PRT reports finding rocket IVO KAF PRT Site.' The *New York Times*, in its literal-mindedness and impatience, couldn't see the narrative, and took a while to understand the forces at work in the material, the sheer statistical and human horde it represented; they were at first disappointed not to see 'the stories'. The *Guardian*'s news reporter, a senior guy, at this point showed his first manipulative little impulse: he said the *New York Times*, in order to stay on board, would need a 'sweetener', and so would the *Guardian* for that matter. He 'understood' that neither paper found the material to be that compelling and they wanted a little sugar on their porridge: namely, they wanted the entire cache of Iraq documents, too. I should have withdrawn at that point, seeing what was obvious: that these people were not gentlemen and did not know how to value significant data and human complexity for what it was. I should have spotted the self-serving glint in the news reporter's eyes and walked away. The world was full of media organisations who would have moved mountains to join us in the work we had been doing. But these papers, even at the earliest stage, were on a fault-finding mission, looking to exploit us as best they could. This *Guardian* reporter was stimulated, you could see, not by principle, but by the chance to please his bosses and score one last scoop before he retired.

But we marched on. I liked the *Guardian* and wanted to believe it would come good. It knew what these leaks represented and I saw no real problem with the 'sweetener', other than the manner of its being asked for. In any event, I supplied them and the *New York Times* with the Iraq logs. It was all to the good, I kept saying, we're not in this for gratitude. If they put their resources behind both sets of logs, then the basic cause of openness and freedom of information will have been served. My only real job now was to work with them to get the best out of the material. Well, not my only job: I also had to keep them honest, which quickly proved to be a full-time occupation. It's really an unsavoury tale and I wish I didn't have to tell it, but they have at length, and in gross personal terms, so we must go on. What I can tell you is that I was under the greatest pressure of my life. I was being surveilled; I was living out of a rucksack; when I was sleeping at all, I was sleeping on sofas; people beyond my reach were being arrested; and I was fighting to keep the whole vast dreadnought on an even keel. I was tired. I wasn't always accommodating. I wasn't always conventional.

Not always nice. But I thought these were men of action and principle, not weaklings with a crush, and it was difficult to see the way they moved around me so gingerly and sometimes full of hurt, like I wasn't giving them enough attention or showing my best side.

My best side was in the work. I had brought them into a partnership that was about to give them the best scoops of those successive wars. And people had risked their lives, we had to suppose, in order to get that news to the world. In London I spent weeks at the *Guardian*'s offices in King's Cross. There was a moment when it was all working well: we were in a kind of bunker and it looked like a spirit of co-operation had taken hold, although it was sterile when compared to how we put together the Baghdad video. My methods were probably odd to some of them, but we got down to it, myself teaching them to understand the material and clean up the copy, with the *Guardian* people, the *New York Times* in full attendance and *Der Spiegel* coming occasionally. I stayed at the homes of both of the *Guardian* reporters for a while. I was tense and I had to keep moving. But we were getting there, and I wasn't really thinking about the relationships – I thought the material was our relationship – and for a time a spirit of sharing and exploration took over.

I had hoped all along that the papers would share their research with each other, and they honoured that. For instance, one of the early stories I found was on Task Force 373, a US Special Forces assassination squad that was working with a list of 2,000 people. It might sound reasonable enough to people who have watched too many episodes of *Generation Kill*, but this JPL (or Joint Party List) is actually a totally barbaric, extra-judicial nightmare. You saw how

people could just get on the list, no judicial review, nothing. Some governor in Afghanistan could just not like you,
and nominate you for the JPL, and next minute a drone
comes in and bombs your house. With patience and care,
you could follow the repercussions of the task force's work
through the logs. An entry from 2 May 2007 looked ahead
to a meeting with the deputy governor scheduled for the
next day. The first item on the agenda was 'discuss repercussions of recent TF 373 ops and address village grievances'
and the next item was 'provide relief to the district and the
school that was bombed'. Task Force 373 was a secret squad
until we named it, and the story made the front page of *Der
Spiegel*. Interestingly, according to a source the story about
it in the *Guardian* was partly written by Eric Schmitt of the
New York Times. His own paper were alleged not to have
had the stomach to publish it.

I was keen, as were others, that the publications should
be in sync but that the *New York Times* should steal a march.
We felt this would best protect the sources: that the US
government were less likely to go for the *New York Times*,
and that the paper could effectively use its prestige for
strong journalistic ends, on behalf of all the participating
bodies. But, true to form, another gleam appeared in the
eye of our collaborators: the *New York Times* would prefer
that we went first. This was nothing but a piece of strategic
cowardice on their part, a piece of work, indeed, and one
that is so ingrained in that paper's self-protective sense of
itself that they likely can't even see it. They dressed it up
as caution and responsibility: they wanted the stories, had
been working for weeks on the stories, but didn't have
the balls to go out there and run it first. They wanted
WikiLeaks to go first, which, we now see, was part of their

strategy – to hide behind this 'maverick' outfit whose story they were just 'reflecting'. Bill Keller, the editor, could puff himself up with self-belief, but in fact he did not have the courage of his journalistic convictions, was fearful of the Pentagon, and he did what a six-year-old playground swot would be decried for doing, and hid behind the coat-tails of the school's bad boy while scoffing the spoils of the tuckshop. It would be painful to watch them, once the material was bagged, to stray and spew their guts up, never ready to stand up for the part they had played in partnering us. The cock crowed three times, and Bill Keller shamelessly denied us, throwing in a few volleys of personal abuse to keep himself clean.

Disgusting. But a smarter media player than me would certainly have seen it coming. Being first is everything in journalism, but here was the biggest newspaper in the world asking point-blank to go second. Keller's cowardice will be his lasting legacy: for these cables reveal terrible events in Afghanistan, and a stronger man, a better journalist, would have leapt to add his paper's imprimatur to the truth they revealed. Instead, he played it safe and let us take it on the chin, which, of course, we are always ready to do, anyway. But by that point I was a bag-lady and a smelly old nutcase, according to him, while he was Bill Keller, the weakest and most self-protecting man ever to edit the *New York Times*. Infamy comes in many guises, and sometimes, even, it comes wearing a sports jacket and an old school tie, asking us to forgive him what he does, for he only does it in the name of propriety. Next to Ben Bradlee, who stood by his two maverick reporters during Watergate, or Robert West and Gobin Stair of Beacon Press, who were subpoenaed and would have gone to jail rather than sell out Daniel Ellsberg over the Pentagon Papers, this man is a moral pygmy with a self-justifying streak the size of the San Andreas Fault. WikiLeaks, a small, not-for-profit Web start-up, would be standing alone as usual at the last post.

Coincidentally (or not), all the ducks we had spent months lining up began to quack with self-interest when the hour came. Thirty-six hours before publishing, I agreed to let *Channel 4 News* send round an interviewer to the *Guardian*, who would be going live with the story on their website at 9.30 p.m. Channel 4 would go out with a story on their late bulletin at 10.30 p.m. But by now the *Guardian*, too, were bellowing their own tune, not thinking 'This is all to the greater good', but 'What about our exclusivity!?', 'What about our credit!?' The television people were not just television people, they were led by Stephen Grey, a journalist with vast experience in the area who had written a much-admired book about Afghanistan and who the *Guardian* had wished to work for them. Grey had always been on the periphery of our plans, though the *Guardian* later claimed we brought in Grey as a competitor to them. This was nonsense, but for some reason it galled the *Guardian*. They had got themselves into a position of worrying about their credit and their slice of the pie, and this was not only inappropriate, it was troubling, given that my whole relationship with the special investigations reporter was based on the idea that he was an activist who really cared about the material. The *Guardian* would say I was difficult and obstructive, but this was merely part of the bitching and hissyness that make Britain's premier liberal paper the thing we know and love.

Still, the results were impressive. Seventeen pages in *Der Spiegel*, some thirteen in the *Guardian* and eight in the *New*

York Times. The reaction was instant and massive: each of these papers found themselves, for the first time in a long while, at the forefront of a discussion as to the real nature of modern warfare. I was thrown into a maelstrom of publicity and I attended to it as best I could, keeping to the plan, citing the material, pointing all the while to the larger issues of press freedom. You can always tell, however, when you're working with people hungry for more than the upholding of the principle will supply. The *Guardian* people couldn't stop themselves from yacking at their dinner parties, and the senior news reporter, especially, couldn't keep his mouth shut, endlessly wanting to tell everyone his 'how we did it' story. I don't think he ever quite understood the security implications, and he was always looking to big himself up with his colleagues, which is presumably why he blabbed to the *New York Times* about the cables we were holding. As part of his showing off, he let it be known that I had stayed at his house and at the other reporter's house, even though that was a dangerous thing to reveal.

You could see the sun shifting off our patch as soon as they knew they'd had what they came for. At first, they held off on this, because they realised it would be in their interest to have the cables, but it was evident to me. As Orwell would have understood all too well, these things appear in the language. The *Guardian*, along with the *New York Times*, increasingly wanted to characterise me as a hacker, as an unstable source, but in this they were only revealing their own anxiety. You should always be careful of questioning people's motives: you only reveal your own. And this slow deracination of me and of WikiLeaks was merely a way for these organisations both to protect themselves against prosecution and claim more credit. Children behave with more grace under pressure, and although I must often have been high-handed in my protectiveness and in my steering of this project, it could possibly be considered part of their job to understand why. Instead, they went to war with me and totally forgot what the opposition was.

There was a very personal element, too. The special investigations reporter and I had got on well when it was just us. In Brussels and Stockholm, and initially in London, we were friends, and he made me feel that I was some younger version of himself. He sort of fell for my idealism, if you'll allow the possibility, and before I knew it he was behaving erratically and needily, like a besotted person, claiming he had done the most work and everything was his idea. To use some of those mixed metaphors the *Guardian* is so fond of, he wanted to be the star who brought home the big fish. It was somehow a matter of honour for this man with his colleagues. I didn't particularly care who got the gong, but the twelve angry men were not looking at the evidence. They were looking to themselves, their positions, their late careers, and while this is all very human, it got in the way of our work.

The real test of journalistic mettle comes with the counterattack. You always know it's coming. People wanted to drink champagne the night of the big leak, but I was thinking, 'Hold the corks. The White House and the Pentagon are coming back at us and it won't be nice.' Their first move was to say the material was insignificant. 'There is not a lot new here for those who have been following developments closely,' said the first (unnamed) government rent-a-quote on the *Washington Post*'s speed dial. That's standard. And the next wave, led by Rupert Murdoch's rival British daily *The Times*, suggested that the material we had published had already led to the death of a Taliban defector. It turned out the man they named had been killed two years earlier. But as soon as the first criticism arrived, the *Guardian* reporters began to panic.

With hindsight, I can't fault the *Guardian* for the initial work they did in making the documents ready. It was an excellent job, done in the best traditions of their paper, and I felt that some of them – Ian Katz, the deputy editor, and Harold Frayman, the systems editor – brought a level of normality and hard graft to the proceedings. The senior news reporter, of course, scuppered some of that easiness by telling me some of the workers on the *Guardian* had asked for 'danger money' because they were being followed. Over the years I had worked with journalists all over the world, but I had never before encountered a group with so little coolness in the face of threat, so little confidence in the manner of working with people who weren't exactly like them, and so little evident experience in handling basic issues of security. When Alan Rusbridger called Bill Keller to ask if he knew how to set up a secure telephone line, the New Yorker was not fit for purpose. He had no idea. And despite the efforts of some of their respective staffs to enjoy the moment and make the collaboration work at all costs, there were others, the twelve angry men, who were embroiled at every turn in their own careerist dramas, which naturally turned on me as the supposed figurehead of the operation.

I felt I had a clear strategy in going with the Afghan war logs first and following with those from Iraq. The Afghan stuff was less voluminous, and I wanted to see if we – meaning WikiLeaks in collaboration with the media partners – could set up systems for reading and publishing the data, training the journalists and graphics people in how to do it before bringing that experience to the more complicated job of dealing with the hundreds of thousands of documents from Iraq. The two main papers, as I said, had asked for the Iraq material as a 'sweetener': they had gone after it with almost sinister levels of zeal, which caused me to think they would go all-out and make a good job of unwrapping the cache for the public. I can be mono-minded and fixed on an objective, so I was sure the next big push would be happening over the following three weeks. What I hadn't factored into the thing was a high level of journalistic ennui: Iraq wasn't as 'sexy' as Afghanistan, a present and ongoing war. I had thought the various staff would do a better job on the Iraq material, having learned how to do it, but they were burnt out, and many of them went on holiday immediately. You can't, of course, blame people for feeling exhausted, but there was a strong sense, at least to me, that the momentum had gone. They were not doing a good job with the new material yet they wouldn't hand it over to other journalists to get on with it. They were stuck.

In time, our disagreements would take on a darker hue, and this was especially true with the *New York Times*. Bill Keller would wish to characterise me as a 'source', which bodes badly, by the way, for anyone who might see him or herself as a potential future source for the *New York Times*. It used to be a matter of honour, if not merely journalistic and legal good sense, not only to protect sources but to look after them at every turn – as we speak, journalists all over the world are on their way to jail to protect their sources. Bill Keller's treatment of this 'source' has been undignified and aggressive to a degree that shames him and embarrasses his former office. In what world, you might ask, is it okay to work closely with a 'source', allow him to organise an international syndicate, of which you are part, for the publication of the year's biggest story, only to turn on that source as soon as the party is over, and write of him in terms of personal abuse – 'he smelled as if he hadn't bathed in days'. That's right, I wasn't at the bathroom mirror much that week, since I was up all night for three days straight, preparing the material his paper would soon be splashing under their famous rubric, 'All the news that's fit to print'. Even more ungracious, not to say psychotic, was Keller's decision then to characterise me as a person from a Stieg Larsson thriller, a man who is half-hacker, half-conspiracy theorist, using 'sex as both recreation and violation'.

Ladies and gentleman, that last statement is actionable. It is a malicious libel, and one intended – bizarrely – to inflict maximum damage to a person then facing, as I was, allegations of sexual misconduct. He must have known as he wrote and published that line that it constituted the most heinous assault on my wellbeing, my legal standing and my reputation. But he did it anyway. I'll never understand why and I won't speculate. I simply wished to unpack this example for you, so that you could see how they work, how the whole system works with such men, to occasionally destroy the thing they temporarily proclaimed to love. Keller's sordid disavowal is 8,000 words long and it contains many such fallacies. Let this paragraph stand as reply to them all: I would only exhaust myself, and you, and the courts if it came to that, trying to answer each one specifically. They are not the work of a sober, responsible man. We have met these people in literature – conscientious on the top, stagnant at the middle and sociopathic underneath, who will do anything to glorify themselves in the eyes of an unsuspecting public. So, you ask, what sort of man does this? A desperate one, we might say, or a small one, indeed, or an archdeacon who had spent the night on the streets, 'sleeping with panthers', as Oscar Wilde said, only to arrive at his office in the morning and issue a brutal diktat against panthers. The young staff on his paper might blush at his methods, seeing how fast Mr Keller could turn from hungry collaborator to ungrateful avenger in the time it takes to speed-dial the White House.

But you know how it is: part of you is loath to face the fact that a promising working relationship is dead. It's dead now, but at the time I was still, however inexpertly, trying to keep the cartel together to work on as-yet-unpublished documents. Again, I was focused on the work itself: it seemed imperative to get the material out and make it available to researchers and readers. I hadn't gone into this game to store up papers. I wanted to release them, however gradually, so that they would make the impact they ought to have had. In the event, we just muddled through, and I worked with some TV people at the same time on shaping a couple of documentaries to stoke public interest.

The relationship with the newspapers would get more explosive in the coming weeks, and I'll come to that. But let's not lose sight, in all of this, of the leaks themselves. Together, the Afghan and Iraq war logs are a major historical record, and they will not be bossed off the page by squabbling tribes. In some ways, they were the culmination of years of thinking, on my part and on the part of my colleagues, about how to open up the secret worlds that so define our lives and our global politics. For some people, they were just a passing story. But they will live with us

now for as long as we are interested in the vicissitudes of
human conflict. Let us enter into them and see what is
there, before returning to the indignant soap opera of the
modern media.

13

BLOOD

On 28 July 2010, Major General Campbell, a US commander in Afghanistan, said that 'anytime there's any sort of leak of classified material, it has the potential to harm the military folks that are working out here every day'. Major Campbell also admitted that he had not read any of the leaked documents. The following day, at a Pentagon press conference, Defense Secretary Robert M. Gates and Admiral Mike Mullen ramped up this strategic piece of mythmaking. 'Mr Assange can say whatever he likes about the greater good he thinks he and his source are doing,' said Mullen, 'but the truth is they might already have on their hands the blood of some young soldier or that of an Afghan family.'

A member of the press corps asked a question.

Journalist: Admiral Mullen, you have mentioned that the founder of WikiLeaks may have blood on his hands. Do you know, have people been killed over this information?

Mullen: They're still . . . what I'm concerned about with this is I think individuals who are not involved in this kind of warfare and expose this kind of information can't . . . from my perspective . . . can't appreciate how this kind of information is routinely networked together inside the classified channels we use specifically. And it's very difficult, if you don't do this and understand this, to understand the impact, and very specifically the potential that is there . . . that is there to risk lives of our soldiers and sailors, airmen and Marines, coalition warfighters, as well . . . as well as Afghan citizens. And there's no doubt in my mind about that.

Secretary Gates: I would add . . . I would just add one other thing. The thing to remember here is that this is a huge amount of raw data . . . There is no accountability. There is no sense of responsibility. It is sort of thrown out there for take as you will and damn the consequences.

Journalist: With all due respect, you didn't answer the question.

Within hours of these statements, the expression 'Julian Assange has blood on his hands' had entered the language. If you Google the words 'Assange' and 'blood' you will see, by the number of hits, that those two words together suggest that, at least in the media consciousness, I am associated with the concept of 'blood on hands' to a greater extent than Richard Nixon, Suharto and Pontius Pilate put together. That is how the modern world of communications works. Without any evidence – any evidence at all – of casualties resulting from our attempt to let people see what was happening in that war, I was able to be dubbed as a person with 'blood on his hands'. It is one of those statements careless people enjoy, and it has blunt currency, but there is no basis for it in fact. The very sinister thing is how it is then taken up by other commentators, not only as a statement of fact, but as a true reflection of the original statement. It is neither. Look again at Admiral Mullen's statement. He said, 'They might already have on their hands the blood . . .' The words 'they' and 'might' are quickly shaved off by the wider media and suddenly 'Julian Assange has blood on his hands'. And so, something that wasn't true in the first place breeds even sharper untruths, until, by the end, one is forced to embody not only a fiction, but a fictionalisation of a previous fiction, without recourse.

We've become so used to these procedures we've begun to think them entirely normal. But they are heinous. And every day now, if I wanted to, I could spend my time rebuffing the fictions of foes and friends alike, none of whom, it turns out, can be immune from the contaminating force of lies. This is not only a problem for me, of course, and I begin to feel sorry for anybody who was ever stupid or vain enough to think they might do well to live their lives in the public eye. It's a losing battle. One is forced to become like a cypher in the work of Charles Dickens, living out an endless Jarndyce versus Jarndyce of the self, in which evidence can only mount and convolute and breed, without the possibility of a clear true verdict ever being heard or respected. This is my life now, and I bring it to you neither with a shrug nor a whimper. You can only set the record straight where you can and get on with the job of forgetting yourself in the name of bigger causes.

A large part of my job, when not harrying the banks, has been to reveal exactly where the blood has been spilled in modern wars and state-sponsored invasions. It is a large task, and one that can only really be completed by the public at large. We don't splash stories, we convey information, and it is the task – a task that will take years – of individuals, researchers, journalists and lawyers, to look into the data and see what it means. Our work with the newspapers was intended to be a stimulus: the material was vast and was being offered to the public. How it can be us, or the enquiring public, that has blood on their hands, as opposed to the generals and governors who prosecute these wars, is a matter for clairvoyant abstraction. But let us just say that the Afghan logs and the Iraqi diaries cannot be owned by either would-be conquering armies or by evil dictators. They are not theirs to own; they are part of the fabric of the world's reality. Gates and others may not like the fact that they cannot be in possession of that reality, but indeed they cannot, unless they, and their opposite numbers, wish to be known as Big Brother. When forced to tell the truth, in a letter to the Senate a fortnight later, on 16 August 2010, Defense Secretary Gates informed members that 'the review to date has not revealed any sensitive intelligence sources and methods compromised by this disclosure'; the link that was originally inferred between me and 'blood on hands' was falsified from the horse's mouth.

Red herrings and smears aside, the logs make a crucial contribution towards the understanding of the war. They reveal the way the real incidents on the ground unfolded, while also alerting the public to how these incidents were often downplayed in statements about them, whether coming from the military or reported in the media. Again and again, civilian casualties are minimised or misreported. The moral thing to do, and this is moral work for everyone, is to examine the actual field report and compare it with what was said later, and what you find, too often for any kind of comfort, are situations where innocent people were killed and not acknowledged. If a building, for instance, was suspected of being a hideout for Taliban leaders, targeted and bombed, and it later turned out to be a school where a number of children were killed, then this could be gleaned from the logs. And that, I'll maintain to the grave, is a crucial piece of information in the public interest.

Let me give you an example from Iraq. In November 2005 US Marines launched operation 'Steel Curtain' in and around the city of Husaybah, near the border with Syria. After seventeen days of fighting, the Pentagon put out a press release under the headline 'Operation Steel Curtain concludes along Iraq–Syria border'. Have a look, it's still there on their website. After a brief rundown of the objectives of the mission, the report stated 'officials reported that 10 marines were killed in fighting during Steel Curtain. A total of 139 terrorists were killed and 256 were processed for detention during the operation.' There was no mention of civilian casualties. That press release is dated 22 November 2005. Now how about this entry from the Iraq diaries we leaked, dated 11 November 2005: '[Patrol] in support of Steel Curtain reported finding civilian bodies buried in three (3) separate locations in Husaybah. At [first location] 3 females, 3 males and 1 child were recovered. At [second location] 7 females and 10 children were recovered. At [third location] 1 child was unable to be recovered . . . Neighbors positively identified all the remains and the father identified the remains of the child that was unable to be recovered. All casualties were recovered from areas attacked by coalition aircraft on 7th Nov 2005.'

You had to avoid bringing your own bias to the data and just let it speak to you. This was increasingly difficult for the journalists to do, and was one of the reasons that the issue of redactions became fraught. WikiLeaks, you must remember, was learning on the job, and I'm sure we improved, especially when it came to having a better focus on redactions. The data was giant and we might have failed to redact brilliantly at first, but the supposed concern of the United States government for a risk that remains merely hypothetical and unproven is a dishonest attempt to distract the public from the real truth about the Afghan war that the logs revealed.

Another erroneous report emerged at this time that had me saying we weren't responsible for the welfare of informants and that 'they deserved to die'. This is just nonsense: I said some people held that view, but that we would edit the documents to preserve their essential content and not throw harm in people's way if we could avoid it.

Throughout the logs' publication, I was aware that the redaction issue should not become an excuse for censorship. As we saw with Defense Secretary Gates, interested parties, by which I mean Western governments, will often use the redaction issue – or the bogus issue of 'blood on hands' – to justify their calls for the documents to remain secret altogether. Against the grain of modern developments, they are essentially demanding censorship of these documents for political reasons. And my unwillingness to serve in that propaganda war allowed them to dub me as someone who was against redactions. In actual fact, we had been burning the midnight oil on redactions from early on. We didn't prove as squeamish as the governments, naturally, or indeed as squeamish as the *Guardian* or the *New York Times*, but we were judicious, I believe, and to date no one has come to harm as a result of what we published.

Although my view of all this had not changed, I could see ahead of the Iraq release that the myth of WikiLeaks' recklessness was threatening to damage our organisation and our future work. If you are to achieve anything significant in the world, you sometimes have to acknowledge expediencies, and I therefore decided to redact the Iraq diaries much more thoroughly than anything previously. Without the resources to do these redactions manually – especially since our media partners refused to help because they were scared of taking on the responsibility – we wrote a program to remove all names and all other identifying information automatically from the documents. I know that unthinking minds will condemn me for saying this, but I actually believe that our redactions of the Iraq material were too extensive. After the diaries revealed the collusion of American troops in the torture of hundreds of Iraqi prisoners by local forces, the Danish Ministry of Defence started an investigation into the behaviour of their own troops. At first they approached the Pentagon, asking for an unredacted copy of those sections of the diaries that referred to Danish soldiers. The Pentagon flatly refused, so instead the Danes asked us for the material, which we provided. Though some people may refuse to see this, open government is only worthy of the name when it is a real, lived value, not an empty branding exercise, and my attitude to redaction is coloured by this fact.

We had to prepare the Iraq diaries to some extent in an atmosphere of hysteria after the fallout from the earlier leak. The newspaper partners were working at a low energy level, as I said, and they had been slightly rocked by the scale of the response to the previous work. I've seen this before with media organisations: they want big stories, but they can't handle the heat they generate. A lot of these people are just middle-class guys who want to go home to their wives and talk about schools for their kids, and suddenly they're coming to work and it's surveillance and court cases, and the majority just don't have the character for that. But the Iraq material was tremendously important, and I had a fight on, especially after the Swedish sex allegations, in keeping the partners to their agreements and their honour. There were signs. WikiLeaks began organising a joint press conference to announce the leaks. The Bureau of Investigative Journalism, who were also going creepy, were to be involved along with an organisation called Iraq Body Count and various others, including the media partners. The bell tolled, somewhere in my head – betrayal often comes not as a surprise but as a recognition – when the senior news reporter contact at the *Guardian* told my assistant, Sarah Harrison, that the paper did not want to be referred to as a media partner. He said he didn't want the *Guardian*'s logo on the banner behind us, and that he would be there, in the audience, as a reporter only.

Ding dong. Here he comes, holding his ears and claiming he only climbed into the cathedral's belltower so as to get a better view of the man in the street. He told us the *New York Times* and *Der Spiegel* felt the same way: no logos. We rented the Riverbank Hotel down near Vauxhall Bridge, in London, and we had hundreds of press people there.

I brought Daniel Ellsberg over from the States to join me on the dais and we released the data and did a great number of interviews afterwards. Despite many irritations that would only really flare up later on, such as with the media partners and various exploiters, we had set about the release of the Iraq documents with as much precision as WikiLeaks could muster. It was important that we attached an NGO to the release, and Iraq Body Count were right on the nose, ethically speaking, keeping an impressively thorough record of civilian casualties since early in that war. They helped us to create an automatic redactions system for the 400,000 documents. It was also right to bring in *Le Monde*, as we did, as the French had rejected the war in 2003 and suffered as a result. The Spanish daily newspaper *El País* came on board, too. We worked with the Bureau of Investigative Journalism in London to produce documentaries on the diaries for Channel 4 and Al Jazeera. We, and our partners, had a sense that the data would augment (and add detail to) the public's perception that the war in Iraq was a failure and a threat to openness. American troops had already started to leave Iraq, while many other Western nations had already withdrawn their forces more than a year before, and this left the field open politically for a number of NGOs such as Reporters Sans Frontières, Amnesty and Human Rights Watch to examine the material and begin drawing conclusions from it.

The documents consisted of the reports made by American soldiers in Iraq of every incident that they thought noteworthy. All the details were there: the precise location, the time, the military units involved, the number of killed, wounded and detained, the status of the victims, US, Allied, Iraqi military, insurgent, civilian. In short, this was the most significant and detailed history to be recorded, not only of the Iraq war, but of any war.

All of the problems of warfare were there, both at the minute-by-minute field level and, taken as a whole, in grand perspective. Reading through the diaries with our partners, Iraq Body Count, we found 15,000 civilian casualties that had never previously been reported. Modern warfare is not the white heat of technological wizardry and otherworldly precision the Pentagon would have you believe, it's the same old mess of blood and tragedy and injustice. A drone might be able to precisely target a dwelling, but it can't check who's inside, or who just got home from school.

The Iraq documents, and there are still many of them awaiting analysis, reveal the legacy of US human rights abuses, as well as the sad state of the country under Saddam. Some day, historians will be able to piece together an amazing sense of the day-to-day hostilities that made up that war, and these diaries will be the primary source for that. I was proud of the work we had done to make them possible and phoned my mother in Australia. We spoke regularly, but it was good, at a moment like this, to make the connection back to where it all started for me.

In the following days Larry King wanted to interview Daniel Ellsberg and me. The idea was that I would talk about the diaries, and Dan would give his historical perspective. We had to be at the CNN international studio in London at 2 a.m. to sync with Larry King, who, of course, was live in New York, and we watched the rest of his show while we waited. One of his guests was a former girlfriend of the Supreme Court judge Clarence Thomas, who had some unflattering memories of her time with him. The thing that seemed to strike her the most was how ambitious and careerist he had been; he even, she told King, went to do a press interview at two o'clock in the morning! Dan and I looked at each other, and at the clock, and smiled.

But something was on my mind. It was on the mind, indeed, of everyone we worked with. It was to become the main preoccupation of my life at this point, and though we would continue to publish and do the work of WikiLeaks, never halting publication even for a day, the Swedish case would overwhelm the media's interest in our every move, feed a frenzy of speculation and disquiet about me, and see me in prison. I have kept my own counsel about the matter until now. It will be difficult to keep anger out of this account, owing to the sheer level of malice and opportunism that have driven the case against me, but I want to make this argument as much as possible in a spirit of understanding. I have been denied the same toleration by my suddenly multiplying enemies, and, if I cannot beat them, I can surely reserve the right not to join them.

I went to Sweden in August 2010 with the words of the Pentagon still ringing in my ears. Geoff Morell, the press secretary, had given a briefing in which he implied that WikiLeaks, and I specifically, should begin worrying. 'If doing the right thing is not good enough for them,' he said, 'then we will figure out what alternatives we have to compel them to do the right thing. Let me leave it at that.' When asked at the same press conference whether our partners, the *New York Times*, would be similarly compelled, he said, 'I don't know the *New York Times* would describe themselves as their partner . . . I don't know that the *New York Times* or the other publications are in possession of the documents.' This showed that the Pentagon and Bill Keller were thinking along similar lines: let WikiLeaks be blamed and possibly burned, while our partners who published the same material are shown to be somehow immune from the same draconian laws. It wasn't going to play well with First Amendment fans, but what Morell's words proved was that what was freedom of the press for one organisation was not freedom for another. Unlike our partners, WikiLeaks was not to be treated as a publisher but as a spy, and this absurd position came ribboned in threat.

At the same time it was revealed that there was a 90-man Pentagon task force, later increased to 120 men, dedicated to WikiLeaks and working 24 hours a day and seven days a week. The FBI and Defense Intelligence Agency were part of this group. The pot had boiled over and a number of American politicians had called for my assassination. Sarah Palin said I should be hunted down like a dog and one paper even printed a graphic of me with a target painted on my face.

I had not given up on the idea of finding a haven where we might do our work in peace. Sweden looked possible. It was regarded as an independent, liberal country, with a Freedom of Information Act going back to the 1780s and a Constitution that makes special and lengthy provision for the protection of press freedom. Sources are better off in Sweden than in most places in the world: there is a right to anonymity and penalties for journalists who promise but fail to protect the people who privately give them information. To gain protection from prior restraint, it is necessary in Sweden to have both a publishing certificate and to be working for a listed, responsible editor. I went to Sweden with that in mind, hoping to gain a certificate and also to put myself in the position of becoming an accredited editor. You need to have an income for this, so I agreed to become a columnist for *Expressen*, the largest Swedish newspaper.

I hoped we might be able to open a journalistic office for WikiLeaks in Stockholm and began moving towards this. So, Sweden represented two things to me at that point, a future working environment and a safe haven, which makes what happened next taste all the more bitter. Before going, I arranged as usual an invitation to speak, this time for the political party known as the Brotherhood, who are part of the Christian Social Democrats. I arrived on 11 August. And, just at the point of arrival, I received some news from one of our contacts in a Western intelligence agency, confirming what had already been hinted at by the Pentagon press office. The word was that the US government acknowledged privately that I would be difficult to prosecute but were already talking about 'dealing with you illegally', as my source put it. The source specified what that would mean: gaining evidence about what we had in the way of information; unearthing, by whatever means, some sort of link between Private Manning and WikiLeaks; and, if all else failed, deploying other illegal means, such as planting drugs on me, 'finding' child pornography on my hardware, or seeking to embroil me in allegations of immoral conduct.

The message was that I would not be threatened physically. I told Frank Rieger, a supporter in Berlin who is the chief technology officer at CryptoPhone, a company that makes telephones for encrypted secure communication, and he said he would prepare a press release making this information public. He then did so, and I had it with me on a laptop, ready to edit it. The intention was to get it out as soon as possible, as it did no good to put these things out after some damage had been done, or material had been planted. It remains one of my regrets that I didn't turn to it immediately. The same day, my Australian bank card suddenly stopped working. I was being extra careful with mobile phones, only turning them on to receive messages, so the situation was particularly chaotic; but I put it out of my mind and got on with the Swedish tasks, which were towards establishing my editorial position there.

One evening I went to dinner with a few friends and their associates. The Swedish journalist Donald Böstrom, a friend and very experienced news man of about fifty, was there, along with another Swedish journalist and an American investigative journalist and his girlfriend. The American had possibly murky connections, but the girl was nice, and I was chatting her up with Donald frowning across from me. Donald later said I should watch what I was doing: he said the threat of a 'honeytrap' was high at that moment, and I remember he went into detail about how Mossad had captured Vanunu. I guess I must have been up for affection, to put it coyly, because I didn't think very seriously about what Donald was saying. I just made out like I knew how to take care of myself and felt I was so hyper-aware of security that the sort of thing he was describing could only happen to naive people who hadn't had the kind of experience I had. I wouldn't have to wait long to see how massively my hubris would backfire.

The parliamentary duty that had guaranteed me safe passage to Stockholm meant that I was under the care of a group of Social Democrats, many of whom had functions with other political groupings. I was told I'd be able to stay at the flat of a political worker called A——, who was away from her apartment. I went there, and after a few days she returned early. Ms A—— was a political spokesperson for the party and was involved in the arrangements to bring me over. I had no reason not to trust her, and no reason, when she pointed out that there was only one bed and would I be cool sleeping with her, to believe that this was naught but a friendly suggestion. I said yes, anyhow, and we went to bed together that night.

These political engagements are stressful and I was glad of the attention, when it came, of these smiling and affectionate women. It's embarrassing to say so, given that even a single man, as I was, is liable to be thought ungallant even for mentioning what went on with a woman in private. Or more than one woman. But the situation seemed not at all unusual and felt like part of something nice in an otherwise dark time. The Pentagon was calling for my head and many of my friends, and possibly sources, for all I know, were scared or under surveillance. I wanted desperately to protect them and hoped that Stockholm might prove to be the haven I had long envisaged for our work. Speaking honestly, I would have to say I thought A—— was a little neurotic. But our night together was unremarkable. We had sex several times and the next day everything seemed fine between us.

A—— was in charge of the microphone at a press conference a day or two later and there was a lunch afterwards, which she attended, along with other journalists and a woman called W——, who appeared to have assisted at the press conference and who I remember was wearing a nice pink sweater. I won't be winning any prizes for clairvoyant of the year, or, indeed, for gentleman of the year, when it comes to these women, but the situation seemed relaxed and I was not aware of any threat to anybody or any wrongdoing. W—— said she worked at the Natural History Museum and offered to show me some of the private rooms there. I agreed, so after lunch and a quick shopping trip to buy computer parts she and I broke off to go to the museum. Some of the staff in there seemed to know her and we looked around before going to see a movie about life beneath the sea, then going our separate ways.

That night, A—— had arranged a crayfish party, a traditional occasion at that time of year in Sweden, and I went along to meet up with her. This was the day after the day she later claimed I had raped her. A—— was there at the party and seemed totally happy, laughing and drinking with me and my friends and her friends until late. We were sitting outside the party and she sent a Tweet saying she was 'with the coolest people in the world'. It became obvious she had told people about us sleeping together and it emerged, later, that she had taken a picture of me when I was asleep in her bed and pasted it on her Facebook page. I was now supposed to be moving to stay with other people, a couple of guys from the Pirate Party – a Swedish political party that campaigns for copyright reform, among other things – but A—— insisted I come back and continue to stay with her. The arrangement had always been that I would move to the guys' flat after A—— got back to her apartment from her trip, but she said it was cool to stay at hers and I went back with her. And that was how the situation remained for the next five nights.

Some other evenings I spent with W——. But A—— was still working with me on political meetings and so on, including a dinner we went to with Rick Falkvinge, head of the Pirate Party. He was offering to house a server for WikiLeaks, an interesting offer because that meant it would have political protection by being under the custody of the Pirate Party. Another night, after an awards party, I met up with W—— and went back with her to her house in

Enkopping, which is about fifty miles outside Stockholm. My behaviour sounds cold, and no doubt was, which is a failing of mine, but not a crime. I'd spent long enough at A——'s and could see that it would be a bad idea to stay longer. Remember, I was feeling especially paranoid: I didn't like being in one place for too long and the affair with A—— was becoming public, which appeared to be something she wanted.

The thing with W—— was going nowhere, either. She was a little vague, but the night in Enkopping was fun and I thought we'd had a perfectly nice time, albeit one that probably wouldn't be repeated. She didn't seem too fussed herself, as we had breakfast together the next morning and then rode together on her bicycle to the railway station. She kindly paid my ticket – my bank card was still on the blink, though I'm always skint – and she kissed me goodbye and asked me to call her from the train. I didn't do that, and it has already turned out to be the most expensive call I didn't make. I went on to a meeting at the Journalists Union, to see about getting membership: remember, despite all my shenanigans, I was in Stockholm in an attempt to shore up various legal protections that would allow WikiLeaks to conduct its business from there, and, with any luck, for me to live without fear of being extradited to the United States.

As I said, I wasn't really using the phones. (I always carry several at once.) At one point, I did have a short conversation with W——, when she called me, but the phone was low on charge and it ran out while we were still talking. The international situation had me in its grip, and although I had spent time with these women, I wasn't paying enough attention to them, or ringing them back, or able to step out

of the zone that came down with all these threats and statements against me in America. One of my mistakes was to
expect them to understand this: they knew, because we'd
talked about it over the week, that there were said to be 120
people working against WikiLeaks in the Pentagon. So I
wasn't a reliable boyfriend, or even a very courteous sleeping partner, and this began to figure. Unless, of course, the
agenda had been rigged from the start.

One of the nights I was staying with A——, she didn't
come home and said she had slept with a journalist who
was writing a piece about me. This was odd, I thought, and
who was this guy? But I hadn't exactly been Mr Loyalty, and
the whole thing was pretty obviously casual, though I did
notice as I left on the Friday morning that she was a little
strange. Later that day, I got a call from Donald Böstrom,
telling me he'd just spoken to A——, who had just spoken
to W——, who told her she was in hospital. I must say I was
completely baffled. These girls were talking to each other and
one of them was in the hospital? My phones were hopeless,
but on one of them I got another call from Donald, quoting
A—— again, who was saying something about W—— and
the police and DNA testing. I said, 'What on earth is going
on?' So I called W—— and she totally denied these things,
saying she had only mentioned police in relation to perhaps
asking them for advice about tests you could get for sexu-
ally transmitted diseases.

W—— said she wanted me to come down immediately
and have an STD test. I said I couldn't that day, I was dealing with heavy stuff, but I'd come the next day, and she said
that was fine. She then asked me if I'd called her off my own
bat, or because I'd been speaking to A——? It just became
too ludicrous at this point. Donald was ringing me again

and again, saying that A—— was trying to look out for me with this W—— situation, and I was saying, 'No, it's fine, I've spoken to W—— and we're meeting tomorrow.' The whole thing was zany, if anything, and deeply suspicious as the hours passed and the gossip flew. I spoke to A—— and asked her what was all this nonsense about police. She told me I didn't understand how it was in Sweden: you could just ask police for advice like that, about STDs and such like, and there's nothing in it and no formal complaint. Perhaps I should have been more suspicious about what was going on at this point, but, of course, I knew I had done nothing wrong and it therefore didn't occur to me what might happen next with the police.

I wanted to double-check things with W——, so I topped up one of my phones and called her several times that afternoon, with no reply. I needed some time and space to myself, so I then booked into a hotel for the night where I began writing what was to be the first of my Swedish newspaper columns. I had just written that line about the first casualty of war being truth when, about 6.30 p.m., I checked on Twitter and saw there was an arrest warrant out for me for double rape. At first, I thought this must be some tabloid garbage. Completely made up. I just thought, how low can they go, these papers? How far are they willing to go to smear a person? Then I saw, on the website of a more serious newspaper, that the arrest rumour was correct, and my entire belief system temporarily collapsed.

Recovering, I realised that I'd signed into the hotel with a credit card and that several people had seen me. I had to get out of there fast and assess the situation properly and understand what was going on. You mustn't forget how paranoid I was in general at that point, and how conspiratorial.

I couldn't believe A—— and W—— were actually doing this, and couldn't for the life of me work out how it could come about. So I got out of the hotel and went on a train to a friend's house in the north of Sweden. It didn't seem possible to go to the police because I just couldn't trust that there wasn't some general effort afoot to capture me. It seemed so surreal and so unexpected. And it was impossible to say, at that point, whether this had been some kind of set-up, or whether the women were jealous, because, frankly, after pausing for thought and discussing it with friends, I saw that both things were possible, though I understand it had to be one or the other.

I did not rape those women and cannot imagine anything that happened between us that would make them think so, except malice after the fact, a joint plan to entrap me, or a terrible misunderstanding that was stoked up between them. I may be a chauvinist pig of some sort but I am no rapist, and only a distorted version of sexual politics could attempt to turn me into one. They each had sex with me willingly and were happy to hang out with me afterwards. That is all.

But, in modern Sweden, that is not all. In some ways, it might be fair to see Sweden as a place that is isolated from the rest of Europe. It has traditionally had an inclination towards neutrality and is something of an enclosed world, with a population of less than ten million dominated by a few powerful institutions in Stockholm. Sweden has a reputation for political stability and consensus, partly as a result of the Social Democratic Party's dominance of national politics for most of the twentieth century. But things have been changing, and not clearly for the better. In 2001, Sweden, under the SDP, sent troops to Afghanistan, which was the first deployment of troops in an overseas military operation for almost two hundred years. This reflects a turn away from their previous policy of neutrality in foreign relations, and a growing orientation towards the United States. In Cable 09-141, which we later released as part of Cablegate, the American ambassador in Stockholm made clear the extent of American pressure – and Swedish compliance – over the issue of computer file-sharing and government monitoring of computer traffic. Worse still, a Human Rights Watch report published in 2006 detailed Swedish complicity and co-operation in the illegal rendition of two asylum seekers by the CIA. Perhaps I shouldn't be surprised that the day after I was arrested in London in December 2010, the British newspaper *The Independent* reported that the Swedish government had already participated in informal talks with the Americans about extraditing me onwards from Sweden to the USA.

Claes Borgström, the lawyer for the two women, is spokesman for the SDP on gender equality, and you'd have to say, with the best will in the world, that Sweden is one of the few countries in the world where hardcore feminism has entered the mainstream. Indeed, the decision to go to Afghanistan was mainly based on feminist principles: despite the women's movement's traditional anti-war stance, they deplored, understandably, the Taliban's treatment of women and sanctioned, less understandably, bombing as a way of opposing it. The older generation of Swedish feminists can often be heard referring to something called 'State Feminism', and only recently, around February 2011, has the Swedish press begun to look at my case with a fresh eye for what it says about their own system and their own struggles.

A—— is an aspiring political figure in Sweden, and has been for several years, which makes her case especially newsworthy. She is a well-connected figure within the feminist movement, as well as with the Social Democrats, where she was a prominent figure in Broderskapsrorelsen, the organisation that hosted my visit in August. Whatever whirlwind was whipped up, it led immediately to sinister events. I have been informed that A—— has deleted Tweets relating to me. In her last public one, on 12 December 2010, she wrote:

> Am sick and tired of all that's going on, will it ever end? Anyway, I want to send a message to the [conspiracy] theorists that 'the other one' [W——] was as insistent [as A——].

Expressen revealed, on 10 March 2011, that the police officer who first interviewed W—— was a friend of A——'s. The day after the women went to the police, in fact, A—— had given an interview to the same paper, in which she refuted any suggestion that she and W—— had been afraid of me. She said I was not violent and that, in both cases, the sex was consensual. From a police dossier, it appears that the women had not intended to file complaints and were simply seeking advice about STDs. They had said they had threatened me, in the telephone conversations, that they would go to the police if I did not immediately submit to an SDT test. The complainants' lawyer, Claes Borgström, stated in an article in the daily tabloid Aftonbladet that the women did not go to the police with the intention of reporting me; they just wanted me to get tested.

But there are other issues. In a 2006 blog entry called 'Rape?', A—— presents a scenario and finishes with a question: Is there any case in which a man has been convicted of rape even if the woman willingly started having sex? Against recommended protocol, neither of the women's interviews with police officers were recorded. Even prosecutor Marianne Ny believes such recordings should be made, as she stated in her comments to the judicial authority on the new sex offences law. According to police testimony from her friends, W—— only intended to find out whether the police could compel me to take an HIV test. According to one of the witnesses, who had been in constant contact with W—— throughout the time leading up to the police complaint, W—— felt as though she was being pushed around by others who had their own agenda. This conflicts with A——'s story in the *Expressen* article of 21 August 2010, where she is cited, and which claims she was contacted by W—— because W—— wanted to file a report for rape against me, and that A—— gave her support because she had had a similar experience. In the leaked report, which has not been approved by W——, the interviewing officer interrupted the interview because she could no longer concentrate when she found out that an order for arrest had been issued against me, shortly after the interview had started. According to her friend (M—— T——), who was also interviewed by police in connection with the case, W—— felt 'railroaded' by the police and by others around her.

I could go on, but won't. This is not the place to rehearse the entire case for the defence. Suffice to say the accusations were, from my perspective, both ludicrous and sinister. I have prepared a 46-page report on the case, on statements and inconsistencies. It is an exercise in scientific journalism, examining how untruths can feed through a whole pipeline of communication, resulting in an absolute falsehood threatening an individual.

As I said earlier, I claim no prizes for good behaviour during that week in Stockholm, but the rape allegations represent a smear that has already ruined a year of my life and done untold damage to my public standing. Given that the work I have been moving towards all my life has been founded on probity and ethical activism, this campaign against me has only proved useful to my enemies. At the time of writing, I am in the house of one of my bail sureties, under curfew in the English countryside with an electronic manacle on my leg. The use of such electronic monitoring in law enforcement dates back to 1983, when a judge in New Mexico called Jack Love read a cartoon in which a villain attaches an electronic tracking device to Spider-Man. Just like Old Bluey, my life is stranger than any fiction. I have not been charged with any crime, but, in an echo of the 'blood on his hands' manipulation, if you put the words 'Julian Assange rape' into a search engine it will return almost four million hits. The rape allegation was made, withdrawn and then made again, in the course of which I was already criminalised for the horrendous feat of having had consensual sex with two women in Stockholm in August 2010.

They aimed to draw blood, and did. I will not burrow down for you into any more detail: you have the picture. In autobiographical terms, it is strange to have to spend so much time on something so odd. All this happened, and has to be discussed, but it is just not me. It could have been a train crash, or a sudden conversion to Mormonism, or some other gratuitous unlikelihood that came to grab my attention in the middle of the best working year of my life; but it wasn't, it was a double rape allegation, and I have given it all the description I can.

Elsewhere, what passes for normal activity in my life was going on regardless. I remained in Sweden for more than a month after the allegations were first raised, but nothing was happening, and the Swedish prosecutor didn't seem to need to talk to me, so I caught a plane to England and went back to work. A European Arrest Warrant would soon follow hard on my heels, but for now it was time to prepare, along with our jumpy media partners, for Cablegate, the biggest unauthorised disclosure in history.

14

CABLEGATE

Disclosure is not merely an action; it is a way of life. To my mind it carries both sense and sensibility: you are what you know, and no state has the right to make you less than you are. Many modern states forget that they were founded on the principles of the Enlightenment, that knowledge is a guarantor of liberty, and that no state has the right to dispense justice as if it were merely a favour of power. Justice, in fact, rightly upheld, is a check on power, and we can only look after the people by making sure that politics never controls information absolutely.

This is common sense. It used to be the first principle of journalism in every country with a free press. The Internet has made it easier to censor writing, removing the existence of truth at the flick of a mouse (Stalin would've loved it) and monitoring people's private data in ways that would have proved delightful to the demon paper-shufflers of the Third Reich. Secrecy is too often the sole preserve of the powerful, and anyone who says so, these days, is not just taken to be underscoring an old liberal standard and a canard of democracy, but to be revealing themselves as an exotic anarchist bent on 'compromising national security'. The principles laid down in the American Constitution would, if properly examined, look radical to the mindset of a vast number of people living in America today. Jefferson would seem like an enemy of the state and Madison a pinko guerrilla. Likewise, to the modern Chinese, those studious little economists Marx and Engels would appear like madmen who little understood the deep human value of a Gucci handbag and the new iPad.

Information sets us free. And it does so by allowing us to question the actions of those who would sooner we had no means to question them, no right to reply. WikiLeaks, for all its modernism and all its software, is a force for the upholding of liberty that would have seemed quite traditional and quite sensible to the mind of an eighteenth-century figure such as John Wilkes. We come under fire, very often, for upholding those principles that many of the governments that criticise us are elected to uphold. We are a people's bureau of checks and balances, working internationally, and knowing that the things governments and diplomats do behind closed doors is entirely our business. The people elect them, pay for them, trust them, and are bosses of them. And governments who allow themselves to forget that will hear the voice of the people in every chatroom, on every blog, on every Twitter feed and, eventually, from every square, rising from Tiananmen Square to Tahrir Square, from Trafalgar to Times, with ripples through every letter of the alphabet. And governments who stand against this truth are done for.

Early on in our relationship with the media partners, I knew I would, at some point, offer them the chance to join

us in publishing a giant cache of diplomatic cables that had
been leaked to us and were being prepared. I was holding
off, to let the Afghan and Iraq war logs see the light of day
in as measured and careful a way as possible. There was a lot
of material, and it takes time to read and sift, organise and
present, with legal and other considerations always imping-
ing on the judgements we make. Our chief concern is to keep
the promise we make to our sources: if the material fulfils
our editorial policy, is important, new, and suffering some
form of suppression, we will release it as soon as we can and
with all manner of support and fanfare. These latest cables
detailed the activities of embassies all over the world; they
lifted the lid on secret operations, deep-seated prejudices,
national embarrassments and human affairs at every level of
government. Like the previous leaks, they would bring the
world into focus despite the efforts of those who would prefer
it blurred. And they would make a change in our understanding of what our governments were doing, and why.

As a result of the surveillance, and the aggressive attitude of the Pentagon towards me personally, I wanted to
make copies of the cables to ensure their safekeeping. I
was not happy with how things had developed with the
Guardian, and thought the *New York Times* were behaving despicably, but my attitude to the former was rather
'better the devil you know'. The *New York Times* had shown
themselves to be cowards, however, and I was not ready to
work with them again. It felt like there was a massive strike
coming down on us, so I copied the 250,000 documents
and stashed them first with contacts in Eastern Europe and
Cambodia. I also put them on an encrypted laptop and had
it delivered to Daniel Ellsberg, the hero of the Pentagon
Papers. Giving it to Dan had symbolic value for us. We also

knew he could be trusted to publish the whole lot during a crisis.

You have to realise, the material did not only have great value philosophically. If we had wanted to, we could probably have sold the cables for millions of dollars – indeed, I have been offered money for them even after we started to publish – but we do not operate like that. Still, I wanted to impress upon our partners the value of this material, so that they would appreciate what they were dealing with when we negotiated the conditions under which it might be released. The *Guardian* was still the right paper to work with on this material and I put my worries aside. I asked for a signed letter from the paper's editor, Alan Rusbridger, guaranteeing that the material would be kept strictly confidential, that nothing would be published from it until we were ready to go, and that it would not be stored on a computer that was connected to the Internet or any internal network. Rusbridger agreed and we signed the letter. In return, I produced an encrypted disk with a password and they had the material. At which point the senior news reporter went off on holiday to Scotland, all bonhomie and jollity, ready to read the material and keep in touch about the future plan.

With the Swedish case now in the air, there was a definite sense of gossiping schoolgirls among the media partners. It amazed me, because many of them are investigative reporters, and you'd imagine they knew something about smears and hysteria when it came to political outcasts. A man, for example, who worked for the Bureau of Investigative Journalism suddenly told his colleagues he wouldn't 'appear on stage with a rapist', and the fact that the papers didn't want their logo on the banner at the press conference

– well, it was the same old credulousness and suspicion. Some of those men have more skeletons in their closets than Highgate Cemetery but they dived on my troubles with an unmistakeable glee. None of them asked me how it came about, or how I was, or whether I needed anything: they simply responded as if the creepy allegations were 'smoke' that could not possibly exist, despite everything their experience told them, 'without fire'. Such people sit in judgement all their lives, hoping against hope that no one will ever turn the lamp on them. And of course no one ever does, by and large, because these men are the media, and no Fleet Street editor was ever known to dish on another.

Having schmoozed their way to several scoops off the back of our organisation, two of these media partners began to behave as if I represented a moral risk. Nothing had changed in the material, nothing had changed in our passion to reveal it, but false allegations had been made against me that caused these men to increase their bad behaviour and their stereotyping of me to the point where it was crazy. I might have rescued it, and I certainly tried to do so, but, beyond a certain point, one needs talents I don't have in order to negotiate with people who are that insane with self-interest. They were going to do whatever they wanted to do and I had made several mistakes, the latest of which was to have given them a copy of the cables.

There were some incredible stories in the cables: $25 million worth of bribes to politicians in India, given with the knowledge of apparently sanguine US diplomats; signs of continued American interference in Haitian politics; revelations that a Peruvian presidential candidate had taken money from an alleged drug trafficker; unprecedented levels of lobbying of foreign governments by diplomats on behalf of

American corporations; politicians in Lithuania paying journalists for positive coverage; and even spying by American diplomats on their colleagues at the United Nations.

The cables were going to be sensational, but at that point they were not quite ready. Our systems were not yet there with the presentation of the documents, and not ready to cope with the traffic that was bound to follow. We had legal considerations and unresolved sensitivities to do with protecting our source, whoever that was, and this was why I had lodged the material with our partner but demanded an agreement that the material not be published until the green light was clearly given. Any decent publisher would have understood this: it was more important than any scoop that the material be properly ready and that the sources be protected. This was priority number one. But not to the *Guardian*. No sooner had the senior reporter got back to London from his holiday than he began harassing me about publication. He said that a rival journalist, a woman attached to the *Independent*, had a copy of the cables and was a clear threat to their exclusivity.

I investigated that matter. It turned out that our Icelandic colleague, Smári McCarthy, had indeed shared the material with the *Independent* journalist during an anxious moment. He had been asked to work on the cables for a short time to help format them, but, stressed at the workload, he had misguidedly shared them with her – to get some help with the burden of the work involved – under certain strict conditions. He then hacked into the computer remotely and wiped the cables, though it would never be clear whether she had copied them or not. The *Guardian* reporter's argument is that she was shopping them around. I can't tell you how many times we have come across people – people who think of themselves as campaigners – behaving like stock exchange bullies when it comes to a commodity they are interested in. You can hear the snap of their red braces as they go in for the kill. Although we had sorted out the *Independent* thing, the *Guardian*'s senior reporter said it was all very threatening and that a 'rogue' copy of the data might be out there. He wanted to rush towards publication. I told him we weren't ready and we had a written agreement. He went off in a fluster and we didn't hear from him.

It became clear later that he had already copied the material for the *New York Times*. They were moving towards publication with no regard for any of the important issues – matters of life and death – that stood behind the documents. Like greedy, reckless, damn-them-all bandits, they were going to shoot up the town no matter who was standing in the way. The *Guardian*'s reporter had behaved cravenly and lawlessly, and was quite happy to please his newspaper, and his heroes across the Atlantic, while dumping the whole thing on our heads without warning. There isn't a student journalist who would behave in so unprincipled a way, having no care for the story itself, or the people who supplied it, before the onrush of his own dirty plan to stab us in the back. Given how poorly the *New York Times* had supported the earlier leaks, and given how hostile they had become to me, it just didn't make any sense for us to collaborate further with them. It was our work, after all. But the *Guardian* didn't care about any of that: they wanted the *New York Times* to help shore up their own defences, and WikiLeaks could go and hang itself from the nearest tree.

We simply had to have some time. It was deeper than any of them could understand, in their juvenile deadline-mania, but we had to have time to prepare for this. I called Rusbridger and he agreed I should come in for talks. The *New York Times* involvement – which was illegal, remember, given my signed agreement with Rusbridger – was not something anyone would yet admit to, but I came into the *Guardian* offices in high dudgeon. I knew they were double-crossing us, without even having the balls to say that is what they were doing. We came into the building with my lawyer, Mark Stephens, and, as chance would have it, we came face to face with the senior news reporter beside the stairs.

'Hello,' I said.

'Oh-oh,' he said. He looked surprised.

'We'll come down and see you later,' I said. 'We just want to clarify a few things that Alan Rusbridger showed us.'

I've never in my life seen anyone's face collapse like that. He went white. As we walked away, our group said the news reporter looked like a person who had just been caught with a murder weapon.

We went upstairs to see Alan Rusbridger. *Der Spiegel's* editor came in. I was shouting, almost certainly, and I asked him point-blank if they had given the material to the *New York Times*. Rusbridger just dodged the question. 'The first thing we need to do,' I said, 'is establish who's got a copy of the material. Who does not have a copy of the material, and who does? Because we're not ready to publish.' His eyes rolled around the room. He didn't know where to look. 'Did you give a copy of the cables to the *New York Times*?'

All this business with the *Independent* journalist had given them a bit of script to warble on, but it didn't hold, and I just kept pressing them. 'We need to understand what sort of people we're dealing with,' I said. 'Are we dealing with people whose word we can trust or are we not? Because if we're not dealing with people whose written word we can trust, then . . .' It now looked like all their eyes were rolling round the room. It was like a cartoon, all these grown men finding themselves unable to face the truth of what they had done, or to put forward some argument to try to defend themselves. I would later be characterised as some sort of nutcase for shouting at them. But who wouldn't shout, when the stakes were so high? Who wouldn't lose their temper with such lily-livered gits hiding in their glass offices? It was soon clear to everyone that Alan's refusal to answer the question was as good as an admission. It was only for legal reasons that he wasn't saying 'yes' or 'no'. My respect for the man plummeted to nothing. I mean, here's this guy, the editor of an important newspaper, an institution, indeed, a man older than me and with a crucial issue in front of him, and what we get is eyes rolling around the room like marbles on a pogo stick. It was just the most incredible thing and I couldn't believe I was witnessing it.

I'm sure I must have given them some lengthy harangue about honour and so on. You do, in those circumstances. Anyway, we ended up being there debating it for seven hours, then we went downstairs to come up with a plan. The *Guardian* had known all along what it wanted to do – it wanted to publish right away. *Der Spiegel* meanwhile was trying to be friends with everyone. The truth is, we weren't ready to go, as I said, and we were being strong-armed by these people who had been niggling away at us for weeks, and were now ready with the *coup de grâce*. At the centre of their colossal, stained vanity, they had forgotten who we were and how we had got to this room. They now thought of us as a bunch of weird hackers and sexual delinquents.

But we knew our material and we knew our technology; these guys were playing by the oldest rules in the business. I implied that I would immediately give the entire cache of material to the Associated Press, Al Jazeera and News Corp. I didn't want to do it, but I would if they didn't play ball.

They sobered up and began to speak more reasonably about how the publication might be handled. I continued my counterattack, pointing out that I would sue them for breach of contract. My organisation was not-for-profit; we depended on donations to pay our costs, and the fact that our systems were not ready for publication when the news hit would mean that our own revenue would take a beating. They had to realise what they were doing to us: we were not a theoretical grouping but a flesh-and-blood organisation who had worked for years to achieve great goals. What they were doing would threaten to destroy us and I would use everything in our power to prevent it. So we began negotiating. They wouldn't budge at first from imminent publication, but eventually we agreed that a month's delay would give us just enough time to prepare. I insisted at that point that *El País* and *Le Monde* join the mix of 'media partners', that phrase so hated by the *New York Times*. We now knew, more than they, how grubby partnership could be, and, on the spot, I was making ready for a future in which lessons had been learned.

I stressed that the leak should not be the story – we were in the business of leaking stories themselves, and therefore, to keep the heat off us and on the actual material, I insisted we let the stories out one by one. Top stories first, none about Israel, none about Cuba, allowing the possibility that the US wouldn't simply overreact to Cablegate as a whole. They would attend, as they should, and as we all should, to one leak at a time. I also insisted, as part of this enforced repackaging of our relationship, that the *New York Times* agree to stop their rubbishy, self-serving campaign of writing stories against me and against Bradley Manning, a young man they had characterised as a mad, bad and sad little fag. This no doubt kept the Pentagon off their backs, but it was disgraceful by any other yardstick. Thankfully, Keller came back the next day with an agreement to lay off that sort of thing and they did for a while.

It later emerged, via the guys at *Der Spiegel*, that the *Guardian* had been ready to fuck us all along. They were working with the *New York Times* and were willing to go without even telling us, and without giving us a chance to prepare the data properly or prepare ourselves for attack. That's how much the *Guardian* actually cared for the principles involved. Openness? You must be joking. A new generation of libertarians? They couldn't have cared less. A new mood of popular uprisings in the world and a new spirit of speaking truth to power? The *Guardian* – the most ill-named paper in the world – may carry picture after picture from Tahrir Square, but they were willing to sell all the principles that movement stood for, and that we stood for in helping them, straight down the river. The senior news reporter's attempt to give his paper one last leg-up before retirement left his paper gasping for its liberal breath. When American right-wingers were calling for me to be killed, the *Guardian* didn't run a single article in my defence. Instead, they got my old friend, the special investigations reporter, to write a dirty little attack on me.

'Strewth,' as we used to say. Life was easier when it was just sugar ants running up my legs and biting me to death. At least in those days I had the sun on my side. But in our new kind of business, you soon get over the old guard kicking you when you're down. We had a month to get the cables in good order, and doing so would be the most exhilarating month of my life. The cables would show the modern world what it really thought of itself, and we worked through the nights in an English country house to meet the deadline. The snow had begun to fall and it lay evenly over the Norfolk countryside. There was no way to know back then that the house was soon to become my prison for the foreseeable future.

AFTERWORD

*Julian's autobiography ends here, but the work
of WikiLeaks continues.*

*

14 January 2011 President Sine al-Abidine Ben Ali dissolves the Tunisian government and declares a state of emergency, then flees to Saudi Arabia. In Libya, his ally Colonel Gaddafi makes a speech condemning the uprising in Tunisia and claiming that protestors were led astray by WikiLeaks disclosures that had detailed corruption in Ben Ali's family and government.

22 January The Peruvian newspaper *El Comercio* receives a phone call from WikiLeaks offering them around 4,000 cables from the Lima embassy. Similar deals are made with media organisations around the world, as Cablegate goes global.

28 January As protestors begin a 'Day of Rage' in Cairo, Mubarak's beseiged government cuts off cellphone, satellite and Internet connections across Egypt. The eyes of the world are firmly upon the Middle East, as WikiLeaks continues to release cables from the region.

15 February In a speech at George Washington University, Hillary Clinton proclaims that Internet freedom is a 'foreign policy priority' for Barack Obama's government. She adds that, 'in order to be meaningful, online freedoms must carry over into real-world activism'. On the same day, the US government goes to court to try to force Twitter to reveal the account details of three WikiLeaks employees.

16 February After the resignation of Mubarak on 11 February, WikiLeaks continue to support the protestors in Egypt, releasing more than 450 cables from the Cairo embassy in one day.

25 February Former President George W. Bush cancels his forthcoming appearance at a 'Global Leadership Summit' in Denver when he learns that Julian Assange – 'who has wilfully and repeatedly done great harm to the interests of the United States' – will appear.

4 March WikiLeaks employee, Kristinn Hrafnsson, wins 2010 'Journalist of the Year' award in Iceland.

15 March Coverage of Cablegate begins in the Indian newspaper *The Hindu*. Over several weeks *The Hindu* reveals stories of bribery in the Indian parliament, the use by America of arms sales for political leverage, alleged links between the Pakistani intelligence services and the Taliban, and many more.

20 March The US ambassador to Mexico, Carlos Pascual, resigns after clashing with President Felipe Calderón over his criticisms of Mexican security forces in leaked cables.

7 April The Israeli paper *Yediot* begins the latest staggered release of cables, shedding light on familiar topics such as the close links between Israeli intelligence and the CIA, as well as more surprising stories such as the close relationship between Mossad and the King of Bahrain, and negotiations over arms-smuggling into Gaza with members of the former Egyptian regime.

8 April Cables concerning the Middle East continue to be released, while protests continue across much of the region. A number of cables from 2009 and 2010 show that the US embassy in Yemen was repeatedly informed by local contacts about the weakness and unpopularity of their ally President Saleh, who now faces angry protests.

21 April A cable from Dubai details claims that Iranian President Mahmoud Ahmadinejad is grooming his chief-of-staff Esfandiar Rahim Mashaei as a future replacement. Mashaei is seen as a rival to Iranian hardliners, opposing greater clerical involvement in politics.

25 April WikiLeaks and nine other media organisations begin to release the Guantánamo files – a dossier of 'Detainee Assessment Briefs' kept by the Joint Task Force Guantánamo. The documents, which cover 765 out of 779 prisoners, reveal records of health assessment, the story of how they came to be detained, the reasons for their continued detention, and the evidence against them.

Dozens, perhaps hundreds, of prisoners, are detained on extraordinarily flimsy evidence, and sometimes no evidence at all. One man is detained because he worked for the news channel Al Jazeera, and therefore thought to have useful information about the channel or people he had met in the course of his work; another man because he might know about terrorist activities in a certain region as a result of his work as a taxi-driver. Other detainee assessments speak to deeper issues with American strategy – having a link to Pakistani intelligence services is listed on the 'matrix of threat indicators', despite the fact that Pakistan is a key American ally in the War on Terror.

As American journalist Glenn Greenwald writes, 'How oppressive is this American detention system, how unreliable the evidence is on which the accusations are based . . . the idea of trusting the government to imprison people for life based on secret, untested evidence never reviewed by a court should repel any decent or minimally rational person, but these newly released files demonstrate how warped is this indefinite detention policy specifically.'

11 May The US government opens a Grand Jury hearing in Alexandria, Virginia. The hearing, which will sit in secret, is to decide whether to prosecute WikiLeaks.org and its founder under the Espionage Act. On the same day, Julian is awarded the Sydney Peace Foundation's gold medal for 'exceptional courage in pursuit of human rights'.

13 May Amnesty International singles out WikiLeaks and its media partners for praise in its annual report, as catalysts for a series of uprisings against oppressive regimes across the Arab world: 'The year 2010 may well be remembered as a watershed year when activists and journalists used new technology to speak truth to power and, in so doing, pushed for greater respect for human rights.'

23 May Cable coverage begins in the El Salvadorean paper *El Faro*. Their coverage sheds light on negotiations over the Central American Free Trade Agreement, on deportation of El Salvadorean migrants from the US, on the attempts of left-wing former guerilla group FMLN to improve relations with America, and on American opinions of local political figures. *El Faro*'s coverage begins: 'In El Salvador there are dozens of diplomatic missions, but only one Embassy, or at least only one that does not need to be named, the flag need not be named . . . For years, prominent public officials, party leaders and businessmen have visited the embassy to share their concerns and personal opinions with US diplomats, their hidden political strategies which they would not confess in public to the citizens of El Salvador.'

31 May Coverage of cables concerning Northern Ireland and the Republic of Ireland begins in the *Irish Independent*. Several stories concern the IRA, with a cable from Honduras claiming that they operate there, and another from Dublin quoting former Irish justice ministers as saying that a Sinn Féin politician outed as a British spy, and then later murdered in an apparent revenge attack, had in fact been outed by the British. Other cables give details of how US diplomats are involved in monitoring Irish Muslims and claims that Ireland is being used by the CIA to secretly render terror suspects.

1 June WikiLeaks continues to draw the media into new partnership arrangements, this time setting up a deal between the American magazine *The Nation* and the Haitian newspaper *Haïti Liberté* to publish cables concerning US relations with the Caribbean island. Cables reveal how Haiti's wealthy elite armed and deployed police in pro-Aristide neigbourhoods after the 2004 coup, effectively using the police as a private army; another suggests that American diplomats lobbied to keep Haiti's minimum wage as low as possible, opposing a move to raise it to $5 a day, while yet another confirms that the US, like other Western governments, were well aware that the 2010 Haitian elections were fraudulent.

2 June Julian wins the 2011 Martha Gellhorn prize for journalism. The judges describe Julian as 'brave, determined, independent: a true agent of people not power . . . WikiLeaks has been portrayed as a phenomenon of the hi-tech age, which it is. But it's much more. Its goal of justice through transparency is in the oldest tradition of journalism. WikiLeaks has given the public more scoops than most journalists can imagine: a truth-telling that has empowered people all over the world.'

21 June A November 2002 cable from the Vatican indicates that Venezuelan Catholic bishops were an integral part of the April 2002 attempted coup against President Hugo Chávez, even defying the Pope himself, who had asked the bishops to 'cool it' on political activism.

2 July Julian appears in London with the Slovenian philosopher Slavoj Žižek and the American journalist Amy Goodman. Žižek compares the impact of Cablegate to the story of the Emperor's new clothes: the power of the leaks comes not only or not even from the information they reveal, but from the fact that the information is confirmed for the first time from the horse's mouth and can no longer be denied. 'We all know that the emperor is naked, but the moment somebody says the emperor is naked; everything changes.'

13 July, Julian's biological father, John Shipton, travels to London to support his son at his latest extradition hearing. He describes Julian as 'a great dissident . . . There are many intelligent people in the world, but most seem to be wicked, while Julian seems to have the moral courage and ability to carry his vision through. He seems to have an immense desire for justice in the world.'

As this book went to press, Julian remained under house arrest at Ellingham Hall, Norfolk.

*

You can follow the work of WikiLeaks at
wikileaks.org
or
twitter.com/wikileaks

You can make a donation at
wikileaks.org/donate

APPENDIX

THE LEAKS

The following pages show examples of the most noteworthy leaks, as mentioned in the autobiography.

I: SOMALIA AND THE UNION OF ISLAMIC COURTS

In 2006, when this document was leaked, the Union of Islamic Courts was the dominant political force in Somalia. The Union evolved out of the local courts that developed to administer Sharia law in the 1990s. These courts, each of which was supported by its own militia, formed a loose alliance in early 2006 and began to take control of much of the country, including the capital Mogadishu. Given that Somalia had been without an effective government since 1991, the rise of the Union seemed to be an interesting development. This secret order, purportedly written by the most important man in the Union, Sheik Aweys, came to WikiLeaks from a Chinese source who had received it from the UN-sponsored Transitional Federal Government of Somalia, who are effectively the Union's opposition. When releasing the document on 28 December 2006, WikiLeaks drew attention to their doubts about its provenance and authenticity. The Union has since been broken up and many of its leaders exiled after an invasion by Ethiopian troops that took place around the time of this leak.

ISLAMIC REPUBLIC OF SOMALIA
Islamic Courts Administration, Office of the Chief of the Imams
Dhusamareb, November 09, 2005

In the Name of Allah, The Most Gracious and The Most Merciful

To: The representatives of the Islamic Courts in Northwest Somalia
 : The Representatives of the Islamic Courts in Northeast Somalia
Cc: The Committee of the Somali Religious Leaders, Mogadishu

Subject: Secret Decision

Brothers in Islam,

Right from the sixties, when Somalia realized civilian government and the
military regime led by Siyad Barre which was defined by injustice, the practice of the Sharia law was undermined and grossly violated. The Sharia law
ordains the path of righteousness and warns against bad deeds.

In the same vein, the over 10 years of disintegration marked gross
violation on the teaching of Islam. The population was divided by the
warlords who caused pouring of the human blood in large numbers and
weakened the belief of the people.

As you are all aware, the so-called Transitional government formed for
Somalia is hunting the Somali religious leaders and the Muslims in general.
They have influenced the International Community to believe that the Somali
religious leaders are Al-Qaeda. You very well know that its agenda is to bring
the Ethiopian troops in order to use them and kill the Somali population. As
you are aware, there are faction leaders who are fighting this government
without subscribing to our vision but would be vital in using as a bridge.

In order to react to the threats posed by the plan of this government,
which is aimed to inflict sufferings on the people of Somalia who are
Muslims, we have decided the following agenda points as shown the on
the next pages for your implementation.

Following the tangible progress made by the Islamic Courts in expanding its political programmes that restored just administration founded on
Sharia law.

In view of the findings on the programme contents used in the aware-ness campaigns, and the reception hailed by the population on plans to establish Islamic State that would herald justice and unity.

In view of the findings on the dire need for expansion of the Islamic Courts Administration to all parts of Somalia to refocus public attention on justice.

In view of the findings on the need to derail the so-called Transitional Federal Government and the Regional Administrations who are holding the population as a hostage.

The following decision was made:

I. To open Islamic Courts in all districts of Puntland and Somaliland in collaboration with the clan elders and the Traditional leaders.

II. That the representatives of the Islamic Courts in Puntlan have to obstruct Militias and arms flowing to the TFG from Puntland and the Ethiopia border

III. Plots to mar the existing relationship between the TFG, Puntland, Somaliland and Ethiopia have to be employed

IV. Penetration into the armed forces of Puntland and Somaliland has to be made and clan used as an instrument to unfasten the cohesion

V. The heavy and the light weapons used by Puntland and Somaliland armed forces have to be purchased with hard currency in secret deals.

VI. If that fails, the custodian of the heavy weapons should be approached with an offer.

VII. Cooperation has to be made with criminals and hard currency provided as motivations to assassinate the officials of the administrations (TFG, Somaliland & Puntland)

VIII. A traditional leader has to be crowned for each and every Sub-clan and the required financial support extended.

IX. Religious lectures indirectly influencing the public should be put in full gear

X. Friction with these administrations should be avoided and instead the taxes paid as required

XI. Strong allies should be identified within the cabinet of each of the administrations using clan elders and the traditional leaders as an entry point while flexibility is maintained and support provided.

XII.   Generous support should be given to the Oromo's and the ONLF to weaken the capability of Ethiopia which is our primary enemy as well as the administrations they are using to pursue their agendas.

XIII. The minority clans who are marginalized by those administrations should be welcomed and influenced.

XIV.   The Wagerdha'a sub-clan of the Marehan should to be supported and hostilities promoted within other sub-clans of the Marehan.

XV.   Fully fledged support should be extended to Gen. Morgan as a tool to destroy and disconnect the clan powerbase of the Key leaders who wield significant power within Somalia.

XVI.   The political animosity with the Religious leaders who are in support of those administrations should be minimized.

XVII. The representatives in Puntland and Somaliland should furnish ideas on how best to restore the Islamic Courts and implements the enlisted decisions.

XVIII. Care has to be maintained all along to avoid leaking of this information

XIX.   Whosoever leaks this information and is found guilty should be shot.

Finally, the representatives are advised to employ diplomacy in the execution of this decision and report on the activities progress including what was possible and the resources required.

Unity comes from Almighty Allah

Chief of the Imaam of the Islamic Courts

Shiikh Hassan Dahir Aweys (signed)

II: US MILITARY EQUIPMENT DATABASE
(EXTRACTS)

In its raw form, as released by WikiLeaks, this is an extremely large database of around 2,000 pages of information on the provisioning of US troops in Iraq. Analysis of this database by WikiLeaks, released alongside the raw data, led to a number of observations. These ranged from the high material cost of insurgent improvised explosive devices (IEDs) – as evidenced by the amount of relevant equipment being purchased – to the ubiquity of cash in the chaotic post-invasion Iraqi economy, demonstrated by the army's purchase of 39 automatic cash-counting machines.

This extract is part of a much longer list of chemical weapons and US units employing them in Iraq.

———————

MILITARY UNIT	NATO STOCK NUMBER	ITEM NAME	QUANTITY
977TH MP CO (WHMJAA)	1040014541625	DISCHARGER GRSCL XM7	105
128 MP CO (WP71AA)	1040014541625	DISCHARGER GRSCL XM7	99
HHS 1 BN 101 FA (WPFST8)	1040014541625	DISCHARGER GRSCL XM7	90
46 MP CO (WPTVAA)	1040014541625	DISCHARGER GRSCL XM7	68
HHC 2-152 IN (WPPUT4)	1040014541625	DISCHARGER GRSCL XM7	56
A CO 1-178 IN (WP5XA0)	1040014541625	DISCHARGER GRSCL XM7	54
410 MP CO (WHL9AA)	1040014541625	DISCHARGER GRSCL XM7	52
551 MP CO (WCUUAA)	1040014541625	DISCHARGER GRSCL XM7	48
984TH MILITARY POLICE (WGDHAA)	1040014541625	DISCHARGER GRSCL XM7	45
HHC 2 STB (WJLKT0)	1040014541625	DISCHARGER GRSCL XM7	37
23 MP CO (WJJEAA)	1040014541625	DISCHARGER GRSCL XM7	36
B 2-505 PIR (WABVB0)	1040014541625	DISCHARGER GRSCL XM7	35

III: GUANTÁNAMO STANDARD OPERATING PROCEDURE MANUAL (EXTRACTS)

This manual gives the standard operating procedures for Camp Delta (Guantánamo Bay prison) and was meant to be read by staff working there. This is the primary document for the operation of Guantánamo Bay, including the securing and treatment of detainees. The American Civil Liberties Union had tried to obtain this from the Department of Defense, but their requests had been refused.

4-20. Behavior Management Plan

a. *Phase One Behavior Management Plan (First thirty days or as directed by JIG).* The purpose of the Behavior Management Plan is to enhance and exploit the disorientation and disorganization felt by a newly arrived detainee in the interrogation process. It concentrates on isolating the detainee and fostering dependence of the detainee on his interrogator. During the first two weeks at Camp Delta, classify the detainees as Level 5 and house in a Maximum Security Unit (MSU) Block. During this time, the following conditions will apply:

(1) Restricted contact: No ICRC or Chaplain contact

(2) No books or mail privileges

(3) MREs for all meals.

(4) Basic comfort items only:

(a) ISO Mat

(b) One blanket

(c) One towel

(d) Toothpaste/finger toothbrush

(e) One Styrofoam cup

(f) Bar of soap

(g) Camp Rules

(h) No Koran, prayer beads, prayer cap.

(5) Mail writing and delivery will be at the direction of the J-2.

b. *Phase Two Behavior Management Plan.* The two-week period following Phase 1 will continue the process of isolating the detainee and fostering dependence on the interrogator. Until the JIG Commander changes his classification, the detainee will remain a Level 5 with the following:

(1) Continued MSU

(2) Koran, prayer beads and prayer cap distributed by interrogator

(3) Contacts decided by interrogator

(4) Interrogator decides when to move the detainee to general population.

Chapter 5
Detention Facility Operations
5-1. Rules of Engagement (ROE) and Rules for the Use of Force (RUF)

a. References.

(1) *CJCSI 3121.01A ROE, DODD 5210.56 RUF, & USCINCSO SER ONE*

(2) *JTF-GTMO ROE/RUF 30 NOV 02*

b. The physical security of U.S. Forces & detainees in U.S. care is paramount. Use the minimum force necessary for mission accomplishment and force protection.

c. *Right of self-defense*: nothing limits your right to use all necessary means available and take all appropriate actions in defense of yourself and U.S. Forces against a hostile act or hostile intent. Hostile Act is an attack or other use of force against U.S. Forces, or force used directly to prevent or interfere with the mission and/or duties of U.S. Forces.
Hostile Intent is the threat of imminent use of force against U.S. Forces, or the threat of force to prevent or interfere with the mission and/or duties of U.S. Forces.

d. *Defend detainees*: as you would yourself against a hostile act or intent, death or serious bodily harm.

e. *Priorities of force*: when force is necessary to protect or control detainees, follow these steps, if time and circumstances permit:

(1) Use Verbal Persuasion

(2) Use Show of Force

(3) Use Pepper Spray or CS Gas

(4) Use Physical Force, then Non-Lethal Weapons (NLW)

(5) Present Deadly Force

(6) Use of Deadly Force (as authorized below)

f. *Deadly force*: is force that can cause death or serious bodily harm. Deadly force may be used when lesser means are exhausted, unavailable, or cannot reasonably be used; the risk of death or serious bodily harm to innocent persons is not significantly increased; and the purpose is:

(1) Self-Defense

(2) Defense of other in imminent danger of death or serious bodily harm

(3) To prevent theft or sabotage of weapons, ammunition, or other sensitive items that present a substantial danger of death or serious bodily harm to others.

(4) To prevent a violent offense against another person in imminent danger of death or serious bodily harm i.e. murder, assault.

(5) To apprehend a person who committed one of the serious offenses above OR:

(6) To prevent escape of detainee(s) who is beyond the outside fence of the detention camp. If detainee(s) attempt escape, follow these steps:

(a) Shout HALT three times

(b) Use the least amount of force necessary to stop escape

(c) Detainee(s) is escaping beyond the outside fence of the detention camp and there is no other effective means to prevent escape, the use of deadly force is authorized. (If you have another justification to use deadly force-besides escape-you DO NOT have to wait until the detainee(s) are beyond the outside fence)

(7) *NO WARNING SHOTS*

(8) Fire to make the person(s) unable to continue the behavior that prompted you to shoot.

(9) Fire with regard for the safety of innocent bystanders.

(10) A holstered weapon should not be unholstered unless you expect to use it.

(11) Report the use of force to your chain of command.

IV: REPORT ON THE BATTLE OF FALLUJAH

This US Army intelligence report is an examination of the first battle for Fallujah of April 2004. Its purpose was to help the army to learn more about the tactics of insurgents, but it also furnishes many other details about the battle in general.

———————————————

(U) Situation in Fallujah, 29 April 2004

(U) Coalition close air support (CAS) was provided by Marine rotary-wing aircraft (AH-1W Cobra and UH-1N Huey gunships) firing Hellfire and TOW missiles, 2.75 high-explosive (HE) and flechette rockets, and 20-mm, .50-cal and 7.62-mm rounds. Fixed-wing CAS was provided by F-15E, F-16CG, F-16C+, AC-130U, F-18C, and F-14B aircraft that flew over 1000 CAS sorties, dropping 70 GBU-12's, 2 GBU-31's, 1 AGM-65H, 1 Hellfire missile, and numerous 20-mm, 105-mm, 40-mm, and 25-mm rounds. Insurgents feared the AC-130 the most; its firepower, combined with real-time surveillance provided by loitering unmanned aerial vehicles (UAVs), quickly discouraged most insurgent maneuver at night.

(S//REL TO USA, MCFI) Multiple reporting indicates insurgent strength numbered between 500 and 1000 fighters. They fought with primarily small arms, rocket-propelled grenades (RPGs), machineguns (MGs), improvised explosive devices (IEDs), and mortars. The enemy operated in small fire-team-size elements that conducted hit-and-run attacks, moving building to building to remain elusive and falling back on pre-positioned weapon and supply caches.

(S//REL TO USA, MCFI) After two days of fighting, 2/1 had penetrated into the northeast Jolan area, while 1/5 seized a huge foothold in the southeast industrial sector to use as a staging ground for subsequent Marine patrols deeper into Fallujah. Marine patrols began to push up against the south side of Highway 10 (a major road that bisects the city east to west) almost immediately.

(U) Throughout the fight Coalition forces allowed nonmilitary-age men, women, and children to exit through the cordon (at least 60,000) and humanitarian supplies to enter. On 9 April 2004, Marines handed out MREs and water to a caravan of vehicles that stretched over 1.5 miles.

(S//REL TO USA, MCFI) Roughly 2000 Iraqi soldiers and policemen also deployed in support. Most of the Iraqi forces deserted soon after fighting began, forcing some Marine units to reposition to fill their intended spots in the cordon around the city. For example, of the 700 Iraqi soldiers of the 2d New Iraqi Army Bn, 38% evaporated from their posts after taking some fire in a convoy on their way to Fallujah on 5 April. An exception was the 36th Iraqi National Guard Battalion (400 Iraqis, 17 SF advisors), which fought well alongside 2/1 in the Jolan neighborhood.

(U) The insurgents defended in depth and employed asymmetric tactics, firing from mosques, lobbing mortar rounds at American positions on the periphery, and staging hit-and-run attacks from the residential areas (see (U) Iraq: Asymmetric Tactics, Techniques, and Procedures Used at Fallujah and by the Mahdi Army for more information).

(U) Political Pressure Curtails Offensive Military Operations

(U) Political pressure to halt U.S. military operations began to build up immediately for several reasons:

- (U) Muqtada al-Sadr's militia, the Mahdi Army, began attacking Coalition forces on 2 April in response to the Coalition shutdown of his newspaper Hawza and the arrest of a top aide of Sadr. This simultaneous Shia uprising added to the pressure to resolve the Fallujah fight as quickly as possible. American solders and Marines were stretched thin fighting Sunnis across Al Anbar and Shia in Baghdad, Kut, and Najaf.

- (U) Other Sunni cells and groups escalated their attacks in areas outside Fallujah, especially in Ramadi. Twelve Marines were killed in Ar Ramadi on 6 April alone.

- (U) The British argued for a halt to the attack on Fallujah.

- (U) The Abu Ghurayb prisoner abuse scandal became public knowledge in late April and further enflamed Arab and Muslim anger at the United States.

• (U) Al Jazeera was claiming that up to 600 Iraqi civilians had been killed by the U.S. offensive. Images of dead children were being displayed repeatedly on televisions around the world.

• (U) The Iraqi Governing Council (IGC) began to unravel. Three members quit and 5 others threatened to quit, prompting CPA head Paul Bremer to agree to meet with the IGC on 8 April to discuss their concern over VIGILANT RESOLVE. The Sunni politicians considered the operation "collective punishment." The IGC argued that mass demonstrations were about to occur.

(U) By 9 April, the CPA prevailed upon General Abizaid to order a halt to offensive ground operations in Fallujah.

(U) Siege Continues for Three Weeks

(U) The cease-fire was a bit of a misnomer. Despite the unilateral cease-fire by the Americans, fighting continued, punctuated by rest periods. Although the insurgents maintained an operational defensive posture and chose not to attack entrenched Marines with a direct ground assault, they did continue to launch standoff attacks. Mortar attacks remained common. U.S. forces countered with minor maneuvers to strengthen their defensive positions. Coalition air strikes continued. Snipers on both sides made movement hazardous.

(U) Over the next few weeks, Fallujan sheiks and leaders met with representatives from the CPA, IGC, or I MEF to negotiate the conditions for a permanent cease-fire. The American National Command Authority pressed for other options besides finishing the clearing of Fallujah. Given few options, on 30 April I MEF and CJTF-7 terminated the operation and formally turned over their responsibility for Fallujah to a newly stood up Fallujah Brigade, a Sunni militia unit led by former Iraqi Army officers. Many insurgents were incorporated into this unit, and its affect on the security situation in the city was negligible.

(U) Casualties

(S//REL TO USA, MCFI) After 26 days of fighting, 18 Marines were killed in Fallujah with approximately another 96 wounded. In the entire I MEF area of operations (AO) in April, there were 62 KIA and 565 WIA.

(S//REL TO USA, MCFI) I MEF estimates 600 to 700 insurgents were killed and an unknown number wounded. Approximately 150 air strikes destroyed 75 buildings, including two mosques.

(U) Enemy Forces

(U) Strategy

(S//REL TO USA, MCFI) The insurgent strategy to defend Fallujah was designed to accomplish two things: 1) to gain media attention and sympathy and 2) to inflict maximum Coalition casualties by forcing a close-quarters infantry fight in urban terrain. Those cells that remained in Fallujah to fight were intent on dragging the combat out as long as possible to enable political and IO pressure to build to a boiling point.

(U) Operational Plan

(S//REL TO USA, MCFI) The Fallujah insurgents could count on cooperation and support from other networks in the surrounding towns of Saqlawiyah, Ar Ramadi, Amariyah, and Karmah. As a result, VIGILANT RESOLVE stirred up a hornet's nest across the Al Anbar Province, especially in Ar Ramadi, as insurgent cells surged their activity to stretch Coalition forces thin during the operation. They emplaced numerous roadblocks, IEDs, and complex ambushes on the key lines of communication (LOCs) in the area to interdict Coalition supply convoys and patrols. MSRs Mobile and Michigan were especially targeted. Insurgents attempted to damage and destroy key bridges, such as the one crossing the Thar Thar Canal.

(S//REL TO USA, MCFI) Throughout the fight insurgents demonstrated operational freedom of movement. Fighters and supplies were infiltrated through the Marine cordon and into Fallujah in various ways:

• (U) Insurgent local knowledge facilitated using a variety of back roads and hidden trails not blocked by entry control points (ECPs).

• (U) Some contraband was smuggled through Marine checkpoints by "civilians."

• (U) It is likely that Iraqi police voluntarily collaborated or were bribed.

———————————————

V: KROLL REPORT ON CORRUPTION IN KENYA

This report, more than 100 pages long, details allegations of corruption by former Kenyan President Daniel Arap Moi, his family and associates. It was commissioned by Mwai Kibaki after he replaced Moi as president in 2002, but never released. These extracts give examples of the nature, tone and severity of the allegations.

MOVEMENT OF FUNDS

A marked flurry of activity has been reported among ex-President Moi's family and their close associates to pre-empt any possibility of losing their wealth to the government.

In November 2003, ex-President Moi met at his home in Kabarak with his sons Phillip, Gideon, his long-term aide Kulie and his well-trusted household lawyer, Dr Kiplagat. During this meeting, the key topic of discussion was the family wealth, both local and international.

Ex-President Moi's lawyer advised them to secure their assets in overseas countries. He stated that there is no court ruling adjudging their wealth as illegal or corruptly obtained. As such, this would be a prerequisite for the government of Kenya to approach any foreign government to freeze any of their assets. The family was also advised to use proven trusts that are experienced at hiding pursued assets among select jurisdictions with relaxed laundering policies.

It was agreed that Kulei should relinquish all the assets held in trust by him on behalf of ex-President Moi and that this transfer be made in favour of companies controlled by ex-President Moi's children. This matter has brought serious friction between Kulei on one hand and Gideon and Phillip on the other. Physical threats were issued to Kulei during a meeting held at Phillip's house, following which Kulei approached Mr Tum, associated with Kenya Seed Company, to seek his intervention with ex-President Moi. Kulei feels that he is being asked to give more than he holds for and on behalf of ex-President Moi and that the sons are failing to distinguish between his personal wealth and that of their father. It has been reported that Gideon may transfer his assets from South Africa to Namibia where ex-President Moi, whose assets are presonally protected by President Sam Nujoma, has invested heavily.

Following the closure of the Kabarak meeting, each party made various moves, all geared towards securing their wealth as agreed. On the surface, it would appear that their individual plans are unrelated, but on the contrary a very well coordinated plan is being executed.

JOSHUA KULEI
Modus Operandi

It has been reported that over the years, Kulei has represented ex-President Moi in over 50 companies operating in Kenya, across all sectors of the economy.

The local companies in which Kulei has presided as director could not have generated enough dividends to account for liquid cash and assets that he is believed to control. Going by the dividend payout and based on the profits declared for tax purposes, his actual wealth does not relate in any way to his source of income.

Kulei is a very wealthy person in his own right. About three years ago, Kulei encountered serious problems with the Mois when Gideon kept convincing his father that Kulei may have more money than him as a result of using ex-President Moi's name. It is understood that this was during the time that Kulei contemplated leaving Kenya to live in London.

Kulei was warned after December 2003 by the DPP that the Moi brothers had a contract out to have him killed. According to client information, he was nearly arrested in relation to the Kenya Pipeline fraud.

NAME OF COMPANY	OWNERSHIP STRUCTURE
Trans-National Bank	Moi, Biwott, Nyachi, Kangwana, Gideon and five others
A Laikipia ranch	Moi 100%
An Eldoret farm	Moi 100%
A Rift Valley dairy farm	Moi 100%
The Kabarak farm	Given by Moi to University of Kabarak
The Mau farm	Given to AIC (church) by Moi
The Cherengani farm	Now owned by government
The Kilgoris farm	Leased by Moi
American Life Insurance Company	Trans-National Bank, Moi, Biwott, Kulei
Kobil and Kenol Petroleum	Moi 50%, Biwott 50%
Nairobi Airport Services	Moi, Mungai, Ndegwa
Rai Plywood of Eldoret	Moi 6%, Rai family 94%
Safaricom Kenya	Biwott, Charles Field Marsham, Gideon, 40%. The Post Office, 60%.
African Cargo Handling	Since sold to Kenya Airways
Kenchic Ltd	Moi, Charles Njonjo, P.K. Jani, J. Kiereini
Morris and Company	Kulei used to be a director but left in 1992
Capital Project Transport	Boinett 50%, Philip Murgor 50%.
MDI Consultancy	Miles Donnelly
Anhalt Road Apartment	Miles Donnelly

GIDEON MOI
Modus Operandi

In November 2004, Gideon travelled from Kenya through a circuitous route that took him to South Africa, Namibia, the United Kingdom and eventually Luxembourg.

Gideon spent a night in Namibia. Ex-President Moi enjoys a private and very cordial relationship with President Nujoma. During his visit, Gideon was meant to meet Nujoma privately under intervention of his father. It is not known whether the meeting actually took place.

Ex-President Moi has invested heavily in Namibia and Nujoma personally protects his investments. It is understood that Gideon is not comfortable with South Africa and all his actions are aimed at transferring his assets from there. There are indications that such a transfer is most likely to be to Namibia.

Gideon has been known to frequently visit the Grand Cayman and Cayman Brac in the past, travelling via Miami, USA.

VI: 'CRY OF BLOOD' REPORT INTO EXTRA-JUDICIAL MURDER IN KENYA (EXTRACTS)

This report outlined, at great length and with supporting detail, allegations that the police in Kenya had engaged in the extra-judicial murder of hundreds of men on the suspicion that they were members of the Mungiki, a local criminal organisation. These extracts give the background to the report and its findings, and the reaction of the Kenyan police and government, as well as some examples of the personal stories told in the report.

———————————

BACKGROUND TO THE INVESTIGATIONS

1. The Kenya National Commission on Human Rights (KNCHR) has, since July 2007, been investigating complaints in respect of alleged executions and disappearance of persons attributed to the Kenya Police.

2. Pursuant thereto, on 5/11/07, the KNCHR released a preliminary report indicating that the Kenya Police could have been complicit in extra-judicial executions of close to 500 people between June and October 2007 and the bodies deposited in various mortuaries in the country, some left in the wild and others dumped in various locations such as forests, desolate farms, rivers and dams.

3. This report was transmitted to the President of the Republic of Kenya H.E. Mwai Kibaki and made available to all the relevant Government departments asking that the concerned authorities act on its findings. The KNCHR was therefore surprised that instead of acknowledging the gravity of the issues raised in the report, the Police Commissioner, Maj. General Hussein Ali reacted by calling the KNCHR a meaningless busybody which had engaged in baseless accusations against the police and further accused the KNCHR of lacking expertise in carrying out investigations. The Police Commissioner also challenged the KNCHR to "provide any evidence to these rather infantile accusations". Subsequently, the Kenya Police issued its official rejoinder to the KNCHR report. The Police rejoinder does not deny the fact of the deaths but merely states that inquest files have been opened.

4. Be that as it may, the KNCHR proceeded with further investigations to complete its report and the ensuing findings confirm the substance of the preliminary report and reveal egregious violations of the law and fundamental human rights by the Kenya police in dealing with suspected Mungiki members and other alleged criminals.

5. While the KNCHR in no way condones the atrocities attributed to Mungiki and other illegal gangs (see Annex 1 for a background on the Mungiki Movement), it condemns the use of extra-judicial killing of

suspected members as a strategy to deal with the illegal group. Methods attributed to the Police and chronicled in this report amount to a serious violation of human rights especially the right to life and the right to a fair trial before a court of law.

6. The KNCHR continues to receive an alarming number of complaints of ongoing disappearances and extra-judicial killings attributed to the police and urges the government to urgently intervene to stop these human rights violations.

DETAILS OF FINDINGS OF ALLEGED EXECUTIONS, TORTURE AND OTHER VIOLATIONS

EYEWITNESS ACCOUNTS

The KNCHR has since July 2007, received witness testimonies where relatives, friends of the victims as well as independent witnesses gave accounts of arrests by police officers known to them or others seen driving police vehicles. Witness accounts indicate that soon after the arrests, some the victims disappear without a trace while others are found dead in mortuaries. The KNCHR has documented these accounts from the witnesses as enumerated below:

Benson Mwangi Waraga (55 years) a tailor along River Road, Nairobi was found dead at City mortuary on 19/5/07, two days after he was arrested by police after a shoot-out near his workplace. The shoot-out between the police and gangsters occurred on 17/5/07 at around 1.00 pm during which three alleged gangsters and a police officer were killed. The incident was prominently covered in both electronic and print media and Mwangi was captured being bundled into the police vehicle (see below). Two eyewitnesses to the incident recorded their statements with KNCHR. They gave an account of how, while working in the deceased tailoring shop in River Road, Githaku House, policemen raided their building at around 2.30pm on 1/5/07.The said police were allegedly looking for thieves in the building. One of the police officers ordered the two eyewitnesses and the deceased to lie down and after about 15 minutes, the three were bundled in a police Land Rover where 15 other suspects had already been bundled. The group was taken to Kamukunji Police Station and was counted to be 18 in number. The eyewitnesses further report that while awaiting to be booked at the Occurrence Book, (which they eventually were not), Waraga was ordered by one of the policemen to report to the Crime Office upstairs. The rest were released the following day,18/5/07. The KNCHR further received reports from Waraga's family that upon receiving the report of his arrest, Waraga's brother went to Kamukunj Police Station on 19/5/07 to see him but he was denied access since it was after 6.00 pm. The next day at 9.00 am, he went back to Kamukunji police station but could not trace Waraga. Together with other family members, they fruitlessly searched for him in all police stations within Nairobi. The following day (19/5/07), they went to City Mortuary where they found Mwangi's body. Attendants at the mortuary told the relatives that the deceased was brought by officers from Parklands police station having been shot as he was running away at City Park. A postmortem conducted by Dr. Peter Ndegwa revealed that Mwangi died of *'multiple organ injuries due to multiple gunshot wounds'*. According to the pathologist, *'the fatal bullets were shot from behind. The victim must have been about 20 cm from his attacker. He also seems to have been on the move (e.g. the bullet traveling parallel to the femur). The other gunshot on the leg seems to have been shot at a closer range and from the front. Could he have been shot once and asked to run?'*

Geoffrey Kung'u who sold shoes for a living disappeared on 8/10/07 at around 11.00 am after he had met his wife at the Country Bus Station, Nairobi. According to the wife, Kung'u was going to buy shoes then leave for upcountry (Murang'a) on the same day. A few minutes later, the wife tried calling him severally but the phone went unanswered. At around 5:00 pm, she called again but the phone was switched off. The next day, the wife went to several police stations including Kamukunji, Shauri Moyo, Makongeni and Central to no avail. On Wednesday, she went to the Industrial Area prison with no success. On Thursday and Friday she went to search for him in Langata and Ruai police stations still with no success. On Friday the 12th of October 2007, while watching news on

KTN at 7:00 pm, she identified all the items and clothing belonging to her husband, more specifically his green jacket with patches of white and orange (see below) which had been discovered earlier in the day by officers of the KNCHR who were accompanied by the media to Kiserian after some bodies had been spotted by area residents. She told the KNCHR that Kung'u had previously been arrested twice by the Kwekwe police squad on accusation of being a member of the illegal "Mungiki" sect. Upon the first arrest, Kung'u paid Kshs 2,000 to secure his release after the arresting officers threatened to kill him. He was reportedly arrested for the second time on 7/9/07 and taken to Makongeni Police station. When she went to visit him, a Kamba officer identified only as a **Mr. Muli** and another one called **Peter** asked for Kshs. 10,000 in exchange for his release or else they would kill him. She pleaded with the police to give her time to mobilize the money, which she brought on 9/9/07 securing his release. A postmortem on the remains of Kung'u was conducted on 24/10/07 at the City Mortuary. The body had significantly been gnawed by predators. The whole left leg was missing from the hip-joint. All the muscle and tissue of the right lower limb and all abdominal organs were missing leaving bare bones and some ligaments. According to the pathologist, the cause of death was 'severe head injury due to double gunshots to the head. These gunshots were fired at very close range suggesting execution'.

Patrick Mwangi, a conductor of a Matatu along Route 45 Githurai, disappeared on 17/10/07. On the day he went missing, he was standing at Githurai 44 stage waiting for his driver to come pick him as he was from lunch. Suddenly persons who identified themselves as policemen arrested him together with another man known as Daniel Mutahi (see profile above) and took them away in a small white personal vehicle registration number KAM 294R. The driver together with his father fruitlessly searched for him in several police stations and mortuaries. The matter was reported to Kasarani police station. He was still missing at the time of compiling this report on 11/7/08.

VII: BANK OF JULIUS BAER

Bank Julius Baer is part of the Julius Baer Group, a private banking group with its headquarters in Zurich. WikiLeaks published a number of documents relating to accounts held in Baer's Cayman Islands branch, resulting in a legal suit against WikiLeaks in the USA, which it successfully defended.

The extracts quoted here include part of a statement given by Rudolf Elmer, the former Baer employee who leaked the information, as well as a document relating to an individual bank account.

From Rudolf Elmer's statement:

Bank Julius Baer is systematically moving taxable funds to the offshore-island Cayman Islands (as well as Luxemburg or the tax-haven Guernsey), to minimize or reduce to zero their tax burden and that of their customers. I call such entities "bellevue-griten (little whores)". I sometimes felt like the guard of those "ladies" who essentially are being abused. The story is about the following limited liability companies of the Julius Baer Holding AG, which offer their services as offshore-entities of Julius Baer Holding AG in the Caymans Islands:

- Julius Baer Bank and Trust Co. Ltd, Cayman Islands (the bank)
- Julius Baer Trust Co Ltd, Cayman Islands (the administrative company)
- URSA Ltd., Cayman Islands (the insurance company)
- Baer Select Management Ltd, Cayman Islands (the investment manager)
- CreInvest Ltd, Cayman Islands (the hedge fund)
- shaPE Ltd, Cayman Islands (the private equity company)

The common goal of these companies is to:
- establish transactions only possible because of the lack of financial regulation and jurisdiction on the Caymans, as compared with well-regulatedcountries,
- reduce the taxable revenues of the Julius Baer groups in Switzerland and other countries for itself and its customers,
- offer vehicles to Swiss and foreign customers for tax evasion or even tax fraud,
- offer the ability to Swiss and foreign trustees to found companies on the Caymans (as well as Guernsey and Luxemburg) in order to profit from this situation,
- protect investors,
- and naturally reduce taxes for the Julius Baer group.

Only the mother company Julius Baer Bank and Trust Co Ltd, Cayman Islands (the bank) is owned directly by Julius Baer Holding AG, Zurich. All other companies are owned by Julius Baer Bank and Trust Ltd, (directly or indirectly) and therefore only Julius Baer Bank and Trust Co Ltd., Cayman

Islands (the bank) appears to the outside. This is effective, as all other companies stay hidden. Neither the Eidgenoessische Banken Kommission (Swiss federal banking commission) nor the tax administration are ever shown the balances or profit calculations of these companies due to the Confidentiality Law on the Caymans (similar to the Swiss banking law), under which there is no right for examination.

The estimated quantum of the tax reduction can be determined from the calculations at the end of this document. This is not about an exact figure of the loss of tax revenue in Switzerland but an order of magnitude and especially the methodology of offshore entities. The numbers presented represent the beginning of this decade and are very likely much higher today in light of the growth of the group.

The following letter relates to an American resident's account in the Cayman Islands. Rudolf Elmer claimed that it represents one example of customers using Baer accounts for the purposes of tax fraud, with the collusion of Baer. (Note highlighted text.)

Date: 12 May 1999

From: Valerie Mullen, Trust Department
Telephone: 345 949 7212
Fax: 345 949 0993

Subject: Winston Layne Trust

I had occasion to speak with Winston Layne today concerning amongst other things, the taxation of the Trust. I explained to him that following the Grantor tax changes in 1996, the actual requirements on beneficiaries and trustees had been clarified recently. I explained that while I am no tax expert, I understood that if you were a US beneficiary, you had a duty to report this fact whether or not you receive a distribution.

Winston Layne thanked me for bringing up the matter and for sharing what I knew with him. However, he advised that he did not want to disclose anything to the US tax people. He confirmed that we had done our duty in advising him of the tax changes but that he wished to keep the trust and the beneficiaries confidential.

While speaking with Mr. Layne, I ascertained that he would rather wait until the final version of the deed had been received from Maples & Calder before receiving a copy for review.

Finally, he confirmed that he would rewrite the letter of wishes for us in full.

Valerie Mullen

VIII: NADHMI AUCHI

Nadhmi Auchi is a British citizen of Iraqi origin. He was convicted of fraud in France in 2003 for his involvement in the Elf Aquitaine scandal. Martin Bright of the British magazine New Statesman *wrote a blog post drawing attention to Mr Auchi's use of litigation, or the threat of litigation, to remove newspaper articles that were critical of him from Internet archives. The* New Statesman *itself then received a letter from Auchi's lawyers, and Bright censored his own blog post.*

WikiLeaks published the original post and the censored version. Both can be seen at:

http://www.wikileaks.ch/wiki/Eight stories on Obama linked billionaire Nadhmi Auchi censored from the Guardian, Observer, Telegraph and New Statesman

or

http://tinyurl.com/3edqwed

IX: SOUTH AFRICAN COMPETITION COMMISSION REPORT (EXTRACTS)

The Competition Commission is a statutory body in South Africa whose responsibility is to promote and regulate fair competition in the South African economy. This extract is part of a 590-page report by the Competition Commission into competition in the South African banking industry. When originally released by the Commission, crucial portions of the report were removed at the request of the banks concerned. WikiLeaks published the full, unredacted version.

———————————

In assessing the profitability of banks in the provision of PTAs and related services we have reference to financial data provided by Absa for its Flexi Banking Services (FBS) and Retail Banking Services (RBS) segments . . .

Absa provided data showing profit growth in the FBS segment at a compound average growth rate (CAGR) of 24 per cent per annum over the period 2002 to 2005. Revenue (operating income) in this segment grew at a CAGR of 23 per cent per annum – i.e. at roughly the same rate as profit – and expenses at 22 per cent. This implies that the growth in the amount of profit in the FBS segment "was due primarily to increases in volume and not to an increase in profit margins (measured as a percentage of revenues)".

In the RBS segment, the amount of profit grew even faster – at a CAGR of 40 per cent per annum over the period 2002 to 2005. Here, however, revenue (operating income) grew at a CAGR of only 9 per cent per annum, and operating expenses at 5 per cent. Thus it is clear that profit margins did increase. Given that the number of RBS customers also grew at an annual average rate of only 5 per cent over this period, higher transaction volumes at lower unit costs provide the fundamental explanation for the increased profits. Absa concluded, and we agree, that "[t]his means that the growth in profit margins at RBS between 2002 and 2005 can be attributed largely to economies of scale." In short, unit costs came down sufficiently to provide the main basis for a 40 per cent compound annual growth in profits over the whole period.

It is evident that Absa failed to pass on these unit cost savings to any significant extent to its customers by way of price reductions, choosing instead to retain most of these savings as profits. Absa was able to increase prices on its main transaction account products over the period 2002 to 2005 at a rate roughly in line with or slightly below inflation during those years – despite benefiting from substantial unit cost reductions as a result of economies of scale.

We were not able to conduct the same specific analysis for the other banks, primarily because they did not provide data on operating expenses going back far enough in time to be useful for this purpose. However, there can be little doubt that in the prevailing conditions of market expansion, all the major banks benefited from economies of scale. As evidenced in the figures provided by Absa, there has been no real competitive pressure to reduce prices from other banks – indicating that they too have retained the greater portion of savings from unit cost reductions as profits rather than pass them on to consumers through lower prices. Indeed, effective competitive pressure on prices has generally been lacking from rivals in this market.

If the market were characterised by effective competition, then surely competitive pressure, either from potential entrants or existing competitors, would have compelled Absa to reduce its prices in order to maintain its relative share of the market and grow its business in this segment. The fact that it did not do so suggests that banks are sheltered from effective competitive pressure when it comes to pricing of PTAs, particularly in the retail banking or middle-market segment.

X: ALTANTUYA SHAARIIBUU

Altantuya Shaariibuu was a Mongolian national who was murdered in October 2006, near Kuala Lumpur. This document released by WikiLeaks consisted of a sworn statement, signed by the editor of the website Malaysia Today, Raja Petra, concerning the murder. The statement was also published on the Malaysia Today website. Around the time of publication a close associate of the Malaysian deputy prime minister was on trial for abetting the murder. He was later acquitted.

Petra's statement can be found at:

http://www.wikileaks.ch/wiki/Raja_Petra_Kamarudin_statutory_declaration_on_Altantuya_Shaariibuu_murder

or

http://tinyurl.com/3ele19y

XI: ICELANDIC BANKS (EXTRACTS)

Kaupthing was an Icelandic bank, with its headquarters in Reykjavik, that operated internationally. From October 2008 Kaupthing, like other highly leveraged Icelandic banks, was unable to meet its liabilities. The bank was taken over by the Icelandic Financial Supervisory Authority, and is currently being wound up.

This is Kaupthing's 'Large Loan Book', which is a record of the largest sums of money that were lent by the bank. Many of the loans detailed in this document raise a number of very serious questions about Kaupthing's practices, particularly given that large sums of money were loaned to individuals with close links to the bank, often with little security. A number of individuals have been arrested, in Iceland and abroad, following the collapse of the Icelandic banking system. This document was leaked at the end of July 2009.

These extracts give Kaupthing's assessment of the loans made to companies in the Exista Group. These loans total around €1.43 billion, much of which was unsecured. Given that Exista was a major shareholder in Kaupthing, owning around 23 per cent of the bank, this raises serious questions about the way the Kaupthing board (mis)managed its assets, at the expense of depositors.

Exista Group hf.

mEUR	Loans	Unused	Equity	Bonds	Derivat.	MM	Total
Exista hf.	627.4	4.7	34.1	51.5	40.4	33.1	791.2
Bakkabraedur Holding BV	252.5	-	-	-	-	-	252.5
Exista Invest ehf.	-	-	-	-	0.9	-	0.9
Lýsing hf.	-	2.5	-	-	-	-	2.5
Ufsastaðir ehf.	0.9	-	-	-	-	-	0.9
Vátryggingafélag Íslands hf.	-	0.2	-	-	-	-	0.2
Fiskifréttir/Framtiðarsýn	0.9	0.2	-	-	-	-	1.1
Guro Leisure Ltd. (KS&F)	193.1	5.0	-	-	-	-	198.3
Bakkabraedur Group (KBLUX)	128.7	-	-	-	-	-	128.7
Exista Sub Group (KBLUX)	35.4	-	-	-	-	-	35.4
Gudmundsson & Reynisdottir (KIOM)	13.6	-	-	-	-	-	13.6
Total	1,252.5	12.6	34.1	51.5	41.3	33.1	1,425.3

Exista - Exista hf.

Exposure	Loans 627.4 Unused 4.7 Equity 34.1 Bonds 51.5 Derivat. 40.4 MM 33.1 **Total 791.2**	Exista operates in the field of financial services and has a focus on insurance and asset finance. Exista is the largest shareholder in Sampo Group, Kaupthing Bank and Bakkavor Group. Skipti, VIS and Lýsing are 100% owned by Exista hf. Exista's business model is effectively based on utilizing income from cash-generating businesses to support highly selective investment activities, made by specialist investment teams and monitored and serviced by centralized Finance, Risk Management, Legal Council and Communications. Exista's operation is therefore based on two foundations; the Operating Businesses and the Investments Businesses. Exista is listed on the Iceland Stock Exchange with the largest shareholders being Bakkabræður Holding BV, Kista-fjárfestingafélag ehf, Gift fjárfestingafélag ehf. and Gildi lífeyrissjóður.
Collateral & Guarantees	Overall LTV: NA	Bulk of the loans are unsecured and with no covenants. The exemption is a EUR 100 million revolving facility which is secured with an equal amount of deposits.
Financial Performance	Net turnover 105.7 Total assets 6,924.7 Equity 2,284.2 - 30.6.2008	EBITDA 23.4 Curr. Assets 1,096.4 Equity ratio 32.99% Credit Rating: BB
Risk Factors		The main risk factor is market risk and a possible prolonged downturn and volatility in global financial markets. Exista is as such exposed to liquidity risk, as it could prove a challenge in current environment to refinance current loans or to liquidate current stakes in the abovementioned companies to secure liquidity. Further on, given the concentration in Exista's asset portfolio on the large financial stocks, the company is subject to financial sector risk, which has been particularly volatile recently.

Exista - Bakkabræður Holding BV

KAUPTHING BANK

Exposure	Loans 252.5 Total 252.5	Bakkabræður Holding BV is a holding company around shares in Exista hf. The company is owned by Ágúst Guðmundsson and Lýður Guðmundsson. The company is the largest shareholder in Exista.
Collateral & Guarantees	Overall LTV is around 89%	As security Kaupthing Bank pledged 6,408 million shares in Exista. Current market value of the shares is around EUR 283 m.
Financial Performance	NA	Credit Rating: NA
Risk Factors	Share price and operations of Exista hf. See separate presentation on Exista and the risk related to Exista.	

Exista Group hf.

KAUPTHING BANK

Exposure	Loans 193.1 Unused 5.0 Equity Bond Derivat. Total 198.3	The rationale for undertaking this business is the underlying ownership of the counterparty by Exista. This is a Reverse Repo transaction where we have financed the purchase of shares in JJB Sports, a UK retail group.
Collateral & Guarantees	Shares in London quoted Co. valued at €107.9m	Subjective rating of the overall security: unacceptable
Financial Performance	N/A	Not rated.
Risk Factors	The value of the shares purchased has fallen by more than half and we are thus reliant on the underlying break – up value of JJB which is significantly higher than the market price.	

Exista - Bakkabraedur Group (Kaupthing Luxembourg)

Exposure	Loans 128.72 Unused 0.00 Equity n/a Bonds n/a Derivat. 0.01 **Total 128.73**	The Bakkabraedur Group is owned and controlled by Agust and Lydur Gudmundsson, who are the founders of the Icelandic listed company Bakkavor Group hf. and the largest shareholders of Exista hf. (with regard to Exista sub group please refer to separate report). Substantial part of the exposure is aligned to the group's investment companies; beside that KBLUX established in favour of: 1. Barello Global S.A. - GBP 12.75mn property financing in UK 2. Jukebox L.P. - USD 23mn aircraft financing 3. Agust Gudmundsson - EUR 7.5mn + EUR 1.4mn property financing in France
Collateral & Guarantees	1.Personal guarantee L. Gudmundsson 2.First priority mortgage on aircraft (market value USD 28.5mn/LTV c.80%) 3.Undertaking to establish mortgages on the properties	There are no direct pledges between the different investment companies and some of the facilities are neither secured by personal guarantee nor by any other assets qualifying on the standard terms and conditions of KBLUX. Taking the lack of gross guarantee into account real short position amounts to EUR 43.67mn. Securities portfolio of the group is widely spread with the major parts being the shares held in Exista (EUR 371.4mn) and Bakkavor Group (EUR 63.5mn, market values).
Financial Performance	Financial situation of Exista sub group is outlined in the report attached.	Credit Rating: no rating Due to changed framework regulations regarding the UK linked operations (which require domestic payment sources for servicing debt), the group structure needs to be partly reorganised.
Risk Factors	The performance of the group might be affected by an ongoing adverse market environment, as the majority exposure of the group is linked to the investment business.	

Exista - Exista Sub Group (Kaupthing Luxembourg)

Exposure	Loans 35.37 Unused 0.00 Equity n/a Bonds n/a Derivat. n/a **Total 35.37**	Exista sub group -being a part within Bakkabreadur Group- was founded in June 2001 by a group of Icelandic Savings Banks and Kaupthing Bank hf.; in December 2002 Bakkabreadur became the majority shareholder of the company alongside the founding companies. Exista's business model is effectively based on utilising income from cash-generating businesses to support highly selective investment activities. In 2007, Exista successfully converted from a pure investment company to a financial services company with operations in the areas of insurance and asset financing. The switch is supporting the diversification in income streams as well as the direct generation of cash flows. Up to now KBLUX arranged and syndicated two deals in favour of Exista: 1. Exista B.V.; in 09/2005 a EUR 150mn Secured Syndicated Loan Facility, with an own commitment of EUR 29mn. Maturity in 09/2008 (bullet). 2. Exista hf.; in 11/2006 a DKK 300mn Syndicated Term Loan Facility, with an own commitment of DKK 47.5mn (EUR 6.37mn). Maturity in 11/2009 (bullet).
Collateral & Guarantees	1+2. First priority pledge of shares in Kaupthing Bank hf. 2. Guarantee given by Exista B.V.	1+2. Security Cover Ratio 150% (pledged shares to loan); in case of non compliance, borrowers are contractually obliged to deliver additional shares.
Financial Performance	Interim Financial Statements 06/2008 (in EUR mn) Turnover 105.7 EBITDA 24.4 Total assets 6,924.7 Curr. Assets n/a Equity 2,284.2 Equity ratio 33.0%× (×w/o taking into account goodwill EUR 341.4 mn)	Due to business nature, financial performance was significantly impacted by challenging market environment. Mainly due to revaluation of shares (EUR -237.2mn) and substantially lowered income from associated shares (c. EUR -482.9mn; compared to 06/2007), Exista had to report a net loss of EUR 82.2mn for the period under review
Risk Factors	The financial performance of the group is intensely exposed to the (investment) market development and might be affected further; the EUR 150mn syndicated transaction due for repayment in September 2008 will not be refinanced but repaid.	

XII: COLLATERAL MURDER

WikiLeaks received a copy of a video shot from the cabin of an American Apache gunship during two incidents in Baghdad on 12 July 2007 that claimed the lives of at least twelve people. The full 39-minute version of this video can be seen alongside the edited 18-minute version at www.collateralmurder.net, where accompanying resources are also available.

XIII: AFGHAN WAR LOGS (EXTRACTS)

These logs consist of a short report on every incident regarded as noteworthy by American troops in Afghanistan between January 2004 and December 2009. Around 90,000 incidents are reported in the document passed to WikiLeaks, though only around 75,000 were released.

These seven entries detail incidents of civilian casualties caused by British troops in October, November and December 2008. Like other similar reports throughout the logs, they give an insight into the chaotic nature of the battlefield and the constant risk – and consequences of – mistakes by coalition troops. Some of the information in each report has been removed and some acronyms have been expanded for the sake of readability, but each original report can be identified by its number and read in full on the WikiLeaks website. Some of the logs were redacted by WikiLeaks on release.

9923276D-082E-4116-97FC-98ED3B4CF007

14th October 2008

Y Coy 45 CDO manning a VCP when 1 x Local National motorcyclist approached VCP and ignored stop signals. Friendly Forces fired 1 x warning shot into the ground in front of the motorcyclist. The round ricocheted off ground and hit the rider in foot. The casualty was escorted to FOB INKERMAN, MO assessed casualty, gave money for taxi and sent to BOST Hospital. BDA: 1 x LOCAL NATIONAL wounded (CAT UNK).

UPDATE
FRIENDLY FORCES fired 1 x warning shot 5.56mm
UPDATE 150112D*OCT08
RC(S) reports that the motorcycle is at PB EMERALD. RC(S) is not antici- pating any more compensation will be paid. 1 Wounded afghan(AFG) Local Civilian

733A452F-C9F3-4A25-AEAA-980BC16FDA1E

22nd October 2008

Afghan National Army (2/3/205) with GBR OMLT while conducted a ground domination patrol. 1 x Local National on a motorbike was driving at speed towards Friendly Forces and the LOCAL NATIONAL failed to stop after warning shots were fired. FRIENDLY FORCES then engaged the motorcycle, killing Local National. FRIENDLY FORCES have confirmed that the LOCAL NATIONAL was not a suicide bomber, and are taking the body to SANGIN hospital. Casual- ties reported.

UPDATE 1352D*
The LOCAL NATIONAL has been refused by SGN hospital and returned to SGN DC.
It is confirmed that an OMLT Soldier fired the shot.

UPDATE 1644D*
***Event re-written IAW First Impression Report*

The purpose of the patrol was to clear the route from PB NABI to a Red ISO container (GR 41 SPR 7355 5012) in order to link up with IEDD team moving from SANGIN DC and guide them into PB NABI for a UXO task. At 1203D*, the foot patrol consisting of 10 x GBR OMLT left PB NABI for the red ISO. When FRIENDLY FORCES reached Red ISO, they established a cordon in order to wait for the IEDD team. At approximately 1255D*, at GR 41 SPR 73706 50328, 1 x OMLT personnel saw 1 x LOCAL NATIONAL on a motor bike approaching his position from the South. He believed the LOCAL NATIONAL was a suicide bomber. For the last two weeks, intelligence has repeatedly reported the threat of two suicide bombers on motorbike in and around the SANGIN Bazaar. When the poss INS was 35-40 meters form his position, he fired 4 warning shots (5.56mm) into the close to the poss INS. The poss INS did not alter his speed or direction and continued directly for the OMLT personnel. At 20 meters away he fired continuous shots (details to be confirmed) into the poss INS centre of mass. The motorcycle crashed into the ditch and caught fire.

On inspection the LOCAL NATIONAL was immediately confirmed as dead and not a suicide bomber. At 1345D*, FRIENDLY FORCES brought the body to SANGIN DC hospital with multiple GSW to the chest and immediately redeployed to their previous position IOT escort the IEDD team to NABI to commence the UXO task.

***Event closed at 1644D*1 Killed afghan(AFG) Local Civilian

4B54C6BD-3057-4C3B-8C74-30342C5D9670

19th November 2008

J COY 42 CDO conducting a admin move to MOB LKG observed 1 x LOCAL NATIONAL vehicle approaching the convoy and fired 2 x Miniflares as a warning. The LOCAL NATIONAL vehicle did not change course or slow down so FRIENDLY FORCES fired 2 x RDS 9mm (WARNING SHOTS) into the ground in front of the vehicle. It swerved and stopped. A visual check of the LOCAL NATIONAL vehicle carried out and the patrol continued on task. Subsequent investigation revealed that a LOCAL NATIONAL child was present in the vehicle and received a fatal Gun Shot Wound. The incident was reported to NDS by HAJJI HAQBIN (An influential BARAKZAI tribal elder) a relative of the child.

***Event closed at 261808D*1 Killed Local Civilian

E8AA01C8-A3FD-467E-85F6-7BF604445A41

29th November 2008

Afghan National Police with GBR PMT conducting police training patrol reported 1 x white vehicle approached the patrol at high rate of speed and failed to stop. FRIENDLY FORCES engaged with SAF. The occupant was ANP (not in uniform). A cordon was established and the QRF was deployed to assist.

UPDATE 291423D*NOV08
RC(S) reports a LOCAL NATIONAL man came to the patrol claiming his daughter had a Gun Shot Wound to the leg which had been caused by the contact. She was currently being treated at BOST Hospital. An investigation is being conducted.

NFTR.
***Event closed at 1950D*1 Died of Wounds ANP

283C7026-A6D2-4A4E-BCD3-5B1E742073F6

4th December 2008

W Coy 45 CDO conducting a reassurance patrol, reported FRIENDLY FORCES observed 1x possible Insurgent spotter at Grid Reference

41SPR72034852 and fired 1x warning shot. Possible Insurgent ignored the warning shot and followed the patrol. FRIENDLY FORCES believed he was a threat to life and engaged with 1x round of SAF.

***Event closed at 05 1530D*

UPDATE 1836D*
RC(S) reports this was a LOCAL NATIONAL not an insurgent. A First Impression Report has been received. Casualty identification has been changed INS --> LOCAL NATIONAL. The LOCAL NATIONAL was treated and sent to a local hospital.

369D999E-F9EC-4C57-9FF0-65B746A19567

24th December 2008

L Coy 42 CDO whilst conducting a clearance patrol ISO OP SOND CHARA were approached by 1x vehicle with 2x LOCAL NATIONAL's which ignored stop signs being given by FRIENDLY FORCES. FRIENDLY FORCES fired 3x 7.62mm MG as warning shots but the vehicle kept moving. FRIENDLY FORCES fired 3x shots into the engine of the vehicle but the vehicle still kept moving. FRIENDLY FORCES then fired 3x shots into the windscreen and the vehicle stopped.

NFTR.
***Event closed at 1803D*1 Wounded Local Civilian

88BE7199-5C88-484E-A5BD-BE6AD0654657

30th December 2008

W Coy 45 CDO conducting NFO patrol reported 1 x vehicle (white van) was travelling at high rate of speed toward FRIENDLY FORCES cordon. FRIENDLY FORCES gave verbal warnings and hand signals to the driver and he did not stop. FRIENDLY FORCES then fired 1 x warning shot into the engine block and the vehicle stopped. A 12 year old male passenger was wounded from a ricochet. The wounded LOCAL NATIONAL was taken by civilian means to FOB SANGIN.

***Event closed at 2115D*1 Wounded None(None) Local Civilian

———————————————————

XIV: IRAQ WAR DIARIES

Much like the Afghan war logs, the records from Iraq also represent American soldiers' reports on noteworthy incidents, this time in Iraq between 2004 and 2009. There are almost 400,000 individual incident reports in the cache. The reports extracted here indicate that when witnessing abuse of detainees by Iraqi army and police, American troops simply recorded the incidents as instructed by their superiors, but, as a matter of policy, no other action was taken to prevent such abuses. As with the Afghan war logs, some material has been redacted.

50A2284C-BF55-E1FD-BEA7B6AED9A0AD20

17th June 2007

WHO: Tal Afer CTU

WHAT: DETAINEE ABUSE

WHEN: 17 June 2007 (Discovered by P-PiTT on 06 May 2009 and reported to 3/1 CAV on 2 Jul 09)

WHERE: Tal Afer CTU

WHY: Discovered by P-PiTT on 06 May 2009 and reported to 3/1 CAV on 2 Jul 09 REPORTED ALLIGATION OF DETAINEE ABUSE TO Khither AbedalJaber Omer Albakaar,by Tal Afer CTU on or around 15 June 2007, REASON FOR DETAINMENT: suspected IED emplacer

Victim received extensive medical care at the Mosul General Hospital resulting in amputation of his right leg below the knee several toes on his left foot, as well as amputation of several fingers on both hands. Extensive scars resulted from the chemical/acid burns, which were diagnosed as 3d degree chemical burns along with skin decay. His medical reports from 30 June 3007 also noted bruises on his back. Photographs of the victim believed to be taken in 2007 are included as well as photographs taken by the P-PiTT team on 5 May 2009, when they observed this victim at the Mosul MTU.

Victim was captured by the Iraqi Army on 15 June 2007 and transferred to the Tal Afer CTU. When questioned about terrorism activities, the victim alleges that LT Ali, LT Adnan and LTC Mohammed tortured him by pouring chemicals on his hands, cut his fingers off, and hid him when Coalition Forces visited the Tal Afer CTU.

The Mosul Major Terrorism Unit (MTU) discovered these events on 8 Sep 07 and began an investigation. Warrants were issued on 11 Sep

07 LTC Mohammed, LT Ali and LT Adnan however no arrests were made. The PDoP was informed of this case in Sep 07, who subsequently notified the Deputy of Police Affairs at the Ministry of Interior (MOI). The victim appears to have been released from the hospital in May 2009, when members of the P-PiTT observed him at the Mosul MTU. He apparently was released from the MTU and his location is currently unknown.

05F55972-0F73-BDDA-C7F69F2EF408DFF1

2nd May 2009

2/1 CAV unit conducting inspection of Riyadh Iraqi Police station discovered multiple detainees who appeared to have been abused by Iraqi Police personnel. The detainees had severe brusies to lower extremities from beatings and were in need of medical attention. Some detainees were handcuffed in offices, others beaten and confined to locked rooms and left in a dyhydrated state with no fluids provided. The unit also discovered the suspected instruments used to conduct the abuse in the office of the Iraqi Police Station Chief. These suspected tools of torture had "blood marks" and were retained by the unit. The unit contacted local Iraqi Police authorities who responded and provided necessary medical attention. When the Riyadh Iraqi Police Chief was confronted about the suspected detainee abuse at his station he responded he was aware of the beatings and supported it as a method of conducting investigations. The unit continues to engage the local Iraqi authorities and provide assistance as necessary.

EC3ED714-64C3-453B-B623-7CCFB4AFF59B

23rd October 2006

AT 231413COCT06 IN QAL AT HADI BAK IVO 38S MB 41100 59300 CPT (NAME WITHHELD) 4/6 IA S2 TRAINER, AND 1LT (NAME WITHHELD) 2/4/6 IA S2 TRAINER, WENT TO 4/6 IA S2 DETAINEE PROCESSING CENTER WHERE THEY CAUGHT THE IA AS2, (NAME WITHHELD) AND IBIF NCOIC, (NAME WITHHELD) BY SURPRISE AND DISCOVERED

SUSPECTED DETAINEE ABUSE. IN THE OFFICE THERE WAS WHAT
APPEARED TO BE A BATTERY WITH OPEN ENDED WIRES, THE END OF
A COT WITH YELLOW ROPE ON BOTH ENDS AND WHAT APPEARED
TO BE PLASTIC TUBING. BEFORE ENTERING THE OFFICE (NAME
WITHHELD) HEARD WHAT SOUNDED LIKE AN INDIVIDUAL BEING HIT
AND MOANING. THE DETAINEE WAS SITTING IN THE CENTER OF
THE ROOM SOBBING. (NAME WITHHELD) STOPPED THE SUSPECT-
ED ABUSE, QUESTIONED CPT (NAME WITHHELD) AND RECEIVED
THE NAME OF THE DETAINEE. ACTIONS TAKEN BY THE REPORT-
ING UNIT: CHAIN OF COMMAND NOTIFIED, SWORN STATEMENTS
WRITTEN, AWAITING 15-6 IOFROM 2-10 BDE, NOTIFIED 4/6 IA CDR

124EE0C7-D4FE-4BE1-DBDF1EED4C2F92DC

3rd May 2009

A DETAINEE CLAIMED THAT HIS INTERROGATORS KICKED, PUN-
CHED, SLAPPED HIM ON THE FACE, STOMACH, LEGS AND ALSO
ELECTROCUTED HIS HANDS, LEFT EAR, AND GENITAL AREA FOR
APPROXIMATELY 15-30 MINUTES. HE ALSO CLAIMS HE WAS QUES-
TIONED WHETHER OR NOT HE PLANTED OR HELPED TO PLANT
IEDS. THE DETAINEE CLAIMED THAT HE DIDN'T. THE DETAINEE
DOESN'T KNOW EXACT TIMES OF DAY THAT IT WAS; JUST THAT IT
WAS LATE IN THE MORNING. DETAINEE SAID THAT HIS MOUTH WAS
COVERED WHENEVER HE WOULD SCREAM AND TOLD TO KEEP
QUIET BECAUSE THE AMERICANS MIGHT HEAR HIS SCREAMS.
DETAINEE DIDNT SEE ANY OF THE ABUSERS. DETAINEE WAS THEN
TAKEN BACK TO HIS CELL AND WHEN HE WAS IN FRONT OF THE
CELL HE FAINTED AND WAS CARRIED TO HIS BED.

ADDITIONAL INFORMATION: DETAINEE DID SHOW HANDCUFF MARKS
ANY OTHER SIGNS OR SYMPTOMS OF ABUSE, AND HE WAS MEDI-
CALLY CLEARED FOR INTERROGATION. DETAINEE DIDNT REPORT
TO MEDIC DURING MEDICAL SCREENING AND WAS LATER TOLD BY
INTERPRETER THAT HE HAD BEEN ABUSED. HE ALSO REFUSED TO
RENDER A SWORN STATEMENT ABOUT HIS ALLEGED ABUSE.

OTHER INFORMATION: THE DETAINEE FEARS FOR HIS SAFETY, SO WE HAVE CREATED A REDACTED VERSION OF THE Situation Report AS WELL. THIS REPORT IS SENT IN FULFILLMENT OF OUR REPORTING REQUIREMENT UNDER FRAGO 273. WE HAVE ATTACHED THE ORIGINAL Situation Report. OUR OPERATIONAL LAW ATTORNEYS HAVE SENT A SEPARATE REPORT TO MNC-1. HOWEVER, MNC-1 WILL HAND ONLY THE REDACTED VERSION (ALSO ATTACHED) OVER TO THE MOI, AND THE DETAINEES NAME WILL NOT BE RELEASED. THE Situation Report WILL BE ENTERED IN THE OSJA DETAINEE ABUSE TRACKER.

A9EDA77A-540C-4058-901D-DBD8AB04DF9D

12th March 2006

1. DESCRIPTION OF INCIDENT/SUSPECTED VIOLATION (WHO REPORTED THE INCIDENT, AND TYPE OF ABUSE): AT APPROXIMATELY 1200 ON 12 MARCH 2006, SERGEANT (NAME WITHHELD) OBSERVED [xxxxx], 2-1-2 PUBLIC ORDER BATTALION, KICK DETAINEE HP031130 ON THE BACK OF THE NECK WITH THE BOTTOM OF HIS FOOT. HP031130 WAS FLEXICUFFED WITH HIS HANDS BEHIND HIS BACK, BLINDFOLDED AND ON HIS KNEES WITH HIS JACKET COVERING HIS HEAD WHEN THIS HAPPENED.
2. DATE/TIME AND LOCATION WHERE ALLEGED ABUSE TOOK PLACE: APPROXIMATELY 1200 ON 1 2 MARCH 2006 AT THE HURRICANE POINT THA IN AR RAMADI.
3. UNIT AND PERSONNEL ACCUSED OF COMMITING THE ABUSE: [xxxxx] OF THE 2-1-2 PUBLIC ORDER BATTALION
4. EVIDENCE GATHERED, AND CONSIDERED IN MAKING AN OPINION ON THE VALIDITY OF THE ALLEGATION: STATEMENT OF SGT (NAME WITHHELD)
5. OPINION ON VALIDITY OF ALLEGATION OF ABUSE: VALID.
6. BASIS FOR OPINION: (NAME WITHHELD) IS AN HONEST MARINE WITH WHOM I HAVE WORKED FOR 7 MONTHS. HE HAS NO MOTIVE TO FABRICATE. IN ADDITION, THERE WERE 2 OTHER MARINES WHO WITNESSED THE ASSAULT.

7. RECOMMENDATION: NO INVESTIGATION REQUIRED. THE CORPS-
MAN NOTED A MINOR RED MARK ON THE DETAINEES NECK PRE-
SUMABLY FROM WHERE HE WAS KICKED. I INFORMED THE COALI-
TION REPRESENTATIVES AT 2-1-2 POB (MAJ (NAME WITHHELD) DSN
302-5212-228 AND MAJ (NAME WITHHELD) DSN 302-3609-131) WHO
HAVE TURNED THE MATTER OVER TO THE IZ BATTALION COMMAND-
ER. RECOMMEND THE POB ADDRESS THIS INCIDENT INTERNALLY.
8. POINT OF CONTACT: (NAME WITHHELD), DSN 302-3609-369

XV: EMBASSY CABLES (EXTRACTS)

The gradual release of American embassy cables, also known as Cablegate, represents WikiLeaks' most high-profile work to date. Around 250,000 cables – short messages by American diplomats around the world on a particular subject, generally around one to two thousand words long – were passed to WikiLeaks by its source. WikiLeaks had released around 20,000 of them by August 2011, initially with its five core partners, but later with an increasingly large coalition of media organisations around the world, now numbering more than fifty.

Unlike the war logs, the cables are written in fluent prose and are meant to convey not only a small number of facts, but also a general sense of wider issues concerning American diplomacy. As such, they are informative not only in what they say, but in how they say it.

The cables presented here demonstrate the extent to which American diplomats saw the interests of large corporations as synonymous with American national interests.

Extract One: These first two cables, from the American embassy in Turkey, concern the possible sale of Boeing aircraft to Turkish Airlines. The Turkish transportation minister implies that Turkish Airlines would be more inclined to buy Boeing aircraft if the American government would help to put a Turkish astronaut in space. Bizarrely, despite lobbying on behalf of Boeing, the ambassador claims to resent the presence of political influence in such a transaction. In his own words: 'Yildirim's conflation of [US Government – Turkish Government] interactions and what is ostensibly a commercial sale between private firms suggests an unwelcome, but unsurprising, degree of political influence in this transaction.' The ambassador also resents lobbying by European governments on behalf of rival aircraft manufacturers, an activity which is widespread and common to all Western governments.

04ANKARA2680
Created: May 12, 2004 12:22

SUBJECT: BOEING FEELS PRESSURE IN THE TURKISH MARKET

1. (C) Summary: Boeing representatives continue to be concerned over attempts by a senior official of the AKP cabinet to pressure the company into hiring one of his associates as Boeing's representative in Turkey. Boeing is currently competing with EADS-Airbus for the potential sale of 19 narrow and wide body aircraft to expand the fleet of Turkish Airlines (THY). In addition to puchasing 19 aircraft and extending lease options for eight B737-400 aircraft, THY anticipates a need for 35 additional planes to meet future demand. End Summary.

2. (C) Earlier this week, Boeing representatives met with Embassy officials to discuss issues of concern to Boeing in the Turkish market. Boeing is

concerned over attempts by a senior member of the AKP cabinet to pressure Boeing into hiring one of his associates as Boeing's representative in Turkey The state-owned Turkish flag carrier, THY, is currently interested in purchasing nineteen planes to expand its fleet. In addition to this fleet expansion, THY is also looking to lengthen its lease on eight Boeing 737-400s, which expire in 2006. THY expects a need for 35 additional planes to meet future flight demand. This project, valued at more than USD 2.9 billion (approximately 85 percent U.S. export content), is one of the largest projects in Turkey in the past several years. The German Chancellor and the French President have raised the upcoming THY acquisitions, on Airbus' behalf, with Prime Minister Erdogan in previous discussions.

3. (S) According to our Boeing contacts, Rafi Harlev, an Israeli national and former Director General of El Al, approached Boeing in March 2004 and introduced Boeing to a Turkish businessman named Mehmet Emin Erkan, Chairman, ERKAN Companies Group, and an Israeli businessman named Ramiz Aydasgil, Managing Partner, ExaGlobal Partnership. Mr. Erkan advised Boeing that the Turkish Finance Minister was interested in meeting with Boeing to discuss THYs acquisition, and volunteered to arrange the meeting with the Finance Minister. (Comment: Senior THY management reports to the Finance Minister. End Comment).

4. (C) During Boeing's meeting with the Finance Minister, the Minister told Boeing that Mr. Erkan understands the airline business well and is fully aware of THYs requirements. Immediately following the meeting with the Finance Minister, Mr. Erkan asked Boeing to retain him as their consultant in Turkey to ensure Boeing's success in this market. Boeing declined Erkan's request.

5. (C) Comment: Post remains concerned about extensive lobbying by senior EU officals and the heads of state of Germany and France on behalf of Airbus. The Finance Minister is scheduled to meet with Airbus in Paris later this week. Post recommends that Washington agencies use all available opportunities to impress their GOT interlocutors on the importance we attach to transparency in THYs acquisition. Post will continue its active advocacy on behalf of Boeing.

10ANKARA74
Created: Jan 19, 2010 05:39
SUBJECT: AMBASSADOR DISCUSSES BOEING SALE WITH
TRANSPORTATION MINISTER

REF: ISTANBUL 17

1. (C) Summary. Minister of Transportation Binali Yildirim confirmed to
Ambassador Jeffrey that price is now the main sticking point in the prospective purchase of Boeing aircraft by Turkish Airlines (THY). Yildirim
stressed, however, that price is not the only consideration and that THY
is looking at the (vague) associated conditions for evidence of a long-
term partnership and commitment. He added that the GOT is also hoping
for a heightened level of civil aviation cooperation with the FAA, and that
progress on that front would improve the environment for Boeing as
well. Finally, he repeated President Gul's request to President Obama for
assistance in sending a Turkish astronaut into space, and hinted that this
was tied into Turkey's consideration of commercial deals. The Ambassador highlighted Boeing's long history of cooperation with and investment
in Turkey, not only through partnerships with local firms but also via direct
investment in the community through its corporate social responsibility
programs. He also promised to discuss the possibilities for cooperation
with FAA and investigate whether NASA could help facilitate the Turkish
space program. End summary.

2. (SBU) Ambassador Jeffrey, accompanied by Commercial Counselor
and Econoff, met with Minister of Transportation Binali Yildirim on January 14 to advocate on behalf of Boeing in the ongoing procurement of
new airplanes for the THY fleet. THY recently announced that it would
be purchasing 20 Airbus single-aisle aircraft with an option for 10 more.
Negotiations with Boeing for a similar number of 737s are ongoing (see
reftel). The value of this deal is approximately USD 3.4 billion.

3. (C) The Ambassador, alluding to the discussions between President
Obama and Prime Minister Erdogan, noted his understanding that the
main sticking point in the negotiations now seems to be on price (as

was expressed by THY CEO to CG Wiener in reftel). Yildirim confirmed that price is the most important outstanding issue and observed that haggling over price is a normal part of any business negotiation. He went on to say, however, that price is not the only consideration, and that THY and the GOT are looking at the offer carefully with an eye toward after-sale service and long-term partnership. Ambassador Jeffrey highlighted Boeing's longstanding commitment to Turkey, its history of cooperative production with local manufacturers, its world-class corporate social responsibility programs, and the superior quality of its products.

4. (C) Yildirim added that the GOT is evaluating the Boeing offer in the context of Turkey's overall civil aviation cooperation with the United States, especially in terms of cooperation between the Ministry and the FAA. He noted that Turkey needs to strengthen both its technical infrastructure and its human capacity to meet the growing demand for aviation services, and expressed hope that the FAA could provide assistance on all these fronts. Cooperation in this area will create the right environment for commercial deals, he said, without going into specifics on what type of assistance is necessary. A frustrated Ambassador observed that FAA has a solid history of collaboration with the Civil Aviation Directorate General and promised to investigate how the USG might best lend assistance.

5. (C) In addition to FAA assistance, Yildirim hinted obliquely that Turkey's desire to send an astronaut into space – expressed in a letter from President Gul to President Obama – is also tied into its consideration of commercial deals, and that NASA assistance to help stand up Turkey's nascent space program would be viewed positively. Ambassador Jeffrey noted that scheduling a Turkish astronaut on an upcoming mission would be extremely difficult, but that other technical assistance from NASA in establishing Turkey's space program might be a possibility.

6. (C) Comment: Yildirim's conflation of USG-GOT interactions and what is ostensibly a commercial sale between private firms suggests an unwelcome, but unsurprising, degree of political influence in this transaction. His comments may also explain the confusing mention of offsets by Prime Minister Erdogan in his meeting with the President - if

the GOT is truly evaluating the sale as a "U.S." offer rather a Boeing offer, then the desired "offsets" may have been from the USG rather than Boeing. While there should not be a link between this deal and FAA/NASA assistance in developing Turkey's aviation and aerospace agencies, such assistance in and of itself could be mutually beneficial and merits further study. We probably cannot put a Turkish astronaut in orbit, but there are programs we could undertake to strengthen Turkey's capacity in this area that would meet our own goals for improved aviation safety in the region. In any case, we must/must show some response to the Minister's vague requests if we want to maximize chances for the sale. End comment.

Extract Two: *This cable also concerns a sale of Boeing aircraft to a national airline. In the words of the cable itself, 'the Embassy's role in Boeing's success is noteworthy for advancing well beyond every-day advocacy'.*

08MANAMA47
Created: Jan 27, 2008 12:25

SUBJECT: EMBASSY ADVOCACY HELPS WIN $6 BILLION BOEING DEAL

------- SUMMARY -------

1.(C) Following months of heavy lobbying by the Ambassador, the Crown Prince and King rejected a Gulf Air proposal to buy Airbus and directed the airline to make a deal with Boeing. Gulf Air signed an agreement valued at $6 billion with Boeing on January 13, in time to coincide with a POTUS visit. The agreement represents a significant Embassy com-

mercial advocacy success. A last-minute French government push for
Airbus included discussion of a visit to Bahrain by President Sarkozy.
End Summary.

------- SMOOTH LANDING -------

2.(C) Post commercial advocacy efforts paid off handsomely on January
13 when Gulf Air signed a deal to buy 16 787s, valued at $3.4 billion,
with options for an additional 8, valued at $2.6 billion. At a press confer-
ence following the signing, Gulf Air Board Chairman Mahmoud Kooheji
said it was virtually assured that Gulf Air would exercise its options on all
8 additional planes. Boeing's stock opened sharply higher January 14,
following the weekend announcement.

-------- BUMPY RIDE ----------

3.(C) Boeing first requested USG assistance in May 2006, when then Gulf
Air president James Hogan announced plans to replace the carrier's aging
fleet with a mix of medium-range and long-range aircraft. Under Hogan's
business plan, Boeing would have supplied up to 25 787s and as many as
22 737s. Gulf Air was then still jointly owned by the Governments of Bahrain
and Oman and Embassies Manama and Muscat each lobbied their
respective host governments on Boeing's behalf. However, Hogan's
managerial differences with Gulf Air's board subsequently led to his
departure from Gulf Air and his ambitious plan was scrapped.

4.(C) With the Government of Oman's announced withdrawal from Gulf
Air in May 2007, Minister of Finance Shaikh Ahmed Bin Mohammed Al
Khalifa took personal oversight of Gulf Air's management with a view
toward stemming Gulf Air's losses, which stood in excess of USD 1
million per day. Shaikh Ahmed stated that either the Airbus 320 or the
Boeing 737 would fit Gulf Air's developing need for high-frequency
regional traffic. "The long-term emphasis for the carrier is narrow-body
instead of wide-body." Andre Dose, Shaikh Ahmed's pick to replace
James Hogan as Gulf Air CEO, soon confirmed to Emboffs that Gulf Air
would downsize to an Airbus fleet (reftels).

5.(C) However, Dose's aggressive downsizing drive, which also led to cuts in routes and personnel, brought him into conflict with the Gulf Air board. In July 2007, after just four months on the job, he resigned his post, leaving Deputy CEO Bjorn Naff to succeed him.

6.(C) The Gulf Air board, now controlled entirely by the GOB, made clear to Naff its vision for Gulf Air as a robust, revitalized national carrier. The airline needed to grow rather than shrink. In October 2007, Gulf Air signed an MOU to purchase Boeing Dreamliners. However, the board reversed itself shortly thereafter, citing concern over being able to justify a decision for Boeing to the parliament in the face of a steeply discounted airbus quotation; the Airbus package was reportedly $400 million cheaper.

7.(C) On December 12 Gulf Air delivered bad news to Boeing – the board had selected the Airbus package. Signaling that Boeing's prospects were finished, Gulf Air asked Boeing to return its deposit. Boeing executives promptly informed the Ambassador and Econoff that the deal was lost and Airbus had won. But from Post's perspective the contest remained far from over. Gulf Air's selection still needed to be endorsed by the government. The Ambassador directly queried senior MANAMA 00000047 002 OF 003 GOB officials and learned that no formal decision had yet been reached. Accordingly, he advised Boeing of his recommendation - it was too soon to walk away.

8.(C) Boeing renewed its request for advocacy. The Ambassador and Econoff persisted in lobbying Gulf Air management, board members, government officials and representatives of parliament. The Ambassador made the case repeatedly that Airbus, lower up-front costs would be eclipsed by Boeing's lower operating costs and product reliability. He made much of the fact that the Airbus A-350 alternative was still on the drawing board.

-------- COURSE CORRECTION --------

9.(C) Kooheji urgently requested a meeting with the Ambassador on December 30 to advise him that the Crown Prince and King had rejected Gulf Air's proposal to buy Airbus, and directed him to make a deal with Boeing in time to coincide with the January 12-13 POTUS visit. Kooheji said he would accordingly seek to come to terms with Boeing. However, if Boeing were to respond that its best deal was already on the table, Kooheji would be unable to justify a revised board recommendation. Boeing would need to show willingness to make some concession(s) that Kooheji could point to as equation-altering.

10.(C) The Ambassador notified Boeing that its representatives would need to return to Bahrain quickly and be ready to finalize an agreement. Somewhat skeptical, Boeing executives initially responded that their obligations precluded a return to Bahrain before January 14. The Ambassador pointed out that this would be too late. Boeing subsequently returned to Bahrain and called on the Ambassador January 3rd. The Ambassador shared that he had spoken directly to the Crown Prince on Boeing's behalf. The Crown Prince had assured him of the Government's sincerity in seeking a deal. This was not merely a last-minute maneuver to wring concessions from Airbus.

11.(C) Encouraged by such a high-level assurance of good faith, Boeing responded by shaving an additional five percent off its proposed sale price. This concession proved decisive in providing Kooheji with the justification he sought to advocate a board decision for Boeing.

12.(U) On January 13, Gulf Air and Boeing signed the $6 billion Boeing deal. Dreamliner delivery will start in 2016. In the meantime, Kooheji said Gulf Air will seek to meet its needs via the leasing market. The purchase will be supported via a blend of commercial and ExIm Bank financing with the sovereign backing of the GOB.

----------- LAST-MINUTE FRENCH RECLAMA ----------

13.(C) GOB officials tell Emboffs that French President Sarkozy, who was visiting the region at the time, made a last-minute call to King Hamad.

Sarkozy reportedly said he would add Bahrain to his itinerary during the week of January 13 on the condition that he could sign a contract for 21 Airbus planes. French officials reportedly canceled the visit on news of the Boeing deal. Foreign Minister Sheikh Khalid told Ambassador that he would be calling in the local French Ambassador to tell her "we don't appreciate being dealt with this way."

------- COMMENT -------

14.(C) Although Gulf Air has just completed a major long-range aircraft purchase, it is not finished shopping. Kooheji has said Gulf Air still needs to replace eight of its mid-range aircraft. Gulf Air has already signed an MOU with Airbus for those planes, but Kooheji notes that bidding remains open. It seems likely that Gulf Air will choose to replace eight of its Airbus A-320s with newer planes from that manufacturer. But as Boeing's recent win illustrates, Airbus is in no position take Gulf Air's business for granted. Post will certainly continue to hail the advantages of a Boeing solution.

15.(C) The Embassy's role in Boeing's success is noteworthy for advancing well beyond every-day advocacy. Gulf Air relied on the Embassy to not only communicate with Boeing, but to get the best possible deal; Boeing turned to us for an understanding of the true facts on the ground (which at times belied appearances) and as a force multiplier, conveying the Boeing advantage at all levels. These efforts resulted in a win-win solution. In a letter of thanks to the Ambassador Boeing stated, "Your continued effort to touch the right leaders and remain a strong advocate for Boeing in this process made an enormous difference in the final outcome. The working together activity between you, your team, and Boeing is a model that we should really aspire to replicate in other countries."

Extract Three: MON-810 is a genetically modified variety of maize made by the Monsanto corporation. A number of European countries have now banned its cultivation. In response to moves in this direction from some European countries, the American ambassador to Paris suggested that the US should 'calibrate a target retaliation list that causes some pain across the EU'.

07PARIS4723
Created: Dec 14, 2007 16:23

SUBJECT: FRANCE AND THE WTO AG BIOTECH CASE

1. (C) Summary: Mission Paris recommends that that the USG reinforce our negotiating position with the EU on agricultural biotechnology by publishing a retaliation list when the extend "Reasonable Time Period" expires. In our view, Europe is moving backwards not forwards on this issue with France playing a leading role, along with Austria, Italy and even the Commission. In France, the "Grenelle" environment process is being implemented to circumvent science-based decisions in favor of an assessment of the "common interest." Combined with the precautionary principle, this is a precedent with implications far beyond MON-810 BT corn cultivation. Moving to retaliation will make clear that the current path has real costs to EU interests and could help strengthen European pro-biotech voices. In fact, the pro-biotech side in France – including within the farm union – have told us retaliation is the only way to begin to begin to turn this issue in France. End Summary.

2. (C) This is not just a bilateral concern. France will play a leading role in renewed European consideration of the acceptance of agricultural biotechnology and its approach toward environmental regulation more generally. France expects to lead EU member states on this issue during the Slovene presidency beginning in January and through its own Presidency in the second half of the year. Our contacts have made clear that they will seek to expand French national policy to a EU-wide level and they believe that they are in the vanguard of European public opinion in turning back GMO's. They have noted that the member states have been unwilling to support the Commission on sanctioning Austria's illegal national

ban. The GOF sees the ten year review of the Commission's authorization of MON 810 as a key opportunity and a review of the EFSA process to take into account societal preferences as another (reftels).

3. (C) One of the key outcomes of the "Grenelle" was the decision to suspend MON 810 cultivation in France. Just as damaging is the GOF's apparent recommitment to the "precautionary principle." Sarkozy publicly rejected a recommendation of the Attali Commission (to review France's competitiveness) to move away from this principle, which was added to the French constitution under Chirac.

4. (C) France's new "High Authority" on agricultural biotech is designed to roll back established science-based decision making. The recently formed authority is divided into two colleges, a scientific college and a second group including civil society and social scientists to assess the "common interest" of France. The authority's first task is to review MON 810. In the meantime, however, the draft biotech law submitted to the National Assembly and the Senate for urgent consideration, could make any biotech planting impossible in practical terms. The law would make farmers and seed companies legally liable for pollen drift and sets the stage for inordinately large cropping distances. The publication of a registry identifying cultivation of GMOs at the parcel level may be the most significant measure given the propensity for activists to destroy GMO crops in the field.

5. (C) Both the GOF and the Commission have suggested that their respective actions should not alarm us since they are only cultivation rather than import bans. We see the cultivation ban as a first step, at least by anti-GMO advocates, who will move next to ban or further restrict imports. (The environment minister's top aide told us that people have a right not to buy meat raised on biotech feed, even though she acknowledged there was no possible scientific basis for a feed based distinction.) Further, we should not be prepared to cede on cultivation because of our considerable planting seed business in Europe and because farmers, once they have had experience with biotech, become its staunchest supporters.

6. Country team Paris recommends that we calibrate a target retaliation list that causes some pain across the EU since this is a collective responsibility, but that also focuses in part on the worst culprits. The list should be measured rather than vicious and must be sustainable over the long term, since we should not expect an early victory.

7. (C) President Sarkozy noted in his address in Washington to the Joint Session of Congress that France and the United States are "allies but not aligned." Our cooperation with France on a range of issues should continue alongside our engagement with France and the EU on ag biotech (and the next generation of environmental related trade concerns.) We can manage both at the same time and should not let one set of priorities detract from the other.

Extract Four: These cables date from the summer of 2009, during which time some members of the Haitian parliament were trying to pass a law that would see the minimum wage on the island raised to $5 a day. The cables make it clear that the ambassador shares the perspective of (mainly American) manufacturers based on the island, who were lobbying to keep wages low.

Created: Jun 10, 2009
SUBJECT: HAITI ANXIOUSLY AWAITS DECISION ON MINIMUM WAGE

1. (SBU) Summary: Parliament's decision to raise daily minimum wages in the commercial and industrial sectors continues to strain relations between President Preval and members of Parliament. Since mid-May, President Preval has encouraged dialogue between members of

Parliament and the private sector to spark consideration of a lower or phased-in minimum wage that would allow Haiti to keep jobs, foster greater investment, and defer his responsibility of signing the current minimum wage law. President Preval has yet to sign the law and Parliament is annoyed with Preval's apparent unwillingness to make a clear decision about the increase. A Haitian Association of Industry (ADIH)-funded study indicated that a 200 Haitian gourdes (HTG) per day wage would devastate the textile sector and noted that it could only thrive with a HTG 100 per day minimum wage. Private sector representatives are convinced that members of Parliament understand the impact the increase would have on employment and Haiti's struggling economy. Members of Parliament, however, are adamant that the law be signed as written. No party to the discussion wants to be tainted by appearing to compromise Haitian workers' progress. End Summary.

Parliament Frustrated by Preval's Inaction

----

2. (SBU) Several leading Senators signaled they are inclined to compromise on the minimum wage law, including Senate President Kely Bastien. During a June 8 speech to the National Assembly, Bastien urged protestors to refrain from violence and echoed a key demand of the students, who called on authorities to release protesters arrested by police June 4-5 (Ref. B). Senator Jean Hector Anacacis called for calm and Senator Joseph Lambert asked protestors to peacefully await President Preval's decision on whether to sign the minimum wage law. According to a key advisor to Bastien, legislators left the June 5 meeting with President Preval unsure of whether he would sign the bill or send it back to Parliament for revisions. (Note: Since Parliament adjourned shortly after the Senate voted the minimum wage bill in early May, Parliament was required to resubmit the bill to President Preval after the opening of the next session on June 8. Preval has 8 working days from that date to sign the bill into law or return it to Parliament with his objections. Senate President Bastien's chief of staff confirmed to Poloff June 9 that the Senate had indeed resubmitted the bill to the National Palace the preceding day. End note.) Minimum wage bill sponsor Deputy

Stephen Benoit summoned industry leaders to a meeting in Parliament June 10, demanding that they produce evidence to support their claims that an increased minimum wage would eliminate their profit margins.

3. (C) Some legislators argue that the bill should be promulgated without a "phase-in" period or any other modifications. Deputy Cholzer Chancy told the press he was unconvinced by Preval's explanations during a meeting at the National Palace June 5, and had seen no evidence that the assembly sector would suffer if the law were enacted. Senator Youri Latortue criticized the President for only belatedly consulting with Parliament on the matter and Senator Rudy Heriveaux voiced his support for peaceful student protests to pressure Preval to sign the law as passed. In a conversation with Poloff June 8, Heriveaux described his failed attempts as president of the Senate's commission on public health to reconcile the students and the university administration. He said he attempted to mediate the conflict the week of June 1, but students' demands escalated as street protests gained momentum. He regretted that the protestors' "rough handling" by the police and the arrest of 24 of them had further radicalized the students.

4. (C) Many in Haiti's parliament seem exasperated by what they consider to be untimely lobbying efforts by President Preval and industry representatives. Deputy Sorel Francois, who voted against the new minimum wage law, told Poloff June 9 that even legislators inclined to moderation would face tremendous public pressure to reject any proposed modifications to a law they have already voted to approve. At a meeting the week of June 1 with industry representatives and 11 deputies, many were receptive to industry leaders' arguments, but argued that the time for lobbying was before, not after, the Parliament approved the law. Senators Heriveaux and Michel Clerie have privately made the same point, and emphasized that recent student protests have only increased pressure to reject any proposed amendments to the law.

Preval Expected to Make the Next Move
----

5. (C) According to legislative procedure established by Haiti's constitution, following the submission of a law from Parliament, the President is expected to sign or veto the law within eight working days. This would force Preval to make a move by June 17. Lionel Delatour (protect) a member of the HOPE Tripartite Commission (CTMO-HOPE) told Econ/ Poloff June 8 that the President is unlikely to make a formal decision on the law and will continue to request that Parliament engage in dialogue with the sector. (Note: President Preval sent a letter to the presidents of the Senate and Chamber of Deputies May 18 requesting that Parliament consider the impact the higher wage would have on employment and the overall investment climate in Haiti. End note) Preval was expected to depart Haiti June 10 for the 6 PetroCaribe Summit (June 10-11) in St. Kitts, however, Ministry of Foreign Affairs Director of International Organizations Azad Belfort reported to PolOff on June 10 that Preval plans to send the Foreign Affairs Minister in his place.

Industry Study: Wage Increase Will Kill Textile Sector
----

6. (U) The Haitian Association of Industry (ADIH) funded a study on the impact of the proposed minimum salary increase on the textile sector. Study author Lhermite Francois interviewed 12 out of 25 factory owners, representatives from the public industrial park (SONAPI), the banking sector and ADIH to discuss the significance of the HTG 200 wage on the sector and its workers,HOPE II opportunities, and the banking sector. Haiti's garment sector employs approximately 27,000 workers. The study found that 53 percent of workers earn an average salary of HTG 154 (from HTG 90-200, USD 2-5, daily). Thirty-eight percent presently receive an average of HTG 218 (almost USD 5.50/day). Overall, the average salary for workers in the sector is HTG 173 (USD 4.33). The study notes that the current salary structure promotes productivity and serves as a competitive wage in the region (Note: The minimum salary for workers in the Free Trade Zone on the Haiti-DR border is approximately USD 6.00. End note) Francois concluded the study by stating that a minimum daily wage of HTG 200 would result in the loss of 10,000 workers in the sector.

7. (SBU) ADIH Executive Director Gregor Avril and HOPE II factory owner Clifford Apaid admitted that the prospect of the law, coupled with the weak global economy, has caused approximately 1,000 job losses during the last month. One factory (a HOPE II legislation beneficiary) closed and other factories have closed down lines and dismissed newly employed workers. According to Avril and Apaid, the garment industry, represented by ADIH, has met with Preval on three occasions and has presented the impact of the HTG 200 minimum wage to over 40 members of Parliament and political parties, who they believed afterward to be sympathetic to the sector's findings.

Comment

----

8. (SBU) Controversy over the minimum wage issue continues to ramp up. Some members of Parliament, notably Benoit, demand that the President sign the law as currently written while they entertain private sector pleas for a reconsidered or phased-in minimum wage even if only to show that they did confer.

9. (C) Despite Preval's meetings with Parliament and the private sector on how to manage the minimum wage legislation without killing investment and job creation, he has said little in the face of continuing student demonstrations. Haitian National Police (HNP) and Ministry of Justice officials are convinced these "students" are being funded and mobilized by interests that go far beyond the university; it remains unclear who is fomenting the disturbances.

10. (SBU) Although the numbers of protestors remain relatively small, numbering 500 to 1,500, the HNP has had to use tear gas frequently to control the crowds and the police appears stretched then. While the demonstrations could peter out as the academic year ends and students leave campus, there are worrying signs that the demonstrations may be picking up steam.

11. (C) With the expected return of the body of former priest and close collaborator of former President Aristide, Gerard Jean-Juste, on June 16 and planned Senate election run-offs on June 21, Haiti is approaching a politically sensitive period. A more visible and active engagement by Preval may be critical to resolving the issue of the minimum wage and its protest "spin-off" – or risk the political environment spiraling out of control.

Created: Jun 17, 2009
SUBJECT: HAITIAN PRESIDENT'S DECISION ON MINIMUM WAGE LAW

1. (SBU) Summary: Haitian President Rene Preval, after intensive discussion with private sector and parliamentary representatives, plans to return the minimum wage law to Parliament with a proposal to modify the bill with a phased-in wage increase for the assembly sector. A 200 Haitian gourde (HTG) minimum salary would be applied to the local commercial and non-textile industrial sectors. The minimum wage law author expressed dissatisfaction with Preval's decision and is not convinced that the wage increase proposed in the bill, as currently written, would significantly damage economic growth or force job cuts. End Summary.
2. (SBU) Following several days of meetings at the National Palace, President Rene Preval reached a compromise with industry representatives and some members of Parliament that would avoid a blow to the assembly/textile sector in Haiti. Industry representatives, led by the Association of Haitian Industry (ADIH), objected to the immediate HTG 130 (USD 3.25) per day wage increase in the assembly sector, saying it would devastate the industry and negatively impact the benefits of the Haitian Hemispheric through Opportunity Partnership Encouragement Act (HOPE II). Recent ADIH and USAID funded studies on the impact of near tripling of the minimum wage on the textile sector found that an HTG 200 Haitian gourde minimum wage would make the sector economically unviable and consequently force factories to shut down.

3. (C) President Preval is expected to return the bill to Parliament with objections on June 17 or 18. Preval's Economic Advisor Gabriel Verret

(protect) told Embassy representatives on June 13 that Preval had brokered a deal with Parliament members. ADIH President Georges Sassine
told Econ/Poloff June 16 that Preval would propose the following modifications to the bill, applicable to the assembly sector only: an increase of
from HTG 70 to HTG 100 in October 2009, a further increase to HTG 125
by October 2010 and then to HTG 150 by October 2011 (Note: Preval
reportedly discussed with industry representatives possible measures the
government could take to help absorb other costs of production, such
as by subsidizing electricity (i.e., providing uninterrupted electricity from
0600 to 1800) and subsidizing taxes on diesel fuel. (Note: many factories,
for lack of outside electricity, are forced to provide their own using diesel
generators. End note.) It is unclear whether these measures would be
offered if the phased-in wage increases were enacted into law. End note)

4. (C) A majority of Haitian private sector representatives support enact-
ment of the law in October, based on reports that wages in the Dominican Republic and Nicaragua (competitors in the garment industry) will
increase also. ADIH member and factory owner Clifford Apaid told Econ/
Poloff June 8 that Haitian Chamber of Commerce President Reginald
Boulos said he supports immediate implementation of the wage increase
to HTG 200 for the commercial and industrial sectors and a phased-in
increase for the textile sector. Some members of the commercial and
non-textile industrial sectors, such as Bernard Fils-Aime, part-owner of
telecommunications company Voila, and Ricky Hicks, owner of Haitian-
American tobacco company Comme Il Faut, welcome the minimum wage
increase and stated that their companies already pay wages above that
proposed in the bill. Sassine told Econ/Poloff that textile sector wages
make up more than fifty percent of factory costs, whereas wages in the
commercial and local industry sectors represent an average of twelve
percent.

5. (SBU) Preval's proposed modifications can be rejected by Parliament.
If Preval returns the bill on June 17 or 18, the Chamber of Deputies would
be able to examine his proposal on June 23. HOPE Commission member
Lionel Delatour told Econ/Poloff that the worst case scenario is that
Parliament returns the original bill unchanged to the President for

signature. Delatour predicts that there is a less than 15 percent chance that this would happen. Although a prospective compromise was brokered between the President and members of Parliament (including bill sponsor Deputy Steven Benoit), Benoit's public criticism of Preval's decision continues, and Benoit is adamant that the HTG 200 per day be applied to both the commercial and industrial sectors – including the textile industry. Senate President Kely Bastien told the press on June 17 that the opinions of the Parliamentarians who met with Preval should not be interpreted as representative of the entire body. Therefore, Preval should not assume that his decision represents a compromise with Parliament as a whole.

6. (C) Comment: Preval's proposed compromise on the minimum wage appears to be acceptable to the textile sector. Recent statements by some members of Parliament, however, may portend a rancorous debate on the issue if and when it comes back to them for amendment. Students continue to demonstrate – sometimes peacefully, sometimes not – for an increase in the minimum wage and its application to all sectors, including the textile industry. Parliament's inconsistent and after-the-fact dialogue with Preval and members of the private sector has only added to the confusion. Because negotiations have been conducted with select Parliamentarians and behind closed doors, it is unclear whether they represent the majority view or are waffling on the issue perhaps to appease Preval and/or industry. Nobody knows for sure how the Chamber of Deputies, which gets the first crack, will respond to Preval's suggestions.

09PORTAUPRINCE881

Created: Oct 15, 2009 11:49

SUBJECT: A MORE EFFECTIVE PARLIAMENT IS SIGN OF DEMOCRATIC (Extracts)

1. (SBU) SUMMARY: A historically discredited legislature greatly improved its performance in the current parliamentary session by passing a record number of laws. For the first time in many years, many parliamentarians are considering presenting their candidacies for a second term. The

professionalization of Parliament comes against the backdrop of emerging populism and increasing influence over the legislature. Popular confidence in Parliament has improved in 2009 as the legislative has shown signs of seriousness and maturity. END SUMMARY.

NOT SO FAST
----

7. (SBU) However as the media and observers pay more attention to the legislative, parliamentarians are tempted to promote increasingly relevant populist proposals as launching pads for creating a national image for themselves (whether for future senatorial or presidential campaigns). Deputy Steven Benoit garnered popularity when he proposed a minimum wage law that did not take economic reality into account but that appealed to the unemployed and underpaid masses. Senator Rudy Heriveaux, seemingly in the footsteps of Benoit, has proposed a law capping both commercial and residential rent at an unprofitable rate. Both proposals have drawn negative feedback from foreign investors and the private sector alike, but have served their proponents' populist political image well.

8. (SBU) COMMENT: The increased productivity and the interest in returning on second terms are signs of democratic maturity. They contribute to legitimizing an institution long deemed irrelevant by the population and the political class. The same Greenberg survey mentioned above noted an improved perception of Parliament's performance between June 2008 and June 2009. Nonetheless, much remains to be done, given that the changes described above are characteristic of a core group only, and the attitudes prevalent in the majority in Parliament remain counter-productive. The next elections will determine to what extent this positive trend in Haiti's institutional development continues. With November elections almost certainly delayed, the credibility Parliament is slowly building with voters may be eroded.

Extract Five: The following cable was written shortly after a devastating earthquake in Haiti, in early 2010.

———————————

10PORTAUPRINCE206
Created: Feb 26, 2010 18:34
SUBJECT: APPAREL SECTOR HIGHLIGHTS HAITI'S ECONOMIC RESILIENCE AND

1. (SBU) Within two weeks of the January 12 earthquake, Haiti's garment manufacturing sector resumed exports to the US, re-routing shipments through Dominican ports. Prior to the earthquake, apparel assembled in Haiti accounted for three-quarters of the country's exports, employing one-fifth of the formal sector. Of the eighteen garment manufacturers in Port au Prince, two must relocate and rebuild from the ground up; one factory that completely collapsed crushed hundreds of workers inside, at least 300 of whom did not survive. Despite the loss of workers and limited access to basic resources, including electricity, many factories have reopened, simultaneously undertaking minor to moderate repairs, clean-up, and reconstruction. Shipping from Haiti resumed in less than a month, meeting customers' expectations of having their orders filled on time. Logistics constraints, while not wholly solved, have been overcome more quickly than expected, and increased international support for the industry aims to create more jobs and bolster the Haitian economy.

2. (SBU) International investors, brands, and manufacturers who expressed interest in expanding production in Haiti before the earthquake renewed their commitment to support the Haitian apparel industry, taking advantage of the trade preferences of the HOPE II Act for duty-free export to the US (reftel A). At the apparel industry's largest trade show in Las Vegas in February, the US Trade Representative (USTR), along with Gap Inc., Hanes Brands, and the US Association of Importers of Textiles and Apparels announced the Plus One for Haiti initiative, urging clothing retailers to "buy Haitian" and source at least one percent of their total apparel

production from Haiti. Representatives from the GOH Presidential Commission for the Implementation of HOPE (CTMO-HOPE) are currently in Washington working with USTR on an additional HOPE extension.

3. (SBU) Given the increased attention to Haiti, investors are giving consideration not only to build more factories but also to create more jobs by supporting infrastructure, such as electricity and water, needed to sustain the industrial parks and free trade zones that would house these factories in Port-au-Prince, as well as other potential industrial hubs, including Cap Haitien in the north. Representatives from high-volume customers, such as Gap Inc. in Korea, are visiting Haiti to explore expansion plans that originated before the earthquake. The World Bank and IMF are conducting port assessments specifically with respect to capacity to handle shipping containers for garments.

4. (SBU) Comment: The apparel manufacturers in Haiti operate on a high volume, thin margin, low capitalization basis where cash flow is extremely important for the business to survive. Industry representatives have told us that the garment sector would greatly benefit from a "soft loan" fund of USD 20 million for their immediate working capital cash needs, granting concessionary loans with an extended grace period and affordable interest rates to enable manufacturers to operate at full capacity as soon as possible, retain the 28,000 workers already employed, and expand production to benefit under the special trade provisions of the HOPE II Act. Combined with other USG initiatives bolstering the garment sector, such a loan would send a positive signal to U.S. retailers and producers in Haiti and the Caribbean, and should also send an encouraging message to the more than 25,000 Haitian factory workers who rely on garment factory jobs to provide for themselves and their families. End comment.

Julian Assange is the editor in chief of WikiLeaks. In 2010 he won *Time* magazine's 'Reader's Choice Person of the Year' poll and the Sydney Peace Prize, and was named *Le Monde*'s 'Man of the Year'. He has also been awarded the Amnesty International 'UK Media Award' and the Sam Adams Award for 'Integrity in Intelligence'. In February 2011, his organisation, WikiLeaks, was nominated for a Nobel Peace Prize after publishing three of the biggest leaks of classified information in history: the Afghan War Diaries, the Iraq War Logs and Cablegate. He is the co-author, with Suelette Dreyfus, of one previous book, *Underground: Tales of Hacking, Madness and Obsession from the Electronic Frontier*.

This book is set in Minion Pro and Helvetica.

The Minion typeface was designed by Robert Slimbach in 1990 for Adobe Systems and was inspired by late Renaissance letterforms, which prized beauty, elegance and readability. The name comes from the traditional naming system for type sizes, in which minion is between nonpareil and brevier.

Helvetica was developed in 1957 by Max Miedinger with Eduard Hoffmann at the Haas'sche Schriftgiesserei (Haas type foundry) in Switzerland. Originally intended as a clear and neutral sans-serif typeface, it has become ubiquitous in branding for corporations, governments, television shows and many other organisations.